NATURE, CULTURE, AND TWO FRIENDS TALKING

NATURE, CULTURE, AND TWO FRIENDS TALKING

KIM ALAN CHAPMAN & JAMES ARMSTRONG

NORTH STAR PRESS OF ST. CLOUD, INC.
St. Cloud, Minnesota

ISBN: 978-0-87839-732-7

First Edition: May 2015

Printed in the United States of America

Published by:
North Star Press of St. Cloud, Inc.
P.O. Box 451
St. Cloud, Minnesota 56302

northstarpress.com

We dedicate this book to our parents,
Al and Marie, Bill and Ellen,
who laid the foundation.

CONTENTS

ESSAYS, PRESENTATIONS AND POEMS (1985-2013)

1. EARLY (1980s-1990s)

2. MIDDLE (1990s-2000s)

3. Now (2000s-2010s)

WHY THIS BOOK?

This book reflects an evolution of ideas about nature and culture for two midwesterners, Jim Armstrong and Kim Chapman, who met as young men in the early 1980s and have spent thirty years in conversation. Like many of their generation, they had to learn how to think about the environment in new ways as their culture evolved, swept along in the current of history. From typical American backgrounds, Kim and Jim, nevertheless, in their twenties arrived at a perspective on culture and the environment at variance with those of most fellow citizens. Theirs were not isolated voices, but neither were they dominant ones in the debate. They sensed that the culture was not embracing its ecological obligations nor accurately forecasting the future, yet they did not want to be revolutionaries. Their political and community leaders often disappointed them by not going far enough in the protection and restoration of the environment. They sought to understand fully what should be done to bring that about and hoped their culture in time would also understand.

Kim's point of view

I don't remember the first Earth Day, or the second, or even the next couple of them. In the 1970s and 1980s, Detroit was not a destination for people wanting to change the world. It was, in fact, where you went if you liked the status quo. I was part of that status quo. My father, like the fathers of many of my friends, worked for the auto industry. We were regular church-going Lutherans—friends and family all living conventional, though not unintelligent, lives. The closest thing I got to environmental activism or direct conservation work was filling dumpsters with newspaper in recycling "drives" that happened once a year. We drove to the drive, of course, as did a couple hundred other people in a metropolitan area of over four million. We made an unnoticeable ripple in the tidal wave of materials being used and then buried in landfills.

My mother was the innovator in the household and recruited me for those recycling drives. Both my parents went to college, engendering a respect for ideas. As a family we vacationed across America, tenting at first, then sleeping and cooking in a pop-up trailer. Sometimes we stayed in hotels. Our destinations were often national parks—Yellowstone, the Smoky Mountains, Yosemite, Everglades—but also state and federal forests in northern Michigan, the Sierra Nevadas, Wyoming, and the Southwest. In those forests I saw clear-cuts where soil flowed down tire ruts and ravines, muddying trout streams. In national parks I sat in our car looking through a haze of exhaust fumes to grand vistas and gigantic sequoia trees. I was steeped in the beauty of our land and took in the minutiae of nature's design. This city kid of ordinary background, exposed to nature and brought up in a household that did not denigrate intellect, became a professional conservationist in 1982.

By the mid-1980s my perspective was transformed, perhaps a little too much, which you can see in the first essays here. At the time I felt my opinions about the environment and culture were far removed from society's, yet in 1988 George Bush the elder declared himself an environmentalist, much like John Kennedy declared himself a Berliner in 1961. Environmentalism had become mainstream, in a superficial way. My coming from the mainstream and becoming an environmentalist exemplified that cultural shift, but also belied it. Our culture's commitment to sustainability is a mile wide and an inch deep. Our culture is decades. . . probably a century. . . away from sustainability in an ecological sense. Read any textbook about environmental science or conservation biology and you will understand how wide the gap is between society's present attitudes and where we need to be in order to continue the human enterprise with the planet comfortably supporting it.

My later essays reflect a shift in the environmental movement itself—not consciously reflected by me, but simply because I was a product of the times. The importance of private enterprise, the idea that we are all in this together—most importantly, that I am as culpable as anyone in my failure to change my lifestyle and give nature the room it needs to do its thing. By that I mean the old IPAT formula for determining humanity's footprint on the land and water—Impact = Population + Affluence (Consumption Rate) + Technology (Capacity for & Efficiency of Resource Use). Two children, check. Middle class American lifestyle, check. Techologically-advanced nation with large carbon footprint, check. With that realization, preachiness pretty much goes out the window, replaced, it is hoped, by a roll-up-your sleeves attitude and compassion for your fellows. Even forgiveness . . . not just of our despoiling race, but oneself for participating in that despoilation.

I am no brilliant conservationist writing eloquently decades ahead of his time. I am an ordinary person, living in a neighborhood with people who are not environmentalists, working with many people who are not in their heart of hearts conservationists, trying to bring about the cultural shift I yearn for. That shift will bring us clean air, soil, and water, healthy lands and ecosystems, and the full restoration of nature's beauty and bounty. The words I write here are my experience, not my concepts, not my recommendations. They show that anyone can become a wild-eyed environmentalist bent on changing the world, without seeming to be one.

Jim's point of view

I first became enthusiastic about the natural world when my family moved to Michigan in 1969. I remember looking at the map and seeing all that blue water—in the middle of the continent! As a family we explored the woods and shores of upper Michigan (Hemingway country) in an Oldsmobile station wagon. We slept by the Lake Superior surf in a canvas umbrella tent that smelled of mildew and pine pitch. Those were the halcyon days of car camping, when there were half the number of people in the U.S. than there are now, and you mostly met families on the road. Campgrounds were quiet, for the most part, and the country seemed enormous. At one point we drove out west. I have fond memories of sleeping under the western stars. At home I was a Boy Scout, and like a lot of boys of my generation I learned how to tie a square knot and sharpen an axe from a Korean War (or sometimes a World War Two) veteran. We went on Jamborees and canoe trips and in the middle of winter (there was winter then, in southern Michigan) we huddled around a pot belly stove in a cabin built by the Rotary Club. Then, in high school, I went several times to the Boundary Waters in northern Minnesota as part of a church trip organised by a local minister, a bull moose of a man whose enthusiasm for the canoe trails was infectious. I still remember that rush of teenage endorphins as we paddled those long, cold lakes—lakes you could, in those days, drink from without fearing giardia. By the time I was in college I was a confirmed devotee of the northland, and my writing reflected that. I won a poetry contest with a poem I wrote about Lake Superior: the prize money was enough for me to afford a tent and a sleeping bag.

Strangely enough, after graduation I didn't head off to the north country. Instead, I saved up my money and went to Europe, where, among other adventures, I walked from the Rhone River through Burgundy and then to Paris, taking French hiking trails through countryside that had been settled since the Iron Age. Every day I would walk through little towns that had once been Celtic hill forts, then Roman outposts, then medieval villages—layer after layer of habitation, displayed as fragments of architecture—a ruined tower, a Roman bridge, a Gothic church. I would buy my breakfast in little boulangeries and walk on paths that had been right-of-ways for a thousand years—so different from the fields and woods of Michigan, which seemed empty of history, or the Michigan towns in which the oldest house was a scant century and a half old. At night I would camp furtively in back fields, or on canal towpaths, living like a gypsy—but never fearing anything more than a scolding from the local gendarme. I met so many friendly country folk, descendents of French peasants who fed me, took me in, cheered me on (French drivers would honk in approval at my *sportif* getup—orange frame backpack, Red Wing boots, walking staff and cloak made from an army blanket). By the time I arrived at the walls of Paris I had gained a new perspective—I had shed my typical American fetish for "wilderness" and instead became a fan of a nature in which humans had a home, a nature which was interbraided with culture. I was not the only one to come to this: the 1980s saw the rise of a more theoretically nuanced understanding of the nature/culture dyad, as many began to realize that by cordoning off wilderness and ignoring the vast spaces between the city and the parks we were essentially embracing the creation of zoos, rather than supporting valid ecosystems. The question became, how can we live in the world in a deeper and more sustainable way? How can we connect the urban consumer to the living countryside in a way that is both practical and sensual? How can we get out of the industrial/suburban nightmare we have created for ourselves—where we don't have a connection to our food, our water, or even our past? Where our greatest environmental problem may very well be an imaginative disconnection from everything around us.

Most of my essays meditate on ways that connection might be reestablished, because we will only save things that we truly love and understand. Thus, my focus has been largely aesthetic and philosophical; through my poetry and prose I have hoped to entice readers into a richer life by celebrating our primal connections to the world. My greatest literary accomplishment, perhaps, was my book *Blue Lash*, which was an extensive meditation on the spiritual power of Lake Superior. I like to think that anyone who has a love for that lake can open my book and find words to celebrate the inexpressible. In my essays I am attempting to lay the groundwork for that kind of sensitivity toward the most local landscape. In essence, I am dreaming of an America where we, like the French, have learned to taste the soil in our wines and the grass in our butter, or where, like the Japanese, we make a point of having parties to view the moon, or the first snowfall, or the blossoming of cherry trees. Where we might find soulful ways of finally, really, settling our land.

Some of that enthusiastic hopefulness has been dampened of late, as the bad news comes rolling in about our situation—every day the predictions about climate change are more dire. I have found yet another challenge here: how to live in an era when, as Yeats says, "many ingenious lovely things are gone."— Coping with the enormity of our predicament has consumed many an anxious night. But that too, is part of the story of our life in nature. I think the final dialogue Kim and I engage in limns that struggle well. We will have to continue to love the world, even as it becomes more frightening.

A WORD OF THANKS

First, we are thankful for this land and its people. From that soil and blood has come the whole cloth of democratic idealism and institutions admired by the world and still coalescing in the body politic of America itself. As important to us are the families that we came from, and the ones we belong to now. Only the people who know and love you despite everything can keep you humble and grounded. Finally there are the influences on us, from those adults we admired when we were young to the young people whom we admire now for their idealism and energy, and including the people not much older or younger than us, but who stand out in our minds for their influence, friendship, and commitment to conservation. In particular Kim wants to mention Lee Schaddelee, Bob Pleznac, Richard Brewer, Con Hilberry, Paul Olexia, Keith Wendt, Peter Reich, Jack White, Robert Jenkins, Rick Johnson, Steve Apfelbaum and Doug Mensing. Jim thanks his father, for taking him camping, and his scout masters for teaching him woodcraft. He thanks Ladislav Hanka, who is an ever-present example of what it means to really live in nature as a metaphysical voyageur. He thanks Kurt Cobb, who is so essential to his thinking on everything from Jung to peak oil, and Chip Blake, who is such a wise editor. Our lives are richer for having met these people and our experiences truer because of their lives of integrity shared with us.

We heartily thank Corinne Dwyer and North Star Press for teaming up again on a nature-themed book, and Elizabeth Longhurst, whose lovely cover design and elegant page layout add a beautiful dimension to our words.

1

EARLY
(1980s to 1990s)

Crosby Lake, an old oxbow of the Mississippi River in St. Paul.

NOTES FROM AN URBAN BIRDER

KIM

I'd been in the Twin Cities three years and, missing southern Michigan, decided to spend more time in the wild places of the urban landscape looking for birds.

April 1, 1989, 6:45 a.m.

I turn out of my neighborhood onto Lexington Avenue where early migrants from the south suburbs, headlights on, ascend the old terraces of the glacial Mississippi to jobs in St. Paul and Minneapolis. This is the route they'll take back tonight, the shortest one to the marshes, sloughs, and prairies of the Minnesota River valley.

I head southwest on old Fort Snelling Road—now Highway 5—and connect with the expressway by the airport. From the bridge over the Mississippi, I look east to its confluence with the Minnesota. My view of the valley is blocked by fog, gray in the pre-dawn light.

Ten minutes later the sun is up when I near the end of old Cedar Avenue. Cedar Avenue is a river that's abandoned its channel, its flowing traffic now surging over a wider stretch a little east of here. I can't see it because of the fog, but I can hear the commuters' symphony coming up the valley. Before plunging in, I stop my car. From up high, the fog forms a sweeping wave, like snow-bound prairieland, its surface out of focus and gleaming as it evaporates. Looking up from inside, it changes to a braided stream of white channels on a gray background, and every once in a while, the sun appears, a pale, dime-sized pearl.

To my right and left in the thickening, thinning fog scraggly cottonwoods and willows emerge and fade. They mark the edge of the marsh. Nearby the cattails, bluejoint, and reed are still. No birds would be out in this weather except ducks, and I'm too far from the water to see them. Even if I tried to walk to the water, the sound of breaking ice and crackling dry plants would drive every floating bird to deeper water. To see ducks, the fog will have to lift.

As I peer through the frosted glass of the morning, it changes. Now the fog looks like it's growing two eyes that squint and cross before I understand they are birds in a long glide coming at me. I see them put their long legs in a dangle while raising heads and thrusting shoulders back to drop themselves into a space of water they know like the sweet certainty of a familiar runway. Great blue herons, here for the day's catch. They do not move. I am too close. Shortly one of them cocks its neck and, spearing its head forward, lifts a long leg and puts it slowly back down, moving without seeming to move. The perfect fisherman that my impulse to travel will send off on loping wings, cruising the tops of marsh plants for another fishing hole. I'm sorry even before I do it. I step, and they fly.

April 2, 1989, 7:45 a.m.

A heavy frost touched the ground last night, and a pulse of warm Gulf air melted it except in the shadows. White hoar on the dark of shade. Ice leavings from my car's windshield collect on the wiper blades, and a veneer of water droplets coats my windows. The sun's been up only an hour, but it's hot on my cheek. I start the car and drive five minutes to Crosby Farm on the Mississippi where it meets the Minnesota.

A station wagon, a sedan, a gray van, and two pickups got here first. A Suburban, roomy and clunky, arrives as I sit in my car. Three fishermen pile out, gather poles and tackle, and head down the slope to the river.

Starting down myself, I hear the staccato honking of Canadian geese and clamorous squawking of mallards, though I can't see the lake yet. When I catch sight of it, only a small section, a fraction of the lake surface is ice-free. Dark bird bodies speckle the ice and water near it. I stop at the lake's edge, by bursting pussy willows, and notice a tawny muskrat head plowing a small furrow that fans out in the water behind it.

April 5, 1989, 9:00 p.m.

Taking out the garbage, the noise of shouting children comes to me. The disharmony mingles with cacophonous traffic on I-94 until I can't tell them apart. By the time the sound is nearly gone, I know what it is—tundra swans— and rush to bring my wife out to hear. Several years before I also thought I heard shouting children until I saw the beating flocks coasting 200 feet above our Lansing home. The underwings flashed brilliant white, then dark, then white again, catching the sunset's afterglow. We stayed up for them, counting their flocks of dozens and hundreds moving northwest in wavering diagonals and gimpy V's. As the night wore on, the swans shouted to us from higher and higher in the sky, in the end sending us their faint calls as we walked down the spiral of sleep to our dreams.

Hoping to see swans, we drive to the river and huddle in a blanket on a bench, the dark and orange towers of Minneapolis's tallest structures a night-light to our vigil by the Mississippi. Jets fly over. Newer designs, Boeing 757s and DC-10s, hiss for a while, then suddenly pop out of earshot, passing through a sound-curtain to the other side. An older 727 comes over. The roar of its three engines searches outward in a cone to find us, muting the night sounds and our conversation. A pulsing grumble trails behind the jet's vanishing wings, randomly censoring our words, the cars on the River Road, and promenading couples, before damping down and freeing sound again. That smothering cover removed, we take a deep breath, and listen. A little "tee-ew" off to our left. Louder now, in front of us. Softer again off to our right. A killdeer flying the river highway north to farmland is here with us now. Like the swans, flowing into and out of our lives, mirroring our own bodies' flow of life northward to a distant place. We don't hear any more swans tonight, but they are poleward bound just the same.

April 6, 1989, 6:00 p.m.

We plan to visit Crosby Farm Park for a short walk before dinner. I don't have hopes of seeing much birdlife since the last two nights were clear enough for winged migrants to fly away north. Last night we heard a flock of tundra swans go over. Driving down Hamline this evening, something catches our eye. A gray bird hovers then dives, fluttering back up to a tree top, its tail held in a long, narrow diamond. Mourning doves are back. In a few minutes we're on the trail at Crosby Farm.

People are still out strolling or fast-walking to get exercise. We turn onto the boardwalk through the marsh. Red-winged blackbirds *congaree* as we pass through their territories. We see other birders. A stocky man, red face flowing into his neck and neck into a brown windbreaker buttoned tight, wheels a small steel cart. The cart holds his photographic gear. His wife walks on ahead. "Seen anything interesting?" he asks. We point and say "Red-breasted mergansers, out there. And some wood ducks." He replies, "Oh, they're back already!" I tell him I saw them last Sunday: factually, not as a boast.

Just then I know what it is to be a serious birder—it is to catch the birds as they first arrive. It's a feeling bordering on the spiritual. I was seeing spring unfold in a moment, though I knew real springs were made of many moments, each feeding the next and tumbling over each other in a pile-up at its end. Right now things were happening slowly enough to see it all. "Yes," says the man, "then spring really is here, isn't it?" Other birders stop and stare into the distance, as if turned to salt. We look no different, binoculars at our eyes, intent on finding indifferent specks.

Later on we stop dead in the trail at the eroding bank of the low-ebb Mississippi. My wife says, "It's a funny duck. Just its head is sticking out. Here take a look." A root tip slowly submerges with the current, then reappears in focus. Yes, a funny duck, I tell her. We laugh and move on, then jerk to a stop again. Birding, like any pleasure, comes in fits and starts. In a wiry pile of blackberry canes something is thrashing in the leaves. We approach and a bird bolts, showing a flash of rust on its tail and giving itself away. The color lingers on my retina. Like its name, the hermit thrush is, if not secretive, at least hard to see. It is one of the first forest birds to reach us in the spring. The northwoods is its home, but the best time to see it is during migration when no leaves cloak its underhanded activities in underbrush. I'm elated. I haven't seen a hermit thrush in years. When the rush of spring becomes a torrent, I will savor this tawny flash as the time when spring stopped even while racing away from me.

We jump out of the way to let a jogger past, ears in a Walkman vice-grip, brain in a headlock by Bon Jovi. The jogger turns a bend and a yellow-shafted flicker yammers nearby. Over the river dozens of tree swallows bend and swoosh. They sashay and allemande past each other, backs catching the last sun rays and burning iridescent blue. A motorboat appears upriver and chases them all downstream.

Juncos stare out at us, waiting for night. Across the river, lights wink on in apartment buildings.

April 8, 1989, 6:45 a.m.

Starting somewhere near my house you can go south to the equator or north to the pole and cover the same distance. Most ducks shuttle half of that in both spring and fall, farther than the average northern snowbird goes by jet to his winter condo. Almost midway through their continental push, ducks descend to rest in backwaters and lakes where Minnesota meets Mississippi. Where the last leg of Lexington Parkway skips over the river and picks up again on the limestone bluffs of Lilydale, ducks find a place to rest.

Crosby Lake is the cut-off channel of an older, larger Mississippi River. Silted in at both ends, this black scimitar of water serves ducks and Twin Citians alike. In twilight, with afterglow on its surface, Crosby Lake bewitches joggers and walkers along its shore. The darkening slice rounds the base of a darker, steep bluff, making lines that seem to follow the earth's curve to a vanishing point.

Six weeks ago, ice fishermen, their families, friends and dogs crawled over the white crust of the lake. This morning I think I see the ghost of ice floating the middle of the lake, but the sun shows the skim to be just mist, retreating at the edge where the sun strikes. Across the lake, a dark mass of aspen ignites and becomes pink trees, while Interstate 35E takes a pounding from commuters and roars like a bored old lion at the zoo. I listen for birds and look for ducks. A flicker's call penetrates the curtain of traffic noise. I see him pumping from one tall tree to another across the lake, ending his flight in a climbing swoop. He calls again. *Wick-wick-wick-wicka-wicka-wicka-wicka-wicka!* More than any of the woodpecker tribe, the common flicker surprises urbanites wherever it has trees to drum and ants to scrounge. Its direct, swooping flight, cacophonous call, and size (bigger than a blue jay) are out of place in the rarified biology of cities. (Yet in my old haunts, in southwestern Michigan, they were a common sidewalk bird.)

I wanted to make this a quick stop, and the birds oblige me. Nothing much is going on. A male and female cardinal chip from a tangled canopy of young ash. Goldfinches roller-coaster by and chickadees flitter among the branches. I see more of these birds than anything else. The high, nasal *eh-eh-eh-eh-eh* of a white-breasted nuthatch comes to me from close by. I hear a killdeer. *Kiddle-DEE, kiddle-DEE!* I'm surprised. This is a shorebird of open farm country, and I want to see it to believe it. Nothing on the shore. The trail and its grassy edge are both empty. Where is this bird? It calls, I look and see a starling, imitating a killdeer. Fooled again by a starling, mynah of North America. Pewee, red-tailed hawk, red-winged blackbird, crow—I forget the times I've looked for these birds in the city and found. . . a starling. Other calls it attempts with mixed success, but better than most other birds.

There's nothing mixed about the starling's success at colonizing a continent. Originally from Europe, its story in America starts with a dream. Call it a midsummer night's dream, because somewhere in William Shakespeare's plays a starling is mentioned and an American admirer of Shakespeare, Eugene Schieffelin, wanted to wake every morning to songs of birds mentioned by the Bard in his plays. In the 1880s and 1890s, he and his fellow American Acclimatization Society members released starlings and other birds mentioned by Shakespeare, into New York's Central Park. Few of them made it. But in 1890-1891 Schieffelin stocked the park with 100 starlings, evenly sexed, and was rewarded. In fifty years the bird traversed North America and became its most abundant bird, the aerial cockroach of the continent.

How can I judge a man's pure dream harshly? The starling is a miracle of nature, the fastest of the perching birds, fast as a swallow. They are impressive as insect foragers. I've watched a phalanx of them cross my back yard, troops on parade, driving bugs ahead of them and picking them off. Starlings live—thrive—in scrub, prairie farmland, city, suburb . . . most anywhere except forests. A recent Audubon Christmas Bird Count reported 600,000 starlings roosting beneath the Ambassador Bridge, spanning the Detroit River. More than half the number of Detroit's citizens perching on a bridge. When I consider how many ducks of two dozen species there are in all North America—forty-five million, less than a sixth of the human population—I cannot deny the superiority of the starling. In its numbers and aggressiveness, it controls the destiny of dozens and dozens of bird species—by out-gunning them for food, out-wrestling them for holes to call home, out-and-out intimidating them simply for space to stand around in. I admire the superiority of starlings. They remind me of us.

But the day moves on, and so must I. I'm disappointed. No ducks. I scan the lake one last time and, there it is, a lone male mallard circling a decoy. The decoy, a Canada goose, has the mallard and me puzzled. What's it doing here? The mallard tries to understand by swimming closer, leaving a short wake like an arched eyebrow. Decoys work, I gather, even on the wrong species.

On my way again, I speed by Runway 29, the workhorse of the airport. Bird sanctuaries and other neighborhoods are at both its ends, and the spiraling traffic volume and decibel crescendo have the neighborhoods up in arms. But who speaks for the residents of the sanctuaries? How does a nesting duck or grebe respond to the daily uproar of hundreds of passing jets? Do great blue herons and great egrets, the long-legged fishermen of the marshes, break concentration while fishing and return to their nesting colonies in the evening with a scant catch? Are nesting bird densities lower in the shadow of the flight path than in similar habitat someplace else?

I don't know of any studies on this topic, but some birds can acclimate to loud noises. Experiments to roust starlings from their landscape-befouling roosts by taping, then playing back, their own alarm calls succeed at first, scaring the birds away. Gradually they became habituated to the sound because it preceded no terrible, or even mildly annoying, event. Crows and blackbirds are well-known habituators to automatic exploding devices that pop off in grain fields and orchards.

Notoriously shy birds, like the brown thrasher, yellow-breasted chat, least flycatcher, and veery, may or may not get used to the cycles of daily thunder in the sky. I've never gotten very close to any of these birds—too skittish. Break one stick, and they're away or down out of sight as fast as possible. A jet lifts free of the ground just as I pass the runway. Instinctively, I duck. Where did that reaction come from? An older time when animals overhead were something to fear? Whatever the answer, the disappearing silver arrow carries part of me away with it.

April 25, 1989, 5:45 a.m.

This morning the white-throated sparrows came back. They are two weeks early, which I know because my in-laws migrate from Florida north to Michigan with the white-throated sparrow, and my in-laws travel in two weeks. For me these birds are John the Baptist announcing the coming of warblers, themselves the true harbingers of summer.

They won't stay here. In a few days the sparrows move north to cut-over aspen land to sing their plaintive song from perches overlooking the young growth: *Poor Sam Peabody, Peabody, Peabody,* they sing in minor key. Forlorn. Lying in bed, hearing this now, I feel sad for Sam Peabody, and for the white-throated sparrow. But they carry on, despite the mournful tune that is their only voice. To them, their song is purposeful and full of meaning: *this is my territory.*

Two white-throated sparrows are engaged in conversation about who owns what. I hear them over the squabbling English sparrows in the shrubbery of the neighbor's yard. Like an insistent child, one English sparrow repeats to himself the only word God gave him to utter: *cheep.* The archetypal bird sound. From Sunday funnies to Kurt Vonnegut novels, all birds say "cheep," though in reality only the English sparrow does. *Cheep, cheep, cheep, cheep,* thousands of times a day.

This immigrant from Europe arrived around 1850 and took up residence in Brooklyn, New York, where well-intended city fathers expected it to improve urban life by eating nuisance insects. Natural history wasn't well-advanced in those days, because no-one realized the shape of the sparrow's bill, like that of all sparrows and finches, was heavy and vice-like, perfect for cracking seeds. And crack seeds it did. Within a few years it was obvious to everyone that, rather than consume insects, English sparrows ate prodigious quantities of stored grain. Within a decade there was a bounty on them. Schoolboys and vagrants killed them by the thousand for a penny a bird. Local governments tried techniques of mass-annihilation. The English sparrow withstood all efforts to exterminate it and today is one of the most prosperous birds in North America, indeed in the world.

How did this bird get so good? Watch a sparrow sometime. It breeds like a rabbit, is wary like a fox, lives in nooks and crannies of the urban fabric, and eats food of all kinds. I've seen them hunched over side-walk cracks munching seeds of carpet-weed, as paltry a fare as can be imagined. They succeed because they live so well with humans, and we are everywhere.

But I was talking about the white-throated sparrow, about two of them trading sob stories outside my window this morning as I lay awake, listening. They didn't wake me up, though. I woke earlier this morning. It was night, actually. No pale band at the eastern horizon contradicted the certainty that it was night. But the American robins knew what was up. If the English sparrow utters the quintessential bird sound, the American robin is the proverbial early bird. They do hunt worms. Worms are abroad at night, pulling leaves into their holes and giving their location away. In fact, last night as I stood on the front porch, one was working like a slow mouse, staying in one place and yanking at a leaf. In last summer's drought, the worms stayed deep in the ground and early robins no longer caught the worm. But robins have it figured out. They know how to make a living in the city. Robins hunt worms where sprinklers run and drive worms to the surface. Through last year's long, dry summer, they cruised the neighborhood, looking for sprinklers.

After robin song, the sparrow started. Now and then a mourning dove called. A cardinal whistled off in the distance, and from farther off came a woodpecker's drumming. Then, just before sun-up, the white-throated sparrow joined in. I want them to stay longer, but I know the city's not for them. They prefer somewhere else. They want to wake fifteen minutes before sunrise and see dark silhouettes of spruces and firs at the edges of their aspen clearings. So do I. But right now I'm lying in my city bed, awakened by birds.

HILL PROSPECT OF KALAMAZOO

JIM

What kept me here, when gravity was on the side
of the thousand-mile net of streetlights
around Chicago, or the New-Jersey-wide exurbus?
Many times I tried to tell it,
standing on Westnedge Hill among petunias
looking out over a handful of buildings rising
above the green mass of summer, the heat
wavering in the air, the swallows chattering
past high pale clouds, the distant river bluffs
a blue promise. It was something I'd seen
in the margin of a medieval painting:
just over a saintly shoulder, the mural crown
of peaked and staggered towers. The ducal kitchen,
brothels, stables, clanging ateliers,
all the prickly heat of the urbane
impounded and made discrete, bright pennants snapping
and rippling in a wilderness of trees.

Even Keats, drowsing on Hampstead Heath
outside the Spanish Inn, or Charles Lamb,
walking fifteen miles through the hedges
for cheese and beer under five-hundred-year-old
chestnuts, both of them knew
they had one buckled shoe in the world
of Wren's domes and columns, sewage, tuberculosis,
and the grime of the canals—
the other hidden in the tangle
of hedgerow and barley, the hawk and
rabbit, the preceding order. Samuel Johnson
roused from bed at midnight by his companions
to wander the shit-smelling streets of the city

drinking sugared madeira in the blue film of dawn,
shivering under his periwig, passed the dim shapes of mongers
walking in from the fields with dew on their clothes,
carrying baskets of turnips and eels . . . and he knew
that in every direction they came from—Greenwich or Richmond—
London dismantled itself on the horizon
and the fields began.

STANDING BY THE PINE:
THE POET AND "TRUEST USE"

JIM

He stands among partial men for the complete man and apprises
us not of his wealth, but of the common wealth.

—*Ralph Waldo Emerson, "The Poet"*

Nearly 150 years ago, Henry David Thoreau traveled to the Maine woods in search of true wilderness. He discovered that the woods were full of lumberjacks; noticing the sudden openings in the green shade, the landscape reduced to stumps, he wrote:

> Is it the lumberman then who is the friend and lover of the pine—stands
> nearest to it and understands its nature best? Is it the tanner who has
> barked it, or he who has boxed it for turpentine, whom posterity will
> babble was changed into a pine at last? No! no! it is the poet; he it is who
> makes the truest use of the pine—who does not fondle it with an axe, nor
> tickle it with a saw, nor stroke it with a plane; who knows whether its
> heart is false without cutting into it—who has not bought the stumpage
> of the township on which it stands. All the pines shudder and heave a sigh
> when that man steps on the forest floor. No, it is the poet, who loves them
> as his own shadow in the air, and lets them stand.

I have fancied this to be the first shot fired in anger against the relentless materialism, which was, even in the 1840s, working with rapacious fury to decimate the natural landscape. In an age of pioneer boosterism, Thoreau is speaking for a different way of valuing the landscape. Yet his alternative seems effete, aesthetic: Can we pit the poet against the lumberjack? And what does he mean by "poet"? How is it that the poet is able to let the trees "stand," and what does it matter if he wishes to "love them as his own shadow?" Years ago when I lived in southwestern Michigan, I spent a lot of time in a small state game area on the outskirts of my town. The preserve was a patchwork of abandoned farm fields and second-growth hardwoods, and included a pine plantation created by the Civilian Conservation Corps in the '30s. My favorite section was a sixty-year-old mixed stand of oak and maple trees growing along a small glacial moraine. I loved to ski through this grove in the winter; with the leaves gone, each tree presented a personality, a unique composite of scars, galls and woodpecker holes, every mark and the attitude of every limb reflecting the history of the tree's struggle for light and room. When I think of that grove now, sitting at my desk in Boston, I think of the wan silence of a Michigan winter afternoon, with huge snowflakes sifting through the colonnaded understory, the flurry of feeding chickadees in the bare limbs. The space around me, defined by gray, gnarled roots, feels shaped, inhabited, as though I were sliding my skis through a hall crowded with brooding giants.

Large-flowered trilliums blanket the forest floor near Marquette, Upper Michigan.

One day I went to the grove only to find it gone, and in its place a field of raw stumps strewn with shattered limbs. A sign stood at the edge of the field, announcing that the Department of Natural Resources had decided to cut the forest in the interest of improving it. The sign noted that regular harvesting was part of good forest management, because it allowed a new generation to grow up straight and tall, freed from the shadows of the older trees. Yet as I stood at the edge of the field, I had a strong intuition of disaster. I thought of all the richness of the mature forest, in all its seasons: its dark, humid smell on summer mornings, its complex procession of wildflowers throughout the spring, its bronzed and rubied canopies in October. I thought of the blue-coated nuthatches, the carpenter ants, the hognose snake, the shelf fungi, the warblers and vireos and hawks—none of these to return, though they might one day be replaced by distant relations. The net result of management seemed to be that a complex world had been replaced with a barren field; what didn't seem to get figured into the management plan was almost everything that had once been there.

I could find no account of this in forest management literature, nor could I find validation for my sense of loss. Following Thoreau's advice, I turned to the poets: to a poem by Gerard Manley Hopkins titled "Binsey Poplars," written in the 1870s. Hopkins is mourning the destruction of a stand of trees he used to visit:

> My aspens dear, whose airy cages quelled,
> Quelled or quenched in leaves the leaping sun,
> All felled, felled, are all felled . . .

The trees had been cut by their owners, presumably for cash, but Hopkins cannot view them as mere objects of exchange. They formed a place for him, a particular location, at the edge of a stream, where the grove

> . . . dandled a sandalled
> Shadow that swam or sank
> On meadow and river and wind-wandering weed-winding bank.

Like Thoreau, Hopkins values the shadows of trees—their "shadow in the air"—as his own; he has brought them into his circle of relation, calling them "dear." He wishes to let them stand because of the way they gather the entire countryside around them—meadow, river, weed—and to remove them is to damage the whole, the unique assemblage. He compares the delicacy of this wholeness to the delicacy of the eye through which it has come to him:

Since country is so tender,
To touch, her being is so slender,
That, like this slick and seeing ball,
But a prick will make no eye at all,
Where we, even where we mean
To mend her we end her. . . .

He is not talking about ecology—the word had not been invented yet. He is not talking about the tenderness of the biosphere. He is talking about his aesthetic experience, before and after the cut. Something serious has occurred on the landscape as a result of the axeman's "strokes of havoc"—something has happened to the way the landscape *means*, as a result of which Hopkins experiences a deep sense of loss. What has been lost is irreplaceable:

After-comers cannot guess the beauty been.
Ten or twelve, only ten or twelve
Strokes of havoc unselve
The sweet especial scene
Rural scene, a rural scene
Sweet especial rural scene.

The foresters who clear-cut my own "airy cages" of oak and maple and cherry were assuring me, with the text they hung in front of their "delving," that I should not read their action as tragedy, that all would grow back, and better. Yet I know, as Hopkins did, that in nature nothing ever comes back: no natural configuration can be repeated, and what goes, goes for good. What I loved was not trees in general, but these trees in particular: and not even these, in themselves, divorced from their surroundings; it was these trees in this place, and the animals and herbs they sheltered. They gathered the land around them, they made an *especial scene.*

Foresters are not devoid of feeling for trees: they are in fact obsessed with the health and reproduction of trees, and they brood over the various diseases that afflict them. They are so convinced that the proper way to care for the forest is to manage it, they often express horror at leaving the forest unattended, to grow on its own. Sigurd Olson, in his book *Listening Point*, dramatizes this managerial mentality in a passage that has the writer discussing a stand of ancient pines with a timber cruiser in the Minnesota woods:

We stood in the shade of a big pine . . . "take this one," said the cruiser
as though reading my thoughts, "this is an old one and overripe, should

be cut to make room for the young stuff coming underneath. Even the seeds aren't as good as they should be, and with the decay inside its a nest of fungus and beetles. That tree is dangerous, ought to come out, and that's true of most of the big stuff left. People don't get any more pleasure from such a relic than they do from a healthy young tree."

The timber cruiser looks to the "success" of the stand, which he defines by the healthy condition of the individual trees. His sympathy lies with the young, vigorous saplings; he seems angry at the old pine for obstructing these new growths. This solicitude is somewhat suspect, we realize—it is the sympathy of the stockman for his cattle, a sympathy tainted by the use to which its object will be put. Moreover, because his purview is only the health of the trees, the health of the forest is peripheral to the forester's consideration. In fact, the complex ways in which other organisms make use of the trees—the colonizing, parasitizing—are repugnant to him.

Olson, a poet, or at least an essayist, has a different kind of sympathy:

As I stood there, I could hear the soft moaning of the wind in the high dark tops and feel the permanence and agelessness of the primeval. In among those tall swaying trees was a sense of finality and benediction that comes only when nature has completed a cycle and reached the crowning achievement of a climax, when all of the interrelationships of the centuries have come at last to a final glory.

The timber cruiser values what the forest produces *for* him. Olson values what the forest produces *in* him—a complex association of thoughts, each of which is traceable in his vocabulary, which varies between the historical, the religious, the scientific, and the poetic. For Olson, the trees stand in relationship to some whole, a "climax" of which they are a part, and their fate has a kind of "glory," despite or because of the fact that they are sacrificed to it. The trees are not there for his benefit, but are part of a "cycle" of "inter-relationships," which gives permanence and value to the site. All of this comes to him, not through analysis of soil pH, but through his immediate sensual perception: he "hears" the moaning of the wind, and "feels" the presence of the primeval. He values the trees for what they suggest about the nature of the universe, and consequently what they say about himself. Because of this value, he wishes to let the pines stand—that they might continue to speak.

Later, when he returns, he finds that the grove has been "harvested" and that the "old skyline" is gone. The vacancy reminds him of "how it was that night when the snow was drifting down and I listened to the great pines for the last time. The beauty and the mystery of that moment was burned into my memory." Olson's willingness to consider what the forest means leads him to an experience of loss, a feeling not available to the forester, who thinks only of gain. The forester is trained not to see the forest for the logs—or the stumps. Here is an example of a professor of forestry's rhetoric, taken from a recent Minnesota symposium on the white pine:

> There are many ways of measuring economic value of the species. One that a forester often considers is stumpage value, the product of stumpage price and production level. For this example, I assume prices for sawtimber at $60 per MBF (International scale), veneer logs at $145 per MBF (International scale), and pulpwood and other wood products at $6 per cord. Converting these to price per MCF, and multiplying by regional production levels of these products, yields $5,307,546. . . . Rounding this estimate, we can say that regional white pine stumpage had a market value of about $5.5 million in 1988. This value includes only market value for industrial raw material and does not include other values, including some other economic values.

What disappears in the forester's evaluation is the forest itself, as a sensual manifold—its greenness, its coolness, its affect of benediction or threat—how it *appears* to him. This is because he has been trained to exclude its appearance as the "shadow of himself in air," an imaginal *projection*. The forester wishes to deny his subjective shadows, to dwell in the clearing of objective reason. The forester attributes value to a thing only in as far as it is quantifiable and useful, for the central tenet of his positivistic science is that things have no intrinsic value, other than quantitative values of size and number.

The forester's method is scientific, and science has always shown a deep distrust of the composite, complicated world given to our unaided eyes and ears, the world that we trust is real—in fact, one of the impulses hidden within science is a kind of mathematical idealism, which has a contempt for the senses. Galileo, the man who, in the sixteenth century, first proposed the scientific method, deeply distrusted the senses; he claimed that objects we perceive as such wonderful assemblages of color and texture "in reality" consisted merely of matter and motion—everything else he called "secondary characteristics" and dismissed as chimerical:

> Hence I think that those tastes, odours, colours, etc. on the side of the object in which they seem to exist, are nothing else but mere names, but

hold their residence solely in the sensitive body; so that if the animal were removed, every such quality would be abolished and annihilated.

Those "things that appear" to our senses, are connected with inferiority, subjectivity, and even with animality. They are insubstantial, like the shadows on the wall of Plato's cave. And Galileo would be in perfect accord with Plato's judgment in the *Republic*, that "that which relies on measurement and calculation will be the best element of the mind." On this basis, poets (whose measures do not measure anything) were to be excluded from the ideal state.

Galileo's contemporary, Sir Francis Bacon, founded British empirical philosophy on the assertion that "the understanding, unless directed and assisted, is a thing unequal, and quite unfit to contend with the obscurity of things." He insisted that "natural philosophy" must address itself to stable principles in nature, not to ephemeral events:

Matter rather than forms should be the object of our attention, its configurations and changes of configuration, and simple action, and law of action or motion; for forms are figments of the human mind, unless you will call those laws of action forms.

The net result is that the senses become conveyors of error, which must be sifted and purified; they must be restricted to that "touching the experiment only"—that is, they must be employed to read the gauges and dials, the meter-sticks and graduated cylinders—those tools with which man becomes the *measurer* of all things. This means that quality can only be expressed by number; and our non-formalized experience of landscape and the objects that make up landscape—our perception of their beauty, variety, composition—has no ontological validity, and is banished, with the "secondary qualities," to the realm of "aesthetics," a ghostly kingdom. The imagination becomes separated from life, and human feeling is excluded from proper judgment.

Empiricism, despite its veneration for experience, leads away from the sensual immediacy of the particular thing, and toward an abstract realm. The goal of Bacon's project was "a road for the human understanding direct from the sense by a course of experiment orderly conducted and well built up," a road which would lead "by an unbroken route through the woods of experience to the open ground of axioms." Down this road, all things become "objects" in the modern sense: devoid of all those qualities which might attract us to them. "Whatever does not conform to the rule of computation and utility is suspect," as the philosopher Theodor Adorno has said of Enlightenment thought, "the multiplicity of forms is reduced to position and arrangement, history to fact, things to matter." In the drive to make them "objective," all things are made the same.

The essayist William Hazlitt once said:

> ...*if we ask what is the real value of any object, independently of its connection with the power of habit, or its affording natural scope for the imagination, we shall perhaps be puzzled for an answer. To reduce things to the scale of abstract reason would be to annihilate our interest in them, instead of raising our affections to a higher standard; and by striving to make man rational, we should leave him merely brutish.*

This well describes the situation of our forester, who has learned to reduce the forest to its constituent organic compounds, which behave in reasonable, mathematically quantifiable ways. Once drained of particularity, the trees become neutral counters, arbitrary compilations of carbon, which can be manipulated "objectively"—that is, without any loyalty to their particularity. Their value is strictly utilitarian. Trees become "lumber." Woods and groves become sites of lumber production. This enables us to determine their economic value: decimals that rank their standing in the marketplace, but obscure their value at home, *in situ*. As Thoreau observes, on site in the Maine woods, "Strange that so few ever come to the woods to see how the pine lives and grows and spires, lifting its evergreen arms to the light—to see its perfect success, but most are content to behold it in the shape of many broad boards brought to market, deem *that* its true success!" But the trees' "perfect success" has no *value*.

Except to the poet, who deals in shadows, in hints and intuitions. The poet, who has been banished from the republic of philosophers and the laboratory of scientists, perversely believes that the world of secondary qualities has some primary meaning. In the words of Baudelaire:

> La Nature est un temple où de vivants piliers
> Laissent parfois sortir de confuses paroles;
> L'homme y passe à travers des forêts de symboles
> Qui l'observent avec des regards familiers.

> *Nature is a temple from whose living columns*
> *Commingling voices emerge at times;*
> *Here man wanders through forests of symbols*
> *Which seem to observe him with familiar eyes.* (translated by Kate Flores)

For Baudelaire, the forest is both strange and *familiar*. It is *related* to him through the senses: the perfumes, colors and sounds "*sé repondent*," correspond, speak to each other and to the experiencing mind, hinting at a "shadowy and profound unity."

This is a romantic truth—meaning, a truth of the philosophical and artistic movement known as Romanticism. Even as the scientific worldview was consolidating itself at the turn of the nineteenth century, an international group of Romantic thinkers—which included scientists, as well as philosophers, poets, and painters—were championing subjective perception. Their "romance" was between mind and world—they insisted on the unity of all knowledge, rational and irrational, not wishing to disregard a whole segment of experience as though it were invalid. Their assumption was that nature was working in us as well as around us, so that our intuitions and emotions told us something of value about the "real" world. "Man is Nature creatively looking back at itself," said Friedrich Schlegel.

William Wordsworth, perhaps the greatest English Romantic poet, celebrated these correspondences between mind and nature, proclaiming:

> *How exquisitely the individual Mind*
> *(And the progressive powers perhaps no less*
> *Of the whole species) to the external World*
> *Is fitted.—and how exquisitely, too—*
> *Theme this but little heard of among men—*
> *The external World is fitted to the Mind;*

Rather than attempting to extricate the world from the mind's perception of it, Wordsworth championed "the creation . . . which they with blended might/ Accomplish." Because perception was cooperative, the romantics believed that one's approach to perception determined the outcome: what one saw depended on *how* one looked. "The ruin or the blank, that we see when we look at nature, is in our own eye," said Emerson, who, more than anyone else, brought Romanticism to the United States and made it part of our culture. "The reason why the world lacks unity, and lies broken and in heaps," he said, "is, because man is disunited with himself. He cannot be a naturalist, until he satisfies all the demands of the spirit. Love is as much its demand, as perception."

The forest I loved was a creation of my perception: yet the rasping of a bronze beech leaf against the snow of late winter, or the appearance, in spring, of a group of rare orchids, or the desultory pecking of a downy woodpecker in a decaying maple—these were not illusory or fantastic; I did not summon them out of the ether. These events appeared on their own time and in all their specific complexity, and the fact of their appearance solicited my wonder and affection—my joy, in fact, the joy which is constantly associated with romantic perception. Such joy springs from a recognition of the inexhaustibility, the spontaneity, of the world; a recognition that the world is not dead mechanism, not atoms and emptiness, but live organism, a place of beings. The world is revealed to the senses as a particular place where we might live, and be at home. Yet such insights are only available to the man re-united, capable of approaching the world with a heart that "listens and receives." This reverses Galileo's argument, and returns us to Thoreau's poet, who knows it is our attachment to objects, in all their secondary qualities, that makes *us* human. The world we build with our senses is the world appropriate to our scale, to our level of action; its beautiful detail makes us moral beings by creating the basis for choosing between one thing and another, one place and another.

The poet within all of us best understands the nature of the pine tree, because the poet will let the pine stand in its uniqueness, and will acknowledge that the feelings it arouses in us are as real as our measurements of its mass or its growth rate.

The poet knows that, while science may help us to discover general laws, only the sympathetic imagination—the poetic force in all of us—can help us to draw near to things, to stand by them and care for them, because only the imagination will let them *be*.

Unconscious Loyalty to Untamed Landscapes

Kim

An essay penned near Breezy Point on the shores of Gull Lake, vacationing with family in summer 1995.

The landscape of my childhood claimed me when I was five years old, old enough to spend time away from my mother and watchful neighbors. In my memory, it is always August. The cicadas whirr in the vaulted canopy of oaks and elms as I bump down gravel roads in Detroit's west suburbs, the muscles of my arms vibrating as my palms bounce against the handgrips.

After the sun rose, before my mother called for breakfast, I listened to mourning doves calling. *A-WOO-hoo-hoo*. That sound, imprinted on my ears as I lay between sleep and waking, compels me, when I hear it, to travel somewhere wild. In farm country that wild was only half-wild, but hidden in the farmland were unused spaces outside human economy, and they felt like the real thing—places of irregularity and unpredictable change. In later years I studied them, understood them as relics of the prehistoric landscape swept away a century before I was born, and valued them for their diverse life, a diversity missing from the settled farm country all around. As a boy I didn't know any of this. I just played, and the remnants were where I played best.

One such place was at my grandmother's cottage on the Canadian side of Lake St. Clair. The lake was the wildest thing about it. One day gray-green swells bulged against the beach under a moody sky; the next, the water was flat as paper, blending at the horizon with the blinding white humidity of air.

Each day was specific. Each day was a tent full of experience staked down at the corners to a place. I was held to that place by buzzing cicadas and grasshoppers clattering against grass stems, by fox squirrels bounding through sunshafts under oaks; the scent of skunk, bitter as burned rubber. I wandered fields where wind blew hot as a sauna, then stepped into the shady reach of a white oak where my skin crawled with the chill until I rubbed the sweat away. Days backed up against each other into the infinite future. The diverse world riveted my attention, and that prolonged my days and my summer—and was the germ of my natural love, the intense leisure I enjoyed unawares living in my landscape.

It had to be unawares, or I wouldn't have learned to love it. If a science teacher summering at the lake had seen my interest and taken the trouble to instruct me, it would have been different. If I'd learned as a five-year-old about the trees and soils, the migration of animals, the phenology of herbs, my activity wouldn't have been my ease, but my unease . . . something more like study. Rather it was in my earliest, unconscious enjoyment and plain existence that a landscape won me over.

Just as we are receptacles for language—and learn it amazingly fast—as children we also are receptacles for the environment. Being small, we take in only essential cues, as we take in simple nouns and verbs when learning language. Like the grooves on a record, I was recorded on: the skittering wind

Bur oaks and marsh fringe McMann Lake, Spring Lake Township, Minnesota.

in upturned leaves, light splashing on glossy surfaces. I lay under those woody giants, watching clouds duck behind branches and the moving green, and I didn't need to know their names. Today when I experience the *impression* of deciduous tree, I feel a tug in my heart that has nothing to do with hard-won knowledge of its species name, rather with nameless experience.

There was a stream overtopped by large trees where I played at age five. I went back a few years ago to find it and drove the entire street without seeing it. I back-tracked and found where it used to be—a gentle fall of ground on both sides of the road snaking under fences, gardens, and garages. I realized that when my old neighborhood's destiny as an uninteresting suburb was fulfilled, the excess run-off forced the stream to flood more often. So the city put it underground. For a long time, I leaned out the car window and tried to restore in my mind the simple culvert bridge edged by black cable through white posts. I saw in my mind's eye the eddies of current, the splashing ringlets from our tossed stones; I felt the delicious cool of shadow thrown down by cottonwoods and willows.

It didn't work. There was the stream, underground, and there was my childhood image, on a high shelf of memory, fading like a photo of unknown relatives. I will never go back there. Taking that fading photo down and thinking about it, slowly a calm excitement for the stream that was comes over me, and I begin to feel a physical passion for the smell of gravel dust and oil, the whistling doves, the bright green fields spreading, the twinkling water. I feel nothing for the place as it is today. That is mere fact. The stream gone underground is still real for me, while the actual place is a depression in the back yards of a Detroit suburb.

I'm talking about loyalty, a powerful personal and cultural impulse. Fans of the Boston Red Sox and Chicago Cubs know it. Corporate managers and army officers demand it. The best families live it daily. Disloyalty might be punished by death—traitors to country, deserters from the field of battle. Corporations and families shoot their traitors metaphorically, but they shoot them just the same. The church excommunicates you. Friends give you the cold shoulder. Nike's shoes and Nestle's baby formula are boycotted. So here's the question: What does a landscape do when you are disloyal? Better question: What do we do to landscapes when we are disloyal?

A good friend of mine, a teacher and writer, is an amateur naturalist. Jim grew up tramping the wetlands and woods of a small town in southern Michigan. Every summer his parents put him in a cramped car with his siblings and drove north for hours, out of the veil of sticky heat, into the northwood's cool charm. That was my childhood, too.

As adults, he and I have gone beyond the simple nouns and adjectives of our landscape—lake, fish, bird, tree, cool, smooth, colorful, fragrant—to an understanding of its ecology. Our language is ripe with complexity: the nutrient-holding power of fallen logs and dead standing trees; the rejuvenating chaos of windthrow, fire, and disease; the helpful redundancy of many species performing similar tasks. We constructed that science on a native love of place, and it is rock solid. This knowledge that a mature mind learns and applies to new situations brings with it a curse of knowing too much. As landscapes go, it is more comfortable to live without knowledge. Learning a landscape's true nature lets you in for a heap of disappointment when the details change, as they must. Aldo Leopold knew it when he said, "One of the penalties of an ecological education is that one lives alone in a world of wounds." When you invest in a landscape, you build an account of information whose value declines as homes are built in woodlots, hay meadows are plowed under, the full-Nelson of development is wrapped around lakes, and streams go underground.

Because I don't like these things doesn't mean I don't like change (the life and wellspring of nature); it means I'm against the specifics of that change. Does anyone really want green algae blooming in streams and lakes, fewer kinds of songbirds in the fields, no wolves, bears, otters, or bobcats, fewer butterflies and wildflowers in our forests? Few want this. Yet everybody accepts these outcomes as the consequence of change, which for me means *taming*.

When we tame oak woods by locking out fire, when we tame a forest by cutting down every stick over nine inches in diameter, when we lay down a bluegrass lawn to tame natural groundcover, when we strive with our road-building to create a landscape where no one needs to walk more than a couple hundred yards to get anywhere, we get a simplified, sterilized, uninteresting, and deadly boring world lacking wildness. All by design. Our cultural concept about what a proper landscape looks like is translated by many small and large decisions into a tamed world. I don't think that's what we want, but most people living in a landscape don't know enough details to recognize the changes set in motion by our decisions, let alone understand the consequences.

I'm so passionate about this because my understanding of what is happening here is anchored to a plunging whale of early experience that will die only when I do. Luckily, my wife and friends are there to say, "Stop obsessing and enjoy yourself." They save me from going down like Captain Ahab, obsessed with a fatal idea.

In our late twenties, Jim and I explored Michigan's wilds doing biological surveys of habitats. On those trips we merged the child's and adult's interest in the landscape. In an old-growth remnant near Seney, we struggled through blow-downs, where disintegrating wood was becoming new life in the ground, shouting, "A working forest! A working forest!" If we'd been children, we would have plunged into its cavernous dark, hid behind trees so wide to make us seem like insignificant beetles, and stood in shafts of sunlight striking the ground with the certainty of truth. Instead, as naturalists we measured the diameters, estimated the standing dead and downed woody debris, documented pileated woodpecker holes, and looked for signs of bears clawing the bark of giants. Finally the child in us couldn't take it anymore, and he leaped out of our eyes onto a catwalk of suspended fallen timber, then jumped from bole to bole twenty feet above the ground. When the distracted naturalists eventually got back to their car, they found they'd forgotten to write down the species of giants that had fallen—a missed scientific opportunity.

Another good friend of mine is, in his own words, not a conservationist. He's a small-town boy, and I'm a small-town-boy wannabee, so we hit it off. We took different directions in our teens. While I lit out for the territories of farmland and wilderness, he struck out for the urban Twin Cities, taking in the details of streets and city-scape. He's a student of cities, understanding not just zoning minutiae, but also how property value determines the number of rental units in a neighborhood. If I argue we need light rail to consolidate urban building and prevent suburban sprawl with its burdensome infrastructure costs, he cites the exact housing density needed to ensure adequate ridership for cost-effective operations.

He ribs me about being a conservationist. "What do we need all those bugs for? They just annoy me—they get in my eyes and mouth. Get rid of them. What, the birds eat them? So what? Birds poop on my car." He's kidding, but he's serious, too. Like most Americans, he's poorly educated about the ecological details of his landscape.

A few years ago he took me to his father's farm. After his dad's funeral the trip had the air of a pilgrimage. It was a typical small farm: manicured lawn, a horse-paddock with a baker's dozen species of plants (not enough to survive a Dust-Bowl drought, for sure); a cow pasture where bones of an American elm sat in a carpet of imported reed-canary grass, and where small wet places were swathed by lake sedge and tussock sedge; lastly the muddy stream with its dredge spoil banks on which box-elder, black willow, and other all-forgiving trees rooted. To him it was entirely beautiful; to me, also, seeing it through his eyes: this is the climbing tree; this is my horse Blackie; this is where the rope swing went; this is where we hid. He played for hours there, and his love for the farmed landscape will never die.

My friend and I are hooked on a basic human urge—to preserve the place where we were young, as we remember it best. The landscape that raised us owns our youth. It has claimed us. Our repeated experience in it has forged an unconscious loyalty. Which brings me back to my question: What happens when we are disloyal to a landscape?

One of the things that happens is we remain children in the landscape. This is good or bad, depending. We enjoy a landscape as a child does, which is good. We ride our mountain bikes over its steep morainal hills and take pleasure in the speed of descent. We enjoy a river for its whitewater, or because we can put our hot feet in it and fool the rest of our body into not minding the humidity. From ridgetops and mountain peaks we hurl our minds over a landscape, taking it all in at a glance. A motorboat drags us across the lakewater until we fall, slicing into its suddenly hard surface. I've done all this. I've played as a child in my landscape. I've been a blur of activity, a frenzied pace, a clamorous noise charging around. I have been pure excitement and joy in nothing but the act of being in my landscape. Whether thirty-five or five, that is the way the child in the landscape behaves. But as an adult you strive for more. I have the strength and physical control to scale a rock wall or push a canoe into a thirty-mile wind that I didn't at five. As a boy I banged around using the simple tools at my disposal—legs, arms, bicycle.

What is it like to be an adult-child in your landscape? Above all, it is fun. Why is golf the fastest growing sport in America? Why are so many baby boomers taking it up? Their growing attachment is a gigantic bulge appearing in demographers' charts. I believe my generation flocks to this sport because it combines an adult's quest for accomplishment with the enjoyment of a physical setting that conjures up buried memories of an out-of-doors childhood. It satisfies unconscious physical yearnings yet requires deliberate work to improve one's game. Golf is a very safe way to be outside. It is entirely without hazards, except for water, sand, and lightning. What is more controlled, more manicured, than a golf course? We take a beautiful natural setting, and tame it entirely. And in taming it, we tame our fears. It wasn't always so: Scottish courses, for example, are nowhere near as refined as ours. As is so often the case, once you scratch an itch, it's hard to stop. Once you begin taming a landscape, it's hard not to take it to the extreme.

Here is the dark side of a child's enjoyment of a landscape. Children want to tame the world in order to understand and feel safe in it. For my daughter, it means killing every bug that invades the house. (Actually, it means getting mom and dad to do her dirty work.) With her watching, I've gone out of my way to catch wasps in jars, snatch flies out of air, pick up plant bugs on pieces of paper, and force ants and spiders to crawl onto my hands so I can throw them ceremoniously out the door—unwanted guests, but not condemned felons for setting foot in the house. It does no good. She and her friends and every other toddler insist on summary execution. Where does this come from? More interestingly, how do people rid themselves of this compulsion to liquidate the unfamiliar parts of their surroundings? I am convinced this urge to eliminate the unexpected and unpredictable is innate in us, and rooted in childhood fears.

I have a friend who cannot swim in lakes. With few exceptions, I would rather swim in a lake than dive into a vat of water infused with the element responsible for biting holes in the ozone layer, but she likes chlorine. It is a smell she understands. A pool is an environment she understands. She sees the bottom, its contents, and they both look like things she's seen before—concrete, tile, blue water. My friend felt this the first time she stared a lake down. None of her brothers or sisters feel this. I would say that her parents let her toddler's fear of the unknown become a grown-up fear. This is how it happens. We grow up clinging to a fear, like a life-boat full of holes, because it is a familiar fear. For the fearful, it is scary to put on goggles and see the striped snails eating pondweed, or feel minnows nipping your toes. However, it is also exciting to discover these things, rather than tame them. Overcoming fear of a landscape's details gives you a more interesting life, in my opinion. On the flip side, avoidance of the untamed seems to me the way that phobias and neuroses begin.

How does that play out in real life, and what does it mean for a landscape? Entering young adulthood, one faces a choice. You can cut yourselves off from your landscape, as most Americans do. Or you can take a conscious journey into your landscape. The landscape that teaches you will be the same one that jazzed your childhood antennae. You will still love what it does to your eyes, ears, nose, and skin. But now you will also enjoy what it does to your critical mind. The information you gather, as a sail captures wind, you will also take pleasure in—it will propel you mentally.

I imagine a bear cub learns in a similar way to enjoy the blackberries and hazelnuts of his mother's territory. When he grows up, his mother chases him away and forces him to learn the specifics of territory he has never seen—the best berry and hazel patches, best water, best rubbing posts. The young adult bear must work, and enjoyment isn't the same as before. Enjoyment now comes by learning competence in the land the bear depends on to survive. Each of us has a chance to become a bear cub testing its emerging powers, plumbing the well of his or her landscape. Some come to it early and some late. Some never arrive, choosing instead to be consumed by the narrow landscapes of human economics, politics, and current events.

I'm thankful that my daughter's generation is coming to it early: they are being taught ecology in the classroom. That wasn't an option for my generation, or my parents'. Ecology is, after all, a young science, about a hundred years old, and it takes a few generations for the arcane knowledge in the minds of researchers to infiltrate the larger population.

In the end, your knowledge of a landscape will serve you well. You will know its details and notice the changes in it. What is the alternative? In your ignorance, you will become obsessive about taming your landscape. If you live on a lake without a deeper knowledge of it, you will wake up one day needing to plant and mow a bluegrass lawn. You then will insist on growing petunias that wither in the sand unless they are watered, and on digging out the wild columbine, dainty hairbell, and other wildflowers of strange shape and unfamiliar color. I guarantee that, in your dotage, you will spend precious time obsessively raking your beach free of driftwood, pondweed and bulrush stems after every storm, and throwing the windrow in your garbage for landfilling. Eventually, you will take a pair of shears and bevel the edge of your lawn where it meets the sidewalk (which you will have poured from the beach to the gravel road). I have seen much of this behavior, in city, farm, and suburb. From an ecological perspective, you will be like a child in an adult body—reacting fearfully to anything that disturbs your sense of order.

Engaged as we all are with refinements to our property, we don't have time to check up on our landscapes. If we live on a lake, we don't have time to get out there and make certain that caddisflies still thrive and the pondweed and coontail aren't growing hog-wild from too much phosphorus and nitrogen. Some of us well-meaning types will adopt a roadside and clean up the trash that our neighbors throw out their car windows. As wonderful as that is, it is but a band-aid on the huge ignorance that wounds the landscapes we live in.

What it comes down to is that a landscape has to have advocates with an intense loyalty to it, and they have to be in the majority. They must know their landscape's details, and what changes to those details means. They will be the adults in their landscapes. When my daughter grows up, she will enjoy being dragged through the water on inner tubes, and will love sunning herself while gossiping with girlfriends. She will continue to play like a child in her landscape. But one of my dearest wishes for her is that she will, as an adult, permit the untamed into her life. The bugs we pick out of her kiddie pool to look at, the bird calls she recognizes, the summer heat dissipated by a jump in a lake. . . all will be familiar parts of her landscape. When she is intellectually able, she may return with a mind to study it. Or at least she will know that there are necessary details to her landscape as deserving of preservation as she is. There will be a foundation to build on. It will be an underlayment of pure love for the place where we were young and spent our childhood. We love what we know best; but what we understand completely, we must *conserve*. If we will conserve, in order to preserve the best of ourselves in our landscape, perhaps we will not act on what we fearfully imagine about a place—and not bring about a deathly taming of that place.

The Echo of the Bees

Jim

Bee, thou must not leave me, I may need thy advice.
—Old Westphalian *"Bee Chant"*

*That buzzing-noise means something. You don't get a buzzing-noise
like that, just buzzing and buzzing, without its meaning something.*
—Winnie-the-Pooh

In a passage from the *Natural History of Selborne*, Gilbert White writes of a peculiar echo that can be heard from the hill at the edge of his village in the south of England: on a still evening, the echo "would repeat ten syllables most articulately and distinctly," he says—adding that he has tested this himself with a line of pastoral poetry from the Roman poet Virgil—a choice which indicates his gentlemanly education. The mention of Virgil reminds him of another of the poet's works, a poem of agricultural lore called *The Georgics*: "One should have imagined that echoes, if not entertaining, must at least have been harmless and inoffensive," he states, "yet Virgil advances a strange notion, that they are injurious to bees." White assures us that "This wild and fanciful assertion will hardly be admitted by the philosophers of these days, especially as they all now seem agreed that insects are not furnished with any organs of hearing at all." The great naturalist then goes on to establish his credentials as a disciple of English empirical philosophy, describing his personal attempt at resolving the question:

> . . . *it does not appear from experiment that bees are in any way capable of being affected by sounds: for I have often tried my own with a large speaking-trumpet held close to their hives, and with such an exertion of voice as would have hailed a ship at the distance of a mile, and still these insects pursued their various employments undisturbed, and without showing the least sensibility or resentment.*

Honeybees cluster around the opening to their hive.

That White should test the hearing of bees by shouting at them through a speaking trumpet presents us with a strange amalgam of the poetic and the rational—yet this is to be expected, as White is guided by a scientific ethos that tries to distance itself from myth and story. Like many educated men of his generation, White has a kind of double consciousness: his sensibilities are deeply imbued with the literature of antiquity, yet he is led by Baconian science to doubt the veracity of any knowledge that isn't mathematical or material. White was born into the Age of Reason, a complex time when men read Ovid in Latin, decorated their homes with statues of the Greek gods, and yet also believed the New Science was going to restore them to a true knowledge of nature, after millennia of superstition.

"It is the hardest thing in the world to shake off superstitious prejudices," White states elsewhere in his *Natural History*, "they are sucked in as it were with our mother's milk. No wonder, therefore, that the lower people retain them their whole lives through, since their minds are not invigorated by a liberal education." The goal of the invigorated mind, according to the empiricists, was to peel away the layers of subjective understanding—the "old wives' tales" we imbibe in our childhood—and get to the object itself, and its true behavior in nature. Such knowledge was sometimes characterized by Sir Francis Bacon as a "marriage" of mind and nature, when human ideas would correspond to the world as faithfully as a mirror corresponds to any object put before it. At one point, Bacon uses an ancient fable of the marriage of Pan, the god of all nature, with the nymph Echo, to express this union:

> And it is excellently provided that of all discourses or voices Echo alone should be chosen for the world's wife. For that is in fact the true philosophy which echoes most faithfully the voice of the world itself, and is written as it were from the world's own dictation, being indeed nothing else than the image and reflexion of it, which it only repeats and echoes, but adds nothing of its own.

It is in the interest of such a clear reflection that White assaults the myth of the bee's sensitivity to sound, for his parishioners held onto that myth with unusual tenacity. It was common belief that a swarm of bees could be attracted to an empty hive by "tanging," that is, banging on old pots and kettles—for the bees were thought to have found such cacophony appealing. Sometimes this noisemaking would be accompanied by spoken "bee charms," magical phrases intended to persuade the swarm to stay, rather than fly off into the wild. Moreover, according to Hilda Ransome, whose book, *The Sacred Bee*, is the authority on such traditions, the custom of "telling the bees" was widespread in England:

> . . . the bees must be told of the death of their owner; if not, they will be offended, dwindle, and die. Sometimes other deaths in the family are told to them, also marriages and other important events. In the case of death in many districts the hives are decorated with crape and portions of the funeral feast placed before them. All news must be whispered gently and politely to the bees.

The "telling" usually had a formula, one example of which Ransome cites from 1840 in Lincolnshire:

> Honey bees, honey bees, hear what I say!
> Your Master J.A. has passed away.
> But his wife now begs you will freely stay,
> And still gather honey for many a day.
> Bonny bees, bonny bees, hear what I say!

Thus, when he takes up his speaking trumpet, the Reverend White is not just addressing the blind adulation of Virgil by men of his own social class; he is also refuting the irrational inclinations of his parishioners. By proving that the bees do not hear, he is making it ridiculous that we should speak to them.

In doing so, he is setting himself against a tradition probably as old as human culture, for humans have been seeking to influence the behavior of bees since the Paleolithic Era. In the caves of La Arana, near the Spanish city of Valencia, an 8,000-year-old rock painting shows men climbing a ladder of Esparto grass to a natural fissure in the rocks, from which emerge flights of wild bees. The men are naked, except for baskets they are carrying to store the plunder of the hive—a strategy still pursued today by tribal bee-hunters in Africa and Asia, who rely on supernatural forces to protect them from the bees' wrath. Why men should be willing to trust their lives to spells and flimsy grass ropes is not hard to explain: modern anthropological accounts testify to the fact that among hunting and gathering peoples, honey is the most prized of all foods, one to which they will go any length to procure. The most salient quality of wild honey is that it is sequestered: always high out of reach, and always *interior*—found in the hollows of ancient trees, or the crevices of rock faces. This secretiveness connects it to the secretiveness of generation in the womb. Yet honey is also *given*: it is always coming forth, available; like water welling up in springs, or plants shooting up from the soil, it is part of the inexplicable fecundity of the earth. As such, it is a sign of the benignity of the land—an echo of which can be heard in the Biblical account of Canaan, the land "flowing with milk and honey." Moreover, fermented honey is so intoxicating it can lead one to see visions or to be possessed by a shamanic spirit—so it is connected with the supernatural, as well. It is a "magico-religious" substance, capable of healing wounds, embalming the dead, and summoning spirits.

Echoes of these associations are preserved in our language—sexual love is "sweeter than honey," we call our lover "honey," and an affair is a "taste of honey." The marriage "honeymoon" is also a general term for a time of ease and good relations. A persuasive person speaks in "honied tones"; a favorable arrangement is a "honey of a deal." Though sugar has long vied for a place in our metaphors, honey remains the more primal substance—we still view it as symbolic of the "givenness" of the natural world.

The Greeks preserved the image of this givenness in their myth of the Golden Age, a time when a race of primitive humans was thought to have "lived without cares or labour, eating only acorns, wild fruit, and the honey that dripped from the trees," and were said to spend all their time singing and dancing. In the Golden Age, we were so imbedded in nature even our death "was like as to a sleep."

After the Age of Gold, said this legend, came the Age of Silver, peopled by "eaters of bread" who were "utterly in thrall to their mothers." This commemorates the time when humans first made a clearing in the forest; grain was sown, houses built; pots were fired and baskets were woven to store the surplus, which enabled men and women to quit their nomadic habits. And thus arose the perceived dialectic between our nature, which lay within fences surrounding our cultivated fields, and the rest of nature, which was called wild; for this agriculture, though it allowed for a new kind of stability, was ever at risk to the contingent forces of blight, drought, and infertility. Beyond the fields, the forest lurked, ready to return should our efforts fail—and at the border of the human and the wild arose the figure of the *Magna Mater,* the Great Mother, who drew all things out of her womb, and who, therefore, had to be supplicated, appeased, and praised. Because the swarm issued from the earth, or from the womb-like darkness of ancient trees, the bee became an emblem of the Mother's miraculous fecundity we had preempted for our own use, but which she was always threatening to withhold. Like the bee, the goddess could bestow sweetness and rich plenty from the land—or could sting in anger, or even abandon the human settlement altogether, returning with her swarm to the wild woods.

The *Magna Mater* was also the goddess of death and of regeneration. The mystery of this cycle was seen in the ear of corn, which died yearly in the field, only to be reborn in spring. During the solstice festival of the Great Mother, a bull, representing the goddess's male consort, was sacrificed and, it was said, a swarm of bees arose from the dead carcass as the resurrected soul of the divine bull. Sometimes a lion was substituted for the bull, a connection dimly preserved in the Hebrew story of Samson, who kills a lion and later finds a swarm of bees in its carcass. He sums up the incident in the form of a riddle: "Out of the eater came forth meat, and out of the strong came forth sweetness"—a pithy summation of the hope offered by the great goddesses of antiquity.

After the Age of Silver came the Age of Bronze—the age of male gods, of warrior kings, of the heroes of *The Iliad.* The principle of organized aggression replaced the principle of fecundity, as the village became a walled city. The great goddesses were remembered in the attributes and mythical histories of the female members of the Greek pantheon—Aphrodite, Hera, Artemis, and Athena—but these goddesses, though powerful, were subject to Zeus, the law-giver. Nature now lived outside the city walls, personified in the nymphs of groves and grottoes, and in the goddesses of the wild places, whose messengers the wild bees sometimes were. Men still visited the ancient chthonic oracles, tended by the bee-priestesses—the chief oracle of Apollo at Delphi, the

Pythian, was called the "Delphic Bee." But the male gods had the ascendancy, especially the sky gods, whose principles were fixity and regularity, rather than metamorphosis and regeneration.

By the Age of Iron, which was also the age of empire, the wildness of the bee was nearly forgotten, as was her association with fecundity and regeneration. When the Romans ruled the world, what interested humans was not agriculture, but power politics. Consequently, what drew them to the bee was not the bee herself, or her honey, but her hive, which provided a handy metaphor for the hierarchy of the state. This can be clearly seen in Virgil's *Georgics*, written at the dawn of the reign of Augustus—when Roman power was consolidated under the absolute command of the emperor. The fourth book begins:

> *. . . I will show you a spectacle*
> *To marvel at, a world in miniature,*
> *Gallant commanders and the institutions*
> *Of a whole nation, its character, pursuits,*
> *Communities and warfare. Little the scale*
> *To work on, yet not little is the glory*
> *If unpropitious spirits do not cramp*
> *A poet and Apollo hears his prayer*

The "world in miniature" is not the world of fields and forests, but the world of Rome. Even the sex of the bee is disguised: Virgil refers to the leader of the hive as a "king," and uses the male pronoun when speaking of the workers. For Virgil, bees are not sacred, but *virtuous* and *civilized*, because unlike all other animals, the bees have *mores*, which enable them to show proper Roman discipline and frugality.

> *Alone they hold their progeny in common,*
> *Alone they share the housing of their city,*
> *Passing their lives under exalted laws,*
> *Alone they recognize a fatherland*
> *And the sanctity of a home, and provident*
> *For coming winter set to work in summer*
> *And store their produce for the common good.*

Virgil states that this "nature" was bestowed upon them by Zeus—implying it was not originally part of their behavior. This reflects the fact that most of the fourth *Georgic* consists of beekeeping advice—how to locate the hive, how to insure the vigor of the colony. Yet much of what he relates shows that the cultivation of bees was conservative, retaining rituals and beliefs that referred back to earlier epochs. For instance, Virgil explains how to get a swarm of bees to settle into the hive:

> *Observe: they make a beeline for fresh water*
> *Always, and leafy shelter. In such a spot*
> *Scatter the scents appointed, pounded balm*
> *And the humble honeywort; and raise a noise*
> *Of tinkling all around, and shake the cymbals*
> *Of the Mighty Mother. Of their own accord*
> *They'll settle in the fragrant quarters, bury*
> *Themselves instinctively in the inmost chambers.*

The "Mighty Mother" Virgil refers to is Cybele, the Phrygian *Magna Mater*, whose priests, called the *Curetes*, were known for their ritual use of the cymbal. According to Greek myth, when Zeus's father, Kronos, was devouring his children, Zeus's mother Rhea hid the infant god in a cave on Mount Dicte in Crete, where, it was said, the *Curetes* drowned out his wails with their "clashing bronzes," and bees, "drawn by the tuneful sounds," fed him with wild honey. Thus the tradition of tanging the swarm, still extant in the days of Gilbert White, unconsciously preserves the age of the goddess cults, and the knowledge that before Zeus was the Mighty Mother, whose power nourished and protected him.

For Virgil, of course, this was just a story: part of the entertainment. In his youth, Virgil was a disciple of Epicurus, whose philosophy of materialism reduced the sacred tales to mere stories—at best, allegories for literal events, at worst, mere literary embellishments. Epicurianism eschewed metaphysics, finding "ample grounds for wonder and joy in the perceptible universe and the omnipotent and omnipresent working of natural law," as classicist Ronald Latham puts it:

> *Epicurus sought to explain everything we perceive without positing the existence of anything other than material objects and the space in which they move, which is simply the absence of material objects. From this primary assumption everything else follows.*

This sounds like a modern attitude, and it is no coincidence. Modern science begins with the same Epicurean assumptions, put forth by Galileo and Descartes—who begat Newton and Locke. No wonder intellectuals of Gilbert White's generation felt they were living in a second Augustan Age: not only was the British Empire a new Rome, the New Science was a fulfillment of the Epicurean promise, and mankind had entered a new secular age, when the myths and superstitions of Medieval Europe could, like the gods and goddesses of antiquity, be banished to literature and art.

With one exception, of course, for the Age of Reason was not, as is sometimes believed, an age of atheism: rather, it was an age of religious materialism. For most scientific thinkers, the profound level of organization they perceived in Nature could only be attributable to the organizing activity of a Deity, whose primary characteristic was felt to be the principle of Reason. At the very heart of their science lies this faith: the world is founded upon an order, and beneath the unceasing chaos of phenomena, a mathematical structure will be descried, if one has the dedication of a Newton. For them, the world was a great machine, cunningly designed.

Thus, for the eighteenth-century naturalist, to study the bees meant to admire them as parts of the great machine. Their significance lay not in what they would say to us, but in how they, unthinking, irrational animals, could have such an intricate social organization—a phenomenon that pointed ultimately to the providence of the Creator. As Alexander Pope stated in his *Essay on Man*, which may be taken as a poetic summing-up of the thought of his age:

> *Who taught the nations of the field and wood*
> *To shun their poison, and to choose their food?*
> *Prescient, the tides or tempests to withstand.*
> *Build on the wave, or arch beneath the sand?*
> *. . . God in the nature of each being founds*
> *Its proper bliss, and sets its proper bounds. . .*

Gilbert White, standing before his beehive in Selborne, stands also at a particular cultural watershed. In pursuit of a true echo of nature, the scientific culture to which he belongs has ceased to believe that nature has a voice; the language of the bees has become the hum of ingenious machinery. There is an acknowledgement of this in the quote White uses to close his essay. It is taken from Lucretius, the Roman poet who, in *The Nature of the Universe*, popularized Epicurean philosophy for the Augustan age, and who was Virgil's first poetic mentor. In Book IV, Lucretius offers a material explanation of the phenomenon of the echo, after which he relates some of the popular superstitions echoes have given rise to:

> *Tales are told of Fauns, whose noisy revels and merry pranks shatter the*
> *mute hush of night for miles around; of twanging lyre-strings and plaintive*
> *melodies poured out by flutes at the touch of the players' fingers; of music*
> *far-heard by the country-folk when Pan, tossing the pine-branches that*

wreathe his brutish head, runs his arched lips again and again along the wide-mouthed reeds, so that the pipe's wildwood rhapsody flows on unbroken.

Lucretius is quick to condemn such peasant beliefs:

Many such fantasies and fairy tales are related by the rustics. Perhaps, in boasting of these marvels, they hope to dispel the notion that they live in backwoods abandoned even by the gods. Perhaps they have some other motive, since mankind everywhere has greedy ears for such romancing.

His own narrative of material causation puts to rest such inane romancing, and thus banishes the rustic fears of nymphs and satyrs. Lucretius assures his readers,

Once you have grasped this, you can explain to yourself and to others how it is that in desert places, when we are searching for comrades who have scattered and strayed among overshadowed glens and hail them at the pitch of our voices, the cliffs fling back the forms of our words in due sequence.

The modern world has inherited the legacy of Lucretius and Epicurus—our preferred narratives refer to chains of material causation, rather than to gods and fauns. Yet with each new causal explanation, we have seen the *Deus* recede ever farther from the Newtonian *machina*, leaving us, not with divine order, but with the whirling of merciless gears. The landscape of scientific realism Lucretius invokes has turned out to be a barren place of rocks and shadows, a wilderness into which the human subject has "scattered and strayed," a place where the human voice—seeking comradeship—is mockingly returned. It is a "backwoods," from which the god has withdrawn—as various philosophies of materialism have drained all the color and richness from nature, and we find ourselves lonely subjects in a labyrinth of unresponsive objects. Thus we have traded one kind of fear for another, and might find we envy the peasants their fauns—for such a world is at least alive.

For in our own century, the Sacred Bee of antiquity has become a faceless machine-being, and the metaphor of the hive has taken on a sinister aspect: it now represents *mindlessness*, the mechanical and soulless activity of chitinous automatons—the swarm, which excites such revulsion. In the twentieth century, especially, humans have fought against the notion of "depersonalization," which has taken the guise of a metamorphosis into an insect. Whereas the bee was once a sign of correspondence with mysterious richness, it now becomes an emblem of the decay of the individual before inhuman forces: the loss of consciousness, the descent into primal incoherence. In our science-fiction nightmares, the industrial city becomes a metal hive in which workers toil mindlessly under the absolute control of the Leader: the workers are expendable to the state, and all thought that is not hive-thought is severely punished. Where for the Romans the city was *mirrored* in the hive— was seen as a natural outcrop of the powers hidden deep in nature—now that very nature is feared as fate; the insect world is the world we descend to when we can no longer keep up the facade of humanity.

Ironically, the assumptions upon which much of this metaphor is based have been overturned. The bee, it turns out, is infinitely more complex than any machine—and so is the world. Science, whose method once promised to reveal ultimate order, has disclosed bewildering complexity instead—a universe that is open, non-linear, indeterminate. A universe not of indestructible atoms, but one of waves and vibrations, where time and space are one substance, malleable as beeswax.

We now know that, while Gilbert White was hailing them with his trumpet, the bees of Selborne were busy talking to each other in a language of their own devising: a language of dance, through which they told each other the quality, distance, and direction of the richest blooms. While it is true that bees and humans may never speak directly, the gap between them no longer seems so absolute, for the bees mastered the use of symbolic language long before humans, and it is this ability to speak to each other that has enabled them to build their rich combs. What the bees may have to say, if we listen closely, is that we are not alone. Nor are we set down in a barren valley that echoes only our own voices—we are part of a humming *plenum* of force, one of many intelligences in a chaotic, but ingenious swarm of life—which was surely what our ancestors wished to say with their legends of oracular and divine bees. Perhaps we have come to a point where we again need a kind of double-consciousness, an ability to see the world with both a scientific and a mythic eye. To quote Virgil once more:

> Blessed is he whose mind had power to probe
> The causes of things and trample underfoot
> All terrors and inexorable fate
> And the clamour of devouring Acheron;
> But happy too is he who knows the gods
> Of the countryside, knows Pan and old Silvanus
> And the sister Nymphs.

THE TRIBAL TAKE
ON ENVIRONMENTALISM

KIM

Around 1995 I was searching for reasons for my unease with the direction of the environmental movement. Those crystallized in recollections of my grandfather's stance toward nature, and those of many others.

Growing up in the 1960s I often went to the great north woods of Michigan to visit my grandfather's farm. "Farm" is a stretch, actually, to describe what he had: a three-room shack and a house trailer plunked down at the edge of scraggly cut-over and burned pineland. The steeply sloping landscape of Kalkaska County was heaped up gravel—or sand, depending on where you stood. My grandfather grew up on a farm near Petoskey, on more fertile soil to the north where sweet cherries, apples, and peaches ripened under the protective weather-making of Lake Michigan. After spending most of his adult life living and working in Detroit, he retired, in the sense of "found his ease," on land that the lords of timber scraped clean, then sold to farmers long on eagerness and short on sense. Ecological sense that is, for the morainal hills, once clothed in white and red pine—cut to become Chicago after the Great Fire or white frame farm houses at the corner of each midwestern square mile—turned out to be about the worst farmland God created. Maybe He created it just to cover it with pines, because that's about all it was—or is—good for growing.

My grandfather took over the burden of planting his ruined acres from the man who sold them to him, whose own imagination had caught fire with the idea of reclaiming the land from abuse. Like his predecessor, my grandfather planted pine, spruce, and fir on bracken-clothed slopes, wind-swept ridges, and other spaces still treeless. As we walked the plantations on our visits, checking the crop, it seemed to me that he knew each seedling individually. "This little fella's having trouble," he declared, bending down to cup the leader in his hand. "Can't get enough water in this blowout. Well, maybe we'll get rain in time." He'd lost the last digit of his right thumb in a factory accident. I stared where it clasped the seedling, the skin of its tip puckering into a dimple. When he let go, the seedling sprang upright, its browning leaves aquiver.

There were porcupines in the area, and from time to time, as will happen, one of them ate a pine tree. They stripped the bark from the branches and upper trunk of a tree, sometimes killing it. They worked on birch, aspen, oak, red maple, and the other pioneers of that droughty land, but young pine seemed a favorite. My grandfather, who also loved pine, saw no common ground. One Friday night when we arrived, he regaled us with the story of an unlucky porcupine. "They'll take the tip of the young pine and nip it right off," he said, gripping his shortened thumb between index and middle finger for emphasis. "Right off! Then they don't grow straight, if at all. The porcupines climb up into the saplings, bend them right over and nip them off. Well . . ." he paused for effect. "We got 'im. Yup. Had a dog and got 'im up in a tree. Then I shot him. Had to keep the dog away, or he'd have gotten a face full of quills. Yup. Treed 'im and shot 'im."

A shallow lake on the old lake plain of Upper Michigan, near the Tahquamenon River.

At that instant I disliked my grandfather, though I knew him well and porcupines not at all. This old man who talked easily of snuffing out a life suddenly appeared cruel, unforgiving and stupid. I wanted to shout at him, blame him for killing an animal that wasn't dangerous at all. How could eating a pine deserve the death penalty? Of course, I said nothing.

Over a decade later I met my grandfather's double. I was a biological surveyor working under contract. I was paid little and camped out to save money, but I was doing what I loved: scouting the land for vestiges of pre-Columbian America. Old growth forests, pristine prairies, undrained wetlands, dunes and swales with nary a trace of human history. Poring over maps and aerial photographs, deciphering land survey records from a century ago, following footstep by footstep the trail of dead naturalists, I played Sherlock Holmes, searching the landscape for clues to natural wonder. As a bonus, I was given a government car to save wear and tear on my own.

One overcast day in late spring I pulled up in front of a fastidious split-level home on a street that ended at Lake Michigan. Somewhere behind the house lay my quarry—forty acres of old forest I had spotted on a 1976 air photo. With luck, it was still there. The plat map showed it to be owned by the county, surrounded on three sides by subdivision. The area was succumbing to vacation and retirement homes like most of Lake Michigan's southern shore.

I got out of my car. The air was tinged with the scent of damp sand. Sand underlaid everything, and the original forests on the flat ancient lake beds and outwash had white pine and red pine in them. These were easy to grab in the logging era, so today virtually none remain, except by roads and railroads where saplings from that time survived and grew to behemoths of nine- to twelve-foot girth. The woods I wanted once had pine, but I'd find only their decaying stumps in a stand of mature oaks. It was public land, and I didn't need permission to walk it, but no road led directly to the woods. I did need to talk to somebody about crossing their land to get to it. This home was as close as I could get by road, so this was the somebody I would ask.

He was in the back yard, visible from where I parked. I waved and called hello as I walked toward him. He looked up from his task, a stocky man about my height, dressed in khaki from head to toe. He wore a billed cap with a low crown. It reminded me of a little black cap my grandfather wore, very much of an old style, not like the modern baseball cap with feed company logos emblazed thereon. The man's work boots were old but polished. He stood erect and nodded as I approached. As I got closer he looked to be about seventy, with a slight smile visible that I took to mean he had a mischievous bent. As I reached him he looked at the emblem on my car and said, "So, the state's sent you out on an errand, eh?" I chuckled and replied, "Kind of. I'm doing survey work. There's an old forest back there that I want to check. It's county land. Could I walk across your land to get there?" He stopped smiling. "What do you want with that woods?"

I replied, "Well, I work with a group doing an inventory of forests, wetlands, prairies, and dunelands. We want to find out how much is undeveloped and where it is. No-one's studied this before." His eyes had narrowed while I talked, but I didn't feel I needed to explain more. I only wanted to cross his land, an innocent request. If he refused, I would drive up the road a couple houses and try there.

He suddenly laughed and said, "Come over here and look at this." I was surprised, but followed him to the edge of his lot. We stood in front of half a dozen white pine saplings, about four feet high, growing thriftily under the shade of the scattered oaks. "I planted these four years ago from roots the state forester gave me." He looked at me for my reaction. "Now these preservationist types, they get on my nerves. We've been doing this kind of thing for years, and now they say it's all wrong. They claim we're wrecking the earth. Hmmmph!" I didn't want to be dragged in, so I asked, "Is that the woods over there?" He glanced in the right direction and frowned. "You know I got more birds coming to my feeder than anybody has a right to. Lookit there now— pine siskins! They've been coming all winter, and now they ought to be thinking about heading north again. Any day now."

This man was like my grandfather. He fed birds and planted pines. Then he powered up a green rider-mower to slash off the heads of oak, cherry and sassafras upstarts expanding their wild world at the edge of the woods, the only patch of unbridled nature in the neighborhood. I put it plainly, "Can I walk out there?" He looked down then waved me on, turning and walking back to the pile of dirt he was digging in when I drove up. The mood had changed, and I hoped I wouldn't see him on my way out.

I finished my survey in thirty minutes. Keeping to my schedule, I gave the living land a stingy half hour to describe the culmination of 11,000 years of changes beginning when the ice sheet melted and filled Lake Michigan to the brim. I'd given it short shrift as usual. Emerging from the scrim of saplings and shrubs at the wood's edge, I spied my conservation friend with his back to me. He was digging. I walked slowly, cracking sticks with my boots to let him know I was coming. I dreaded the encounter. He stood up and turned to face me. I tried to get by him with a quick, "Thanks very much! Sorry to bother you," but he wouldn't hear of it. He blocked my path.

"See here now. That land belongs to everybody around here. We all use it." (I'd noticed the lawn clipping piles and discarded Christmas wreaths, but I kept silent.) "Just who do you think you are? Waltzing in here and walking across my land like you owned it. What are you doing, exactly? Who are you working for?" I looked past him to the car. I said, "I told you. I'm doing a survey. That woods is part of it. It's county land."

His eyes blazed. "No it's not. It belongs to the people living here. It's ours." His eyes ranged, as if searching for a weapon. They settled on me. I held his gaze, trying to understand what was happening. "What's your name?" he said. I told him. "Who's your supervisor. I want his name and telephone number. I'm gonna report you." I looked incredulously at him. "Why?" "Never mind why, you just tell me his name and phone." I shook my head and started walking around him. He leaned in, then thought better of it and let me go. He followed me to my car, shouting, "I'm going to report you. I've got your license number. I know who you are. I know who you are!" I saw him in my rear-view mirror, in the road shaking his fist. I took a deep breath and tried to clear my head to decide where I should drive next.

Green as an aspen sucker, I didn't realize I'd been bent (a little bit) by the windy emotion and attitude of "anti-environmentalism." There was no such name back then, but today it's called the "Wise Use" movement, an ideology that started in the unfocused vastness of America's western lands. This kind of activism says that ordinary citizens should decide the fate of public and private lands in their neighborhood. Innocent enough, until you discover that the movement's national organizers are funded by oil and gas interests, timber and mining companies, and off-road vehicle manufacturers. That said, the recurrent "rebellions" that sweep our country—the "Sagebrush" being the most memorable recent one—surely are symptom of something unhappy on the minds of American people. The huge companies that sidle up to local anti-environmental sentiment, ironically, are the greatest force for destroying a local community's future by exploiting resources for short-term gain. Their vast reserves of cash unleash changes communities are helpless to resist. Yet communities turn to this dark force in their lives for help because the alternative—environmentalists—are viewed as worse.

Why is this so? Are anti-environmentalists telling us something we ought to listen to, and fix? Sometimes I think we come off as bullies to communities, seeming to lack respect for local custom and behavior and demanding that people change and become more like us. Maybe anti-environmentalism is asking us an awfully scary question: Should we environmentalists change and become more like locals?

In the middle 1980s the U.S. Forest Service was reeling from lawsuits filed against it for flagrantly violating its own management plans, a ten-year process called for under the 1976 National Forest Management Act. Though not as virulent as in the Pacific Northwest, the debate in the Upper Lakes States had the potential to become nastier than our polite veneers were used to. To defuse some of the emotion, a committee was formed. The Forest Service regional office out of Milwaukee provided a chairperson and support, while representatives from the timber industry, state and county government, and conservation groups eyed each other suspiciously across paper-strewn tables.

My way of helping was to try to persuade everyone we needed a map showing the capacity of the land to produce trees—an ecological roadmap of the region—assuming that, if we all started with the same basic information, we'd have an easier time communicating about the thorny stuff, like which trees to cut where.

During a break at an early committee meeting, I found myself standing next to an activist from the local Audubon Council. She wore an environmentalist uniform. For women it consists of mid-calf boots that meet a mid-calf skirt, preferably of seasonable cotton or wool, a denim shirt in summer, a largish sweater in winter, and hair worn long and tied back. Sometimes a blouse hinting at exotic locales may be worn. For outdoors work and for men, it's khaki and denim, with hiking boots. Casual shoes and blazer are optional.

She squinted at me sideways biting into a donut. While she chewed I commented, "I think people are warming up to this map idea. It would really help us out, don't you think?" She stopped chewing, swallowed, then spoke, "I think you've sold out." I raised my eyebrows and laughed. She took another bite and repeated her charge. "Why?" I asked. "You're too ready to compromise," she replied. "You don't take a stand. You let them suck you in and you become just like them. You've sold your soul." I looked incredulous, I'm sure. She just smiled.

I think we do have a problem. Environmentalism is accused by some of being a religion. I don't think that's right, because George Bush said he is an environmentalist, yet I know he's Episcopalian. Environmentalism isn't a religion, though it is practiced religiously. That's where we get into trouble. Henry David Thoreau said in his tract *On the Duty of Civil Disobedience*:

> Action from principle—the perception and the performance of right—changes things and relations; it is essentially revolutionary, and does not consist wholly with any thing which was. It not only divides states and churches, it divides families, aye, it divides the individual, separating the diabolical in him from the divine.

When I read these words recently, I dutifully walked to my bookshelf and pulled out the King James Version of the Bible, which Thoreau's words caused to resonate in my head. Jesus said,

> Think not that I am come to send peace on earth; I came not to send peace, but a sword. For I am come to set a man at variance against his father, and the daughter against her mother, and the daughter-in-law against her mother-in-law. And a man's foes shall be they of his own household. (Matthew 10:34-36)

Being revolutionaries, Jesus and Thoreau wanted to change relationships—people to God, people to people, people to the world around them. When someone like my grandfather or his Lake Michigan doppel-gänger plants a pine tree, he creates one kind of relationship with the land that people notice and are influenced by. When he needlessly kills something in nature, out of habit or bad training, that is another matter. When I declined to tell my grandfather about his absurd and useless killing act, I refused to be a revolutionary. But when I say that things have gone far enough, that killing a varmint, or keeping "them weeds" at bay with a mower, opposes nature in a silly and meaningless way, then I urge revolt against what is customary. This plays out in ways that make environmentalists "outsiders," no matter who or where they are.

While in graduate school I enjoyed visiting some old family friends who lived in one of those sprawling developments astride the ancient sand dunes of Lake Michigan. The area felt entirely two-faced, its curb-and-gutter streets running true up the steep cuts in the dune fields and down the backsides, while behind each manicured lawn and ranch-style home the eternal forest crowded in, its wildly undulant floor bestrewn with bead-lily, mayflower, sedges, and a host of diverse flowers. A short walk through these woods brought me to the big lake's front door, its breeze constant under a high pressure system, or its surface flat and leaden beneath a gray sky.

One morning as we stood in the back yard, the family cat—top predator now, with the wolf, cougar and bobcat gone—pounced in the tiny lawn backing up to the woods. It caught a shrew, a common forest animal on nobody's legislative list of things to care about. But to my knowledge it had a place here, just as the barred owl that ate it did. I jumped off the deck at the cat, startling it. The shrew dropped to the ground and scampered. I clapped my hands to rattle the cat and give the rodent the time it needed. "Hey!" shouted my host, a gregarious man, a successful man. "Don't do that! Those moles mess up the lawn!" Considering the sparse shaded grass, its patches of dun sand, his concern didn't register with me.

But I delayed, and the cat was back on the shrew, so I grabbed him. "What are you doing?" shouted the man, "Let him have it!" He'd stepped towards me, anger rising in his voice, his fist pointed at me. No trace of the voluble host who'd welcomed me boisterously the day before. "Let him have it," he repeated.

I didn't. I held the cat until the shrew was back in the woods. My host turned away, ran his hand through his graying crew-cut, then stamped back and forth on his deck, head down. The people around him were uncomfortable, making small talk as they glanced at me coming to them. My wife pulled me aside and said, "Why didn't you just let the cat have the mouse? Now everybody's upset!" Not true, I thought; I'm happy. This well-fed cat, healthy, warm in winter and safe from predators, ate more than its fair share of birds and small mammals that otherwise were food for needier creatures who lived in the woods. It was a recreational killer. From an ecological standpoint, it disrupted the normal relationships in the forest, made them less whole, less perfect. I knew this because I'd read the scientific papers on predation by dogs and cats, my education bolstered by observations over the years. Yet by acting on "my truth" I changed my relations with that family forever.

We environmentalists do have a problem. My small rebellion did nothing to stop development of sand dunes, nor cut down on cats eating shrews. It certainly cast a pall over relations with friends and family, even if only for a moment. It was revolutionary, upsetting the usual course of events in that neighborhood. It depended on somebody knowing the "truth"—about nature that is—and acting on it. That is what environmentalism is about.

Which means that by its nature environmentalism puts people in a bad mood because somebody is telling them what to do, based on an absolute authority residing in scientific fact. How do people affect the natural world? Let me tell you! Human nature just hates a know-it-all. If a person also dresses funny, or doesn't act naturally—fusses about "rats" and "weeds" and "pests"— so much the more grating when they lay down the law. I'm afraid we environmentalists are guilty on many counts of not fitting in, and that gets us in trouble with people who do fit in, namely people who've lived in one place for generations and have a pretty strong notion of what goes on "hereabouts."

At the same time, I don't apologize for saving that little guy's life. He deserved it much more than that pampered cat did its precious carnivore thrill. My host's opinion about the peskiness of the shrew was superficial and wrong. Maybe the shrew did make a mess of the lawn, but the climate and droughty sands made an even bigger mess of it. Living there a dozen years but never seeing really—focused on home as "base of operations" for wider travels—my host knew little about where he lived. I knew more walking among the oaks, maples and beech trees, feeling the cool in the heat of the day, noting the fingers of sand cresting a hill, the beach grass binding against gravity and the wind. I had the greater authority to speak about lawns, soils, and shrews. But for all that, what did I accomplish when I did?

Recently I was at a meeting of the Farm Bureau, a conservative organization that lobbies in Washington for, among other things, the repeal of the Endangered Species Act. When I arrived I was made to feel very welcome by two staff people I knew—we'd worked together on a series of meetings among farmers, environmentalists and government agencies for the continuation of a federal land retirement program, the Conservation Reserve.

After a light lunch, we walked to the meeting room. I was introduced to people who farmed in the area, there to develop local policy for the national policy group who would lobby to make their ideas come true. My place was pointed out, at a table near the podium, and I sat down next to a woman talking animatedly with her neighbors. She was a blond farm wife, hair pulled back in a ponytail, late forties, energetic and accustomed to being listened to. Women actually doing farming are rare in the Midwest, but a woman on a farm often does bookkeeping or runs some essential part of the operation, while directing her children's lives and being active in the community. Many work outside the home. They are modern, yet grounded in tradition.

I couldn't help overhear, and immediately realized she and the man next to her were talking about the Endangered Species Act. "What was it, some kind of a rat?" the man asked the woman. "A kangaroo rat," she said, disgust in her voice. "The agents just walked right into his field while he was plowing and arrested him. Confiscated his equipment and put him in jail. Over a rat!" They all shook their heads. Another woman spoke, "There was a good article on that in *American Farm* last month. I made copies for everybody I knew." People nodded their heads. "There oughta be a law to protect the real endangered species, the farmer!" quipped the blond woman.

I squirmed. This piece of legislation, the most potent tool for habitat preservation we've got, hasn't stopped more than a few dozen projects —out of tens of thousands—in the twenty-three years since enactment. More often it simply forces people to talk to each other and share information. The result is better stewardship of our land. But as with the snail darter at Tellico Dam—a boondoggle to create a recreational lake for big resort development—it's the most extreme case that gets the attention. Here was a notorious new example of the excessive force the Endangered Species Act wielded, and the room was abuzz with this and other affronts to their farming way of life.

The policy session would be sharp-edged, I was sure, but first I was to speak. When the time came, I gamely strode to the front, smiling gently. "You might wonder why an environmental group wants to work with the Farm Bureau," I began. Just then I wondered myself, but I went on, "It's because we both work with the land and care about it." I continued from there, explaining our common ground. After polite applause, I got questions about several festering issues: "Can you help us get the state to control weeds on its land?" "Weren't you the ones who didn't allow spraying on your land to control grasshoppers?" But after I answered, they allowed me to sit down without bringing up what was on everybody's mind, "How can you stand behind unreasonable legislation that tramples people rights and renders them powerless?"

If they had asked, my answer—my righteous answer—would have been "I have true information given to me by careful scientific study, which proves the following . . ." But I would have flunked the test. There's too much history, too much bad blood between the environmental movement and those it would move. Impassioned speeches on behalf of nature do not move the people—kangaroo rats and tiny fish have never been as important to modern Americans as people and their needs. Information doesn't move them. The *Scientific American* pitted against the *Farm Journal*: which carries greater weight amidst corn, soybeans, and straight-line roads strung with small towns like beads on a necklace?

If scientific information isn't to be believed, what is? The anti-environmental movement insists that we rely on common sense to fix our environmental ills. This is, of course, impossible. René Dubos supposedly said, "Ecosystems are not only more complex than we know, they are more complex than we can know." A space shuttle isn't designed using common sense. Prevailing wisdom doesn't lead to breakthroughs in physics. Nature is infinitely more complex than any human construction. Non-science won't help communities manage their natural resources better. The huge mistrust of scientific information used by environmentalists prevents significant change in the way people treat the land.

Early in my career I served on an environmental advisory group to a city's government. We debated the dangers of herbiciding weeds in playgrounds, discussed zoning changes in burgeoning strips displacing woods and fields, and nitpicked around the periphery of the city's business. In those days I knew the enemy. They suffered from wrong values. Nature was grist for their money mill, or a friend's money mill.

At one meeting the city's head engineer, who always surprised me by wearing red socks and bow ties, couldn't understand why I opposed giving the local river a severe dredging for the way it emptied itself onto its own floodplain. Though natural for rivers, flooding was unnatural to engineers and an inconvenience to some of the city's voters. I argued that the floodplain itself held water back, lowering the river's level to the benefit of people living downstream. Scientifically I was right, as recent analysis of the 1993 floods on the Mississippi system proved. But these studies weren't available, much less front page news in the *New York Times* as they are today. As I took different tacks on the same argument, the engineer grew more agitated. He alternately sat up and leaned back, swiveled in his chair, hands outspread as he argued—not to me—to the rest of the committee. In the end we voted not to oppose the dredging.

I don't think the vote went against me because I couldn't muster up the facts. I think the decision was more about who I was, and how I spoke. The man's red socks were a contradictory flight of iconoclasm, in my mind, because he seemed fossilized with his dusty ideas about hydrology. It was easy to think how dense he was, impenetrable even by the bullet of logic. I tried explaining the idea a dozen times, in simple language, in complex, yet he was unmoved. Still in school, wearing jeans and a plaid shirt, I looked young, inexperienced, and came across as an upstart and ignorant of the plain facts of the situation. It was easy for the others to dismiss and be mad at me, as it was easy for me to write my opponents off as rubes and blockheads.

Scientists are part of the problem here. We are by nature researchers, not disseminators of information. Our basic personality is that of the introvert. Research is ultimately a solitary act. We specialize to stay at the cutting edge of our field, we turn inward in a fit of pure thought to posit our hypotheses, invest mightily in rigorous studies, and vie for the approval of our peers and a place in scientific journals. By contrast, we need to face environmental issues by patiently fence-building with local people and governments, discussing the most trivial and mundane of scientific ideas, getting to know and like the people we are educating, and being liked in turn. The local community is a scary place for scientists. It is vague, ever-changing, complex, and defies simple description and analysis. Even scarier, if we advocate that change is needed, even if our research supports it, we fear being accused of bias, which would call into question our credibility as dispassionate observers.

The household shall be divided against itself, yea, even the individual, into the divine and the diabolical. Sure, that's one way to look at it. It's often said—I say it myself—that we need the extremes to keep the center honest. Lined up from left to right, Earth First!, Greenpeace, Sierra Club, Environmental Defense Fund, and so on, are the pit-bull brigade against environmental slippage. Just today I was hit by one of these group's scatter-shot e-mails regarding the weakening of the Endangered Species Act, urging me to call the White House comment line or fax in my opposing voice. And don't forget to send us a check. Honestly, I am grateful to them, and I might call the White House, but I don't think I can send them a check whenever they raise the alarm. Washington is a world and a plane of existence away from everyday America, where most of the environmental problems reside. In the long run can we enviros hope to change America in fundamental ways needed by the environment by squaring off good against evil, and fighting it out? I think not.

Thoreau's British contemporary, John Ruskin, said,

> There are three material things, not only useful, but essential to life. No one knows how to live till he has got them. These are pure air, water, and earth. There are three immaterial things, not only useful, but essential to life. No one knows how to live till he has got them also. These are admiration, hope, and love.

Although he was reduced to confused and lofty pronouncements late in his life, at the height of his powers, this champion of landscape painting, of beauty and art, had an optimistic view of his fellow creatures. A highly spiritual man, Ruskin reminds me of Jesus, who no doubt Ruskin looked to for inspiration: "But I say unto you, Love your enemies, bless them that curse you, do good to them that hate you, and pray for them which despitefully use you, and persecute you" (Matthew 5:44). Jesus was a savvy guy. Knowing that not only would his disciples preach Christianity as a religion, they would preach it religiously, he warned them to get along with people. "Agree with thine adversary quickly, whiles thou art in the way with him; lest at any time the adversary deliver thee to the judge, and the judge deliver thee to the officer, and thou be cast into prison" (Matthew 5:25). "Moreover, if thy brother shall trespass against thee, go and tell him his fault between thee and him alone: if he shall hear thee, thou hast gained thy brother" (Matthew 19:15).

But his consummate advice for being neighborly is "Judge not, that ye be not judged" (Matthew 7:1). For an environmentalist, this is a paradox. In the environmental movement, how can one stand aloof from this world in order to view the world more clearly, from a scientific and ecological vantage, then point out the blatant problems and advocate their solutions without judging? Judging is an essential part of the cognitive process, and we would not be effective on behalf of the environment without it. Yet this advice from an ancient revolutionary asks us to be a walking contradiction—both a compass simultaneously pointing due north and awhirl in a moving magnetic field.

Can the environmentalist maintain a clarity of purpose while "living with the enemy"? I remember a colleague griping that Forest Service staff was no help in enforcing forest management laws. "How can they stand up for what's right?" he said. "Their children go to school with loggers' children. They buy at the same stores. They go to the same church and social events." The point is valid. How can you bring hardship—real or imagined—to the people you constantly associate with?

I would venture to say it is possible, but very hard. The self must be divided into—not the diabolical and divine, which are part of every person—but into the worldly and the celestial, the ephemeral and the eternal, the common wisdom and wisdom of the ages. Holding fast to the ideal of people in more perfect union with the natural world, an environmentalist must be a cagey salesperson for nature, knowing the product inside and out and tailoring it to the personal situation of every prospective customer. Does this sound crass? I think it is, too, but on the one hand we have ecologically purist rhetoric that leaves no room for people to muddle through, and on the other we have compromised problem-solving that gives nature the shaft. Facing up to the ugly truth that our society largely finds nature expendable is the first step in curing Pollyannaism and appeasement both. After that, the only compromise you make is one of style—you basically have to like the person you're selling nature to. For many people this is hard. I wonder sometimes if some environmentalists—and anti-environmentalists—find strength to get up in the morning by knowing they have an enemy to fight that day.

Even when I like the people I'm selling nature to, it's hard to change their minds. My family used to visit some friends who lived on a lake north of Detroit. After graduate school I occasionally dropped in during my survey circuit through the burgeoning northern suburbs. Their lake was caught in a downward spiral of nutrient enrichment; the phosphorus and nitrogen delivered to its waters every rainstorm caused explosions of underwater plants and algae which fell to the lake bottom when they died, where bacteria consumed them and most of the oxygen in the lake. A classic case of eutrophication. The lakeshore owners' answer was to pay into a community pot and hire an aquatic lawn mower to snip off the water weeds and haul the clippings away to be landfilled or spread on a farmer's field.

Fresh from graduate school where I had learned all about eutrophication, I decided on one of my visits to plant a little seed of doubt in the minds of this family. I naively hoped it would take root, flourish, and their behavior would change. One day when the father had just finished mowing the exotic bluegrass sod to within an inch of its life, clear down to the lapping waves, I seized the moment. "When you cut the lawn that short, and put fertilizer on it, you send nutrients into your lake. That's what brings on the weeds," I explained. I expected a reasoned reply, cautious but open to my idea. The father stared at me. His wife was standing nearby, and a funny look came over her face. She said, "We always cut the lawn. So does everybody. The weeds aren't a problem." Slightly taken aback, I continued, a little lamely, "If you'd let the grass get a little taller under the oaks, it would filter the run-off, see?" I had noticed sprigs of native sedges under the oaks, and the lopped off leaves of some wildflowers. All was not lost. Balance could be restored, if they would let it happen.

The father said firmly, "If we don't mow, it looks like hell." That was the end of the discussion. He rolled the mower up the hill. His wife stood nearby, then asked if I needed anything. I said, no, but what I really needed was a lesson in human nature. Inevitably people are inclined to continue what they've always done, rather than take on the untested and unfamiliar. Change comes slowly. Culture changes over decades or centuries. Cultural change doesn't happen with advocacy, although that helps identify the issues.

There is a place I dread going. It's a nature preserve where for two decades my company has waged war with the neighbors. It's a bad neighborhood for nature, and as nature's representatives thereabouts, we are *personae non grata*. Still, each meeting with one of the neighbors gets us all a little more familiar with each other, and a little less likely to yell. At first I believed some of them were born mad, their poor mothers subjected to abuse from the minute they came out of the womb, but now I chalk it up to people protecting their own interests, their own ideas about how the world works, their own ways of doing things. And people fighting and lashing out at outsiders who try to overturn any long-held belief. It's no different, a sociologist would explain, than entering the territory of an Amazonian tribe. You learn the local customs, or risk being killed. Nothing so terrible would happen here, but the impolite equivalent is loosed on the outsider who doesn't behave.

People are instinctively tribal, drawing strength from their close-knit group against other tribes that threaten their interests. As a German with some English in me and a touch of Welsh, I know my ancestors lived in tribes a scant 1,500 years ago. Some of humanity still live in such tribes. Why is it surprising that in America today tribes coalesce for the common defense? Modern tribes are legion: Wall Street brokers, Montana ranchers, Iowa farmers, young inner city African-Americans. How can environmentalists enter these tribes, gain their trust, speak to them in defense of nature?

If you are smart and lucky enough, the tribe accepts you, perhaps as an oddity, but there you are. It happens. I know a man with one foot in the natural world, the other in the urgency of agricultural production. He is a farmer by choice, and by passion an expert in butterflies. I often stopped by his place, 160 acres of bottomland in southwestern Michigan, during my excursions about the countryside in search of biotic relicts from the past. My visits were somewhat of an occasion for him since every last one of his neighbors was in the mold of my grandfather—in their own mind conservationists, in practice, sentimental destroyers. They conserved what they valued—namely their lifestyle and place in the world, certain practices and customs, and especially the idea that they are stewards of the land. This despite proof of the opposite: increasing their use of chemicals yearly, tearing out hedgerows to accommodate bigger equipment, and depending on fewer and more specialized breeds of plants.

He had a place on a stream that he farmed using what are called now "sustainable" practices—cutting back on the doses of fertilizer and chemicals, leaving a wooded cushion around his stream—letting nature be, as much as that's possible while cutting and turning the ground.

On my visits he would ceremoniously pull his flat wooden specimen boxes from under the bed or atop the chest of drawers in the dining room, lay them on the table, and place two beers straddling the boxes, which we'd drink while comparing notes. I usually started by telling him about my forays in his neck of the woods: the undiscovered prairie meadows I stumbled on, the rare plant not seen in fifty years, the disappointment of a 140-year-old oak forest shattered by chainsaws two weeks earlier, where I'd smelled the bittersweet almond of severed black cherry heavy in the air, the smell of regret.

I was fascinated, and a little unnerved, by Bill's situation. One night, sitting in his small dining room around a worn table, the light from a ceiling lamp casting gloom into the corners, he told me about his neighbors. Expecting the high-minded rant I was used to from naturalists and biologists frustrated by the nature-destroying attitudes abroad in the land, Bill surprised me. He swept his right arm across the table, clearing an invisible layer of debris, and brought his hands together, fingers resting on the sides of his bottle of budget beer. "You know," he began, "when I started farming, I was going to change the world. I watched my dad go from using no chemicals, and scarcely a drop of fertilizer, to a man utterly dependent on the sales-person at the co-op, a guy who didn't know a hill of beans from diddly-squat. I vowed I wouldn't fall into the same trap." "Yeah?" I replied, not knowing where this was going. "I'll tell you," he continued tipping his head towards me, "my neighbors can't see it any other way. Every year they get a new corn hybrid, and they need to put a certain herbicide on to control weeds, and a particular pesticide to cut down on root worm, and they need to fertilize it. And if they do all this, they get a big fat crop and get rich. Why would they want to do anything differently? I'll be standing there talking to them, and they've gone and bulldozed a piece of woods, or tiled a wet spot in their field, and I'll say, 'Did you need that little piece too?' And they'll say, 'Hell, yes, that's $1,000 waiting for somebody to claim it.' And they're right, you know. I can tell them that wood frogs live in that pond, or that little woods was the only place I knew where ginseng grows, but what's that compared to money?"

He swept the table again with his hand, and looked at the delta of tabletop visible between his arms. "What about all the money they spend on chemicals and fertilizers?" I asked. "What about all the time and expense to run the tractor? Doesn't that cut their profit?" Bill smiled. "That's just capital expense. You can write that off." He raised his palms, then brightened. "Hey, you wanna see something?" "Sure, what is it?" Bill stood up and disappeared into another room. I heard a sliding sound, then he reappeared with a broad, flat wooden box. He set it on the table, stepped away and beamed. It was a specimen box, two and a half feet square and about four inches high, of a fine-grained varnished wood. A glass lid set into grooves slid away to expose the contents. Bill leaned forward and opened it. "This is my first collection. I took all these when I was just getting started. I was a kid, and didn't know what I was doing. But once I got going, I was hooked."

The reason was plain. The wings of dozens of native butterflies, from the smallest hairstreak and copper to the giant swallowtail, sent back to my eye the transformed light of the overhead lamp. My mind thirstily received the silver spatters on the wings of fritillaries, the orange-and-black contention displayed by the monarch and viceroy, and the graduated indigo night sky of the red-spotted purple. Each species conjured up a place where, learning the trade, I first saw it darting through trees, or disappearing behind a clump of marsh grass. As we stood there admiring, the world shrank to specific moments of recall, each an echo of our happy inventory of the woods and meadows hereabouts. The collection of pinned and dried bugs was not petrified color and form, but time crystallized, whose bottle cork we could unstop so we might again experience the taste of our lives already lived. Bill turned to me and said, "Guess you know where I spent most of my time when I wasn't working on my dad's farm." I understood. The living world was a magnet for people like us, a kind of drug to which we returned again and again. If we took something away with us when we returned to the hardened city, to the scrambled earth of tilled ground, it went beyond specimens and field notes—to the core of our being, where a soul waits for sustenance. It was no less powerful than love we felt for our wives, our children, our home place, yet it was more alien and aloof, able to do without us, while the bonds we formed within the human culture, if severed, damaged many more than just ourselves. Nature did not need me, or Bill, to carry on. And yet, clearly, it needed us. It needed Bill kicking clods of earth while he talked about the flush of geometrid moths that fed warblers passing through everybody's back forty. It needed me heading for unfriendly territory, to dispute over which was better—water backed up in a marsh, or rushing down a drain tile.

When I worry about going over to the "other side," becoming "like them," I reach back to memories of a natural world that needs advocates. Once I stood at the brink of winter, locating myself in the very center of the biggest undrained bog in Kalamazoo County. Around me was the familiar olive green of leatherleaf, hinting of silver, the rising gurgle of amber water in my boot prints, and the casual droop of tamarack branches. Cars and trucks droned distantly on the interstate and the county road that clasped this bog as between pinchers. It was a vestige, really, no more able to withstand future development in the area than a newborn animal can survive separation from its mother. Suddenly the flit of wings, a short stutter in my ears, as a flock of juncos ganged into the clearing where I stood. They were followed by the cheerful scold of chickadees, then the white-throated sparrow's plaintive whistle. Standing stock still, I became part of a marauding flock of birds, moving and feeding together. I could have touched the ones hanging from nearby limbs, leaned and tapped the heads of those who clung to the leatherleaf at my knees. At a few ounces each, this flock of birds didn't amount to much—a handful of feathers, beaks, and bones. The bog amounted to a little more because of the water and space it held, but in ten years, ringed by homes, ditched all around to present the illusion of lakeside living, it would change into something else, something tamer, more familiar to us all . . . cattails maybe.

When I was a surveyor, earning my living by walking the variously firm and spongy ground of the world, and feeling that much more connected to it, I was fervent in my love for the Earth. If I had stood still, my feet would have rooted and my arms become fixed on heaven for light and sustenance. At no time else in my conservation career have I witnessed so immediately the reasons for preserving the bounty and beauty of nature, and at no time since have I been as penetrated by the violence of its destruction, which I absorbed daily. I saw it in the bog water that bled into ruts of caterpillar tractors which hauled 200-year-old cedar boles away for slivering into roofing shingles. I saw it in streams hollowed out and swept barren by mightier flooding that new concrete, asphalt and roofing tiles brought on. It was for all to see at field edges where bulldozers toppled woods to make room for more corn or shoved dirt into wetlands for building space.

Facing devastation that wiped away what I cared most about, how could I admire and love, much less hope for, the good in my fellows? Mortals are not made who can dispassionlessly watch violence at work. If someone told me, "Go live with them, young man," I would have easier forgotten my training as an ecologist and become a tax attorney or car salesman.

That place I spoke of earlier, where I dread going . . . I'll be going there next week to meet with a man who wants something from me. He wants me to help him keep his drain tiles flowing, drying out his fields so he can plant early, by obtaining a legal agreement from my company, a conseservation non-profit. I am justifiably suspicious. When we met two weeks ago he told me "all the permits are taken care of," yet just yesterday when I asked about specific permits, he said he didn't have them. Maybe we were talking past each other, and it was a simple misunderstanding, but maybe not. I can't tell. And being in hostile territory, I'm naturally inclined to be cautious. As we stood by a ditch that received the field drainage before spitting it into the neighborhood creek, talking the details of the tile system, I summed up my position: "We want to be good neighbors, but we don't want to open up our land to damage. What you want could damage it, expose the soil and introduce alien weeds that crowd out the native plants. Just like you want to be good stewards of your land, keeping soil erosion to a minimum, we want to be good stewards of ours. We'll work with you, but we can't give you everything you want." While I was talking he stared at the trees lining the creek bank. When I finished he took a few steps away, then came back to lean on the car. "Now I want to say something. You mention erosion. You ever been to the Grand Canyon?" I averred. "What's the Grand Canyon? It's the result of erosion! Erosion is natural. I get pretty upset when people start talking about farmers creating erosion—not that you said it. It's just a sore subject, is all."

I don't blame him for feeling put upon. In the 1930s soil erosion was public enemy number one, as far as the U.S. Department of Agriculture was concerned. The research their scientists conducted on ways to slow erosion is still valid today. However, in the 1950s and again in the 1970s the USDA reversed its position, encouraging continuous rotations and fence-to-fence plowing, sure-fire pre-scriptions for accelerated topsoil loss but also higher yields. But so the discussion goes with the farming tribe. If I say, "I care about my children's children. I want them to be able to see what I can see today" they will say, "I care about feeding the world, about no-one going hungry." I think opponents naturally run these kinds of shibboleths up the flagpole when staking out territory, preparing to defend their turf. But each side owns only part of the truth.

The greatest service a conservationist can do for society is to help people become whole conservationists. My grandfather saw himself as a conservationist after the wisdom of his day. He was not ecological, rather utilitarian. In his mind, conservation included killing or destroying the parts of nature which were useless or destructive to the parts of nature he approved of. My conservationist friend who wanted to report me so many years ago, had I admired his bond with pine saplings and siskins—as real to him as mine with porcupines and lawn-encroaching oaks—we might have found common ground. Had I taken the time, my last memory of him might not have been his fist flailing the air. Finding agreement is a good place to begin disagreeing.

Yes, the animals, plants, ecosystems, and landscapes of America need saving. But people need saving more. Someone must speak for them. Someone must invoke their desire for a home place, diverse and beautiful, able to support their children's children with delight and certainty of plenitude. For all the environmental education being shunted into homes via nature shows, science programs, brochures, and despite children coming home from school determined to turn mom and dad into fervent recyclers, we are losing ground in preserving habitat and species. It's amazing that all the ducks in North America total eighty-five million—a quarter of our country's population could eat them up in a single day. Or that dozens of common species are shrinking in numbers. The blame lies squarely with groups that cynically play on fear of outside influence in order to gain leverage for resource exploitation that closes options for everyone. That's why the anti-environmental movement will lose in the end. It is not about people's future, but about the future of money-making, a narrowly defined vision of success that forces communities to choose between quality of life and jobs, the environment and an income. It puts forth a false dichotomy that is not at all the choice we must make.

Today, at the precipice, as this next millennium receives six billion human souls, our planet needs advocates. There is work for the person whose soul revives at the whip-poor-will's night chant, a spear of cormorants overhead, the smell of pine and spruce. There is work for the person who will stand outside the mainstream and say, "I speak for nature." There is work especially, for the person who greets his neighbor saying, "We may disagree, but let us talk."

KALAMAZOO COUNTY BY AIR

JIM

Below the riveted wing of the 727
the land is cross-ruled with highways,
filaments of rail. Telephone lines
suture every hamlet to the national ear,
but no field is uniform from the air—
furrows trace purely local contours,
the lighter sand-loam on the high ground
deepens to brown,
occludes to black in the muck bottoms,
gives way to alder and cattails—
beyond which the river drags its coils
through remnant hardwood,
an alley between
productive fields.

In 1830 men in calico shirts
worked their oxen through the waist-high mud,
laboring under the moving shadows.
Each carried a broad-axe, a leather Bible.
In fifty years, the horizon
was easier to see.

The flight attendant walks
up the aisle, counting each seat.
We squint against the blue radiance
as the plane banks south and rises.
The fields, the black vein of the river,
the burgeoning woodlots, all
vanish amid the statuary of clouds.

DUMP

JIM

At the edge of the pasture the farmer has piled
whatever is no longer useful: empty pesticide
drums, an old combine, a roll of fencewire,
rotted plywood, a washtub of galvanized tin,
a plastic lawn chair. Honeysuckle
laces the pile, leaves drift in, rust
blooms. The plastic chair sinks in poison ivy.
Farther in, under the trees, the tube
of an abandoned television lies
face down so its glass stem rises
like a shoot, the green of copper
where the electricity entered, no longer
getting the message—caked in
mud, it is a blind eye,
a bulb in the vegetable mould, a surface shining.

2

MIDDLE
(1990s to 2000s)

Fields Going Wild: Ladislav Hanka's vision of nature's restorative power.

FROM THE DARKNESS, LIGHT: WHAT AN ECOLOGIST AND POET SEE IN AN ARTIST'S WORK

KIM AND JIM

In 1997 Kim and Jim had an email conversation about the environment. Speaking as scientist/conservationist and poet/ teacher respectively, Kim and Jim reacted to Ladislav Hanka's etchings of scenes set in southern Michigan, their former home. At the time Kim lived in St. Paul and Jim in Chicago. Lad remained behind in Kalamazoo, sending Kim and Jim messages in black lines on white paper. Some of those messages, reproduced here, are the springboard for their discussion.

Kim

What I am overpowered by in Lad's etchings is the juxtaposition of light and dark. It's Shakespearian in its approach—opinionated yet absolutely unshakable over the years. At the edges, or in the corners—sometimes in the center—is a darkness where lines and structures are overlaid and combined. Then opposite these visually complex places you find the light. At least that's what it seems on first blush. The light, of course, is where reason, intelligence, linearity, and simplicity concentrate themselves. And that is where I take "the human" to dwell.

It seems to me that these works of Lad have as a central metaphor the intrusion of the human-dominated world into the non-human-dominated. At the same time I think he is saying—hoping more likely—that the human-dominated world will be influenced by the non-human and produce "a more perfect union."

Take the piece *Fields Going Wild* with the pine cones at the top and in the field being overgrown by roots and trees. Look at the furrows, how they're

63

being invaded by a tangled intelligence of roots. You see fully grown trees there, seemingly reflected from ponded water, as if anticipating the future. The trees and roots follow the old furrows, guided and positioned by them to take their place in a new formation, a blending of the "wild" and the "human." Huge white pine cones hover overhead and have fallen in the field, spreading their seed into fertile ground.

White pine is perfectly adapted to reclaim old fields. In the East it was doing this very well until the last few decades as deer populations soared amid suburbia's sprawl—between herbivore teeth and the footprint of a 6,000-square-foot home, there's not a lot of room for white pine to grow.

In Lad's field, at the edges, where corn stubble pokes up, the illuminated ground prevails. There the non-tame world hasn't got a grip—yet. But even after the forest returns, we'll see the evidence of the field. The two will occupy the same space for centuries. You'll run into that line of willow or alder marking the field edge for a long time. Behind us there may be a line of trees and, fifty years from now, somebody will bump into the wires dangling from trunks, an old scar that the trees simply absorbed and grew right on by. Where people abandon their control, wild life will creep in.

I like it when the undomesticated world invades the domesticated. That is as important as the blending of two sets of chromosomes that produces a new magical life—human and otherwise. It also reassures me that "nature" is exerting its influence as it has over the 3.8 billion or so years life has existed on our planet. Though humans dominate huge areas of the planet, the "wild" or "untamed" will gain a toe-hold if we relax our grip on the life-force there.

What kind of life will it be? What blending of wild and domestic? Will it be safer, or more hostile and resistant to people? More or less bountiful than what was there originally? More exciting, or boring? I wonder whether the "new nature" we are creating will be benign or helpful to people.

Now my eyes are drawn to the thick sinewy roots in the lower right. Snake heads! And what's this, a couple of beetle larvae? I study this little corner, and notice the leaf-hopper and other small lives. Here the non-domestic is wilder, more ingenious in its art than people playing the same game. Somebody who restores old fields to prairies by planting the native seeds would say, "We can't bring back the prairie, only suggest its outlines." The non-human life force works towards a more complex system than people can create through their landscaping, agriculture, forestry, and other endeavors at manipulating the wild world.

In the work titled *Reclaiming the Night* lines form a window-pane pattern, maybe a superstructure of some kind. This could be any construct: a perspective

*Sphinx (or hawkmoth) and other moth species move between light and dark
in* Reclaiming the Night.

grid to assist the artist, a framework for creating a building, maybe a scaffolding
to hold something in place. A Polyphemus-like moth and several hawkmoths
dart away from the light, which disintegrates them, causes them to disappear,
as if to say, where humans dominate, the wild is extinguished. Light
extinguishes the intricate dark towards which the moths flee. Filaments of
branches anastomose outward to the light, or perhaps they converge towards
the central dark. It's hard to know what's going on.

Where the wild and human converge, something happens that we can't
predict. We'd like to think we are editing the wild, refining its parlance and
vocabulary, just as Thomas Jefferson believed when he arrayed his grounds at
Monticello with trees and shrubs from around the country and the world. It's
an ancient impulse, wanting to improve nature.

Looking at the etching you finally see the outline of a luna moth aiming
for the dark. The moth, one of North America's largest, has almost vanished
here, obliterated by the light. The message is: two worlds intersect, and they
may not be complementary. One may overpower the other.

*Reseeding the Fields: Hanka sees corn cobs and pine cones blend
where the tame and wild converge.*

Lad's piece titled *Reseeding the Fields* shows rows of corn cobs forming ridges and furrows as in a field. Some of the cobs take on a look of jaw bones from deer, decomposing and melting in the earth. Above them red pine cones scatter their seed. At the interface a bulge of brightness: a sunburst beneath a storm cloud, an ignition of fuel in an engine cylinder, a flash from a lighthouse beacon seen from sea.

There is a fertile flashpoint, a productive collision between the human and non-human worlds. The science of that interface is called "wildlife management." Aldo Leopold's first great work was not his *Sand County Almanac* but the first textbook of wildlife management: *Game Management*, published in 1933. In it he elaborated on the concept of "edge," or the idea that a burst of diversity and abundance comes where otherwise separated entities are brought together and co-mingled.

A wildlife biologist will cut a swatch out of a forest to introduce "edge" where white-tailed deer, ruffed grouse, and other huntable species congregate.

A game manager will carve a patch from prairie, filling it with corn or millet, in order to concentrate the walking and flying protein that otherwise is dispersed over vaster spaces. It's easier to harvest from the edge.

Over a century ago in the Midwest, the edges of woodlands verging prairies bore delicious fruit and nuts: hawthorn, hazelnut, cherry, wild plum, crabapple, and the like. The savanna and prairie-forest borders were rich hunting grounds. Elk, deer, woodland bison, woodcock, and other game stocked its larder. In Minnesota, the Ojibwe and Dakota fought to possess the prairie-forest border running diagonally across the state.

But for all that, the new nature is unnerving, perilous, "edgy." It is experimental, exciting for some, dangerous for others. The edge is explosive, controversial, loud and boisterous. It is the "cutting edge," the "leading edge," and other epithets given to the new. But when all is edge, when everything is constant turmoil, something is lost, something fragile, delicate and beautiful. And in its place, the gregariously prolific generalist, the aggressive colonizer, the over-competitive consumer of space and place.

Jim

On *Fields Going Wild*: It may not be so much a prediction, or hope for the future, as it is a statement of principles; that is, superimposed on the more "realistic" image of the clearing, with its furrows converging on a little line of scrappy woods, are images that tease out the permanent principles which will outlast the transient "scenery." To me it is a little statement of metaphysics, a summary of archetypal principles. For example, mirroring: as above, so below. The root systems and the branch networks are superimposed, so the structure of the pine cone echoes the shape of the tree that formed it. The twisted roots or limbs look like cloud formations. This is the old Romantic idea of Nature's unity of principles—what we would now call the pervasiveness of self-similarities in natural forms. That is, at all levels of scale, the same laws are at work. Some of this is simply related to function: both roots and branches are maximizing surface area for osmosis—air, or water, or sunlight, *machts nichts*. But each tree has its unique way of achieving this task—a method of deploying branches that can be reduced to a fractal number, in fact. The mirroring of roots and snakes is a bit more complex: the way of the root—that is, its tendency to advance by complex sinuosities—can lead one to consider the root a slowed-down snake. Likewise, the curl of the grub seems to be echoing the delicate unspiralling of a fern fiddlehead: these similarities are what gave many of the great Romantics cause to wonder at Nature's mysterious order, and influenced them to dare believe in a kind of primal unity not only in nature but between nature and the mind. The grub also looks like a brain on its stem. Volutes and spires, symmetry and eccentricity—and polarity. Hence the black and white contrasts here. Polarity was the old Romantic engine driving the train of nature, and a figure for the fecund duality of spirit and matter. Dark and light, male and female, animate and inanimate matter: all swirling in the mix, forming complex islands of order and disorder.

Thus the snake is also the old symbol of the natural mind: proceeding by indirection, by sideways movements that always lead forward—and the divided landscape of underground/overground is the conscious and unconscious mind, each mirroring and feeding off the other. As in any good Romantic work, we are led back to the roots of our own consciousness, to the mind itself, that forest of mirrors and masks. That rootwork of neurons, connected to the web of our sensory network.

Of course, Kim, your perspective provides a correction to too much metaphysics. Whatever the state of Nature, our timebound nature is imperiled by an approaching poverty, which is the *real* tale of this millennium: the collapse of the intricate web of species that has woven itself with such labor since the Ice Ages at least. That is to say, if Lad is using a particular set of images to figure the grand schema, Nature as eternal principle and ground of being, you are saying that the species he is employing are heading for a crash.

Still, it is important to differentiate between the transient and the permanent, or perhaps more philosophically, between *natura naturata*—things as they have been, "natural history," and *natura naturans*—nature as process, as becoming: the dark horizon here is the unknowable complexity of nature that seems to be functioning as a kind of cornucopia, out of which come a wealth of writhing and flitting forms.

There is no easy allegory at work of course: In *Reseeding the Fields* the horizon is not dark but light: the light of eternal creation, the "force that through the green fuse drives." In *Reclaiming the Night* the light seems to be the blind or careless energies of our civilization, and the large area of darkness off to the right is that ever-present place beyond our consciousness and control, where the moths are undergoing a kind of transfiguration. Again, these are statements which are true in the large sense: nature as history is now a tale of woe. Nature as process is unshakeable, unassailable.

It seems to me that's what makes these statements brave. Rather than yet another protest against our destructive tendencies, these prints seem to me to be stepping back and making a larger comment: this is what Nature is, this is what *we* are, even. For these images almost seem to be trying to seed us, to penetrate us with some kind of more natural consciousness—especially *Reseeding the Fields*, where those corn cobs are coming at us like a phalanx of vegetable phalloi. They are actually aimed at your sex organs, interestingly enough.

The great problem facing environmentalists is akin to the problem facing historians during the last century: a close scrutiny of our behavior towards nature reveals us to be an incredibly destructive and venal race. This is very important, just as it has been important to debunk the myths of the benign nation/state, of the "progress of civilization," of the "civilizing influence of Christianity." But the problem with a properly acerbic view of human behavior in historical terms is it can lead to cynicism or inaction; and it can also lead to a kind of sentimentalizing of nature (the "not me" in Romantic philosophy). That is, if we can't find good in human history, we will place it in natural history. The only problem is, human history *is* natural history, if we are to believe everything biology has been saying since 1860. Our nasty, brutish past is nature's as well.

And so is our idealism. Everything is nature: our great burden is to be conscious agents in the natural field. If we behave, as a species, like the gypsy moth or spruce budworm, that is perfectly natural. But we'd like to do better. That's also natural, but somewhat more complex. The question is: *can* we? We always used to assume the world was rational and that humans could behave better if properly informed—"follow nature," the Stoics said, and they meant follow reason. But we know nature isn't orderly or disorderly. It's both. It is both as intricate as a wren's nest or a cricket's leg, and brutal as a volcano or a hurricane. Just depends. We are in a kind of Manichean world again, where order and chaos are in constant interchange. But it suits our idealism—our instinct toward order—to orient ourselves to the *right kind* of order. Not the simplistic order of Newton's laws and Watt's steam valves, but the complex order of biology and ecology. Not all of nature, but the kind of nature to take as a guide— sustainable growth, protective complexity. I think that is what Lad is at.

Kim

You're right! Nature is a force for change, and also just the scenery we drive through. It is flooding in the Red River Valley (process), and the aftermath in blankets of sand and mud spread over everything (structure). When drought arrives on the Great Plains and scintillant day upon day beats the ground in hot waves (process), the grasses wither and the tree roots bake, changing the plant life (structure). Fields are plowed and planted (process), come up in corn (structure), then are abandoned to grow up again in vegetable matter. Forest and grown-over cropland give way to shopping centers and subdivisions. Form is not eternal, but shape-shifting is.

Yet we live in a world where the shape and behavior of a thing impresses us as beautiful or ugly. Whether we hate something or love it depends on our individual aesthetic sense, which is a product of experience and instinct—but also it depends on the nature of the thing itself, which we react to. If you like to decorate your house with landscapes and images of the out-of-doors, you won't hang a shot of a 1950s Gary, Indiana, taken on a smoggy autumn day, unless you deliberately cultivate an aesthetic that reviles beauty and celebrates visual injury and bleakness. Rather, people put up paintings of ducks in wild escape from the hunter, the stag on rimrock, or Ansel Adams's *Moonrise, Hernandez, New Mexico* or *Bridal Veil Fall, Yosemite Valley.*

I believe that the natural world has an innate beauty based on function *and* form. The two intertwine as lianas of strangler figs on a tree. They interact in complex and infinitely varying feedback loops.

I see beauty when I behold the dizzying array of wildflowers, wild grasses and sedges covering the dirt of a healthy prairie, or a woodland floor. This beauty grabs you because it commands attention. The detail and unknowableness of the scene is magnetic to our intelligence. We want to know what's going on, but can't comprehend it until we study it in detail, delve into the complexity of the fabric. This is inherent beauty I believe we perceive instinctually; it is not learned.

I also know the grand palette of lifeforms vests that habitat with stability and resilience. In a fierce drought, a prairie containing many species of plants still gives up a crop of grass, still flowers. Animals graze—though not as many as before—bees gather nectar, and so on. After the drought, it bounces back, grass grows abundant, and wildflowers bloom prolific. Your phrase, "protective complexity" describes this well. The prairie will survive and flourish again after weathering adversity because its tremendous numbers of plant species contain some that keep growing despite the drought, some that slow down or go dormant, and some that exuberate in times of good rainfall.

Death and resurgence of individuals and entire species sustains the larger system, seeing it through good times and bad. In elegant fashion, diverse wild habitats sustain themselves despite change. Simultaneously, form supports function, and function influences form. It is not instinctive in me to appreciate this kind of beauty. It must be learned by studying the ecology of wild habitats.

What people spontaneously gravitate towards is the symmetry in pristine landscapes. I mean landscapes untouched by Europeanized cultures elicit a gut reaction from people viewing them: they are curvaceous, subtly patterned, gradual in their transitions, soft-looking, and inviting. Whether viewing them from the ground, an airplane, or on a satellite photo, the texture of the land salves the eyes. Whereas, looking at human-built landscapes, the juxtaposition of angles, asymmetrical structures, small parcels of land in varying states of development—my eyes at any rate are distracted and harried. I love the look of the Chicago skyline, and find the elaborate faces of a street lined by Victorian mansions wonderful to behold. But the impact of the entirety—the rail lines, tenements, waste ground, desolated buildings, industrial sectors—it's all chopped up, fractured and jarring to the senses. The complete opposite impression that wild lands make on a person.

Jim

The relation of form to function in nature: there is a great mystery. It always seems to me there is a surplus, or a superfluity, to form in nature. I have just been outside, looking at a fritillary butterfly feeding on a milkweed flowerhead. I'm sure you know this butterfly, one of the regal queens of the Michigan sky in summer. The complex interaction of color and shape in the butterfly's wing, which is orange-tawny and which features, on the underside, a welter of blue spangles which William Morris would be envious of as sheer design. It is hard to believe all that is necessary for mere survival and reproduction. There is nothing utilitarian about it. Likewise, one can argue that the heady scent of the milkweed flower is important to attract pollinators—yet it has none of the simplistic, cloying brashness of a synthetic dime-store perfume—it is strong but complex, beautiful to the nose as the butterfly is beautiful to the eye. Such aesthetic taste seems innate to nature (with notable exceptions, of course: slime mold, maggots, tent worms, other merely utilitarian forms whose inchoate lines seem innately repellent)—even discounting our predisposition toward them, natural forms seem to adhere to a unity of principles. You rarely see an animal in nature as poorly dressed as the humans who frequent shopping malls—animals are always color coordinated with each other and often with the environment. Again, some of this is explicable in practical terms: camouflage, but not all. It seems more sensible to appeal to the orderly set of blueprints from which animals and plants derive: an aesthetic component imbedded in DNA itself.

One might claim we like only what we are used to, of course; we think nature is elegantly designed because we grew up with it. But that begs the question: why do we then find some things ugly? The exceptions point to the rule.

I am intrigued by the notion that "It is not instinctive" in you or in anyone to appreciate "this kind of beauty." I would claim it is—but that the instinct can be so channeled as to lose sight of its original purpose. That is, part of the love of the beautiful is the love of order, of coherence: our brains are addicted to symmetry, simplicity, clarity. A beautiful form must make order happen for us, that is clear. (As modern art has demonstrated, other qualities are appealing, but we do not call disorderly objects or experiences beautiful—rather, we find them exciting or intriguing or disturbing. A kind of calm is inherent in our notions of beauty, though it is often coupled with an intensity or depth—which may even be disturbing). At any rate, civilized tastes may overexpose us to principles of human order so that we grow unused to the more subtle varieties found in nature, much as children given too many candies cease to like apples. I would say your "education" into ecological principles has served as an aesthetic re-education—teaching you to appreciate subtleties in the landscape your ancestors would have come by just in their daily lives. People who find natural landscapes unappealing are usually simply threatened by the unknown: they can't make sense of what they are seeing, so what they are seeing seems simply ugly. Attention is crucial to the aesthetic response, and the mind cannot attend to what it cannot understand. Here we return to the idea of function, of course: the order you perceive is often functional: you see how the land is operating as process. This is what makes Lad's prints so powerful; he sees this as well. He is sorting out the wildness and making sense of it by putting into dialogue with our tameness: showing us that tameness and wildness define each other at the edge (as you have so eloquently described).

Kim

I wonder if the quest to define an innate, genetic order that accounts for the beauty in nature—which people instinctually perceive—isn't a desire to find God. This is an old idea, but is God ultimately expressed in our genes, and the genes of every animal, plant and other life form of the planet? The most spiritual scientists claim to be seeking the mind of God in their research and deconstruction of nature's complexities. I suppose the destroying sun the Manhattan project scientists discovered in the atom bomb is God's wrath, while the cloned sheep of Dr. Widmuth is God's inventive, life-giving power made obvious through lab technique. Mary Shelley foresaw the danger in seeking God this way, and her caution at the time was ancient wisdom already: Prometheus was punished for stealing fire from the gods, and Galileo was threatened with excommunication for describing the planets spinning around the sun.

The minute silver comma punctuated with a dot on the underwing of the Question Mark butterfly that visited my yard a couple weeks back would only by a miracle be the result of any "selection pressure" in the butterfly's environment. Instead, its namesake marking probably "came along for the ride" as a genetic hitch-hiker on the back of a gene that *was* strongly favored by the environment. At the same time, it gives lepidopterists a handle on the critter and the rest of us a chance to view something curious. It's not every day that the punctuation mark signifying uncertainty is branded in silver on the underside of a butterfly's wing. That is something worth seeing. Likewise the miraculous in geology: Hawthorne's Old Stony Phiz (the "Old Man in the Mountain") staring out over a valley in Vermont, the Grand Canyon, Devil's Tower, Niagara Falls, and so on—millions of visitors yearly are drawn to these curiosities of nature. Can it be said that God's hand is behind the design because we cannot keep from looking at it? At most, God may be responsible for the geological force called erosion, which proximally is responsible for carving these structures. What then do we make of human-created erosion: Crazy Horse Mountain, and the busts of four famous Americans in the Black Hills?

People have, until very recently in their genetic and cultural history, lived in pure nature. Cities are only a few thousand years old, while creatures resembling people have been around for a million years. We spent ninety thousand years as nomadic gatherers and hunters, and only the last two to ten thousand as agriculturalists. The vast human formations establishing human dominance on the planet—agricultural regions, managed forest reserves, megacities, world-spanning transportation and communication networks—have been in place only a few hundred years and are coalescing today because of an ever-expanding population. So our recent innovations are at a slant to our genetic and cultural history—and are forcing a change in our basic nature, I'd argue. E.O. Wilson in his book *Biophilia* claims that, indeed, appreciation of natural beauty and of diverse life forms is genetically inspired, the result of thousands of generations of humans living in a wild nature. What is most strange today is that people are replacing wild nature with a human-created one.

The latest turn of events in this inexorable creep towards human dominance of the planet is animal cloning. Now we can create diversity of any kind we want. Someday we may even be able to reverse the process of extinction—*Jurassic Park* may not be so far-fetched twenty years from now. While I'd like to see a Dodo Bird alive, there's something horrifying about the idea: people as God, I suppose. Scientist as God, specifically.

The belief is widely held that people must use every inch of the planet for human benefit because we cannot afford to do anything else. By making all natural systems "pay their way" and become incorporated into people's global economy, we are indeed on the path to godhood. God as budget director and personnel manager, certainly, but God nevertheless. I think this is foreboding because we are extended this paradigm to humans. In the early 1900s eugenics was chic in leadership circles and inspired the Nazis, which in turn forced even the most insensitive person to send the notion to the cellar. It has been dusted off and presented in a new form now. At least once a week a scientist discovers a gene that controls some behavior, some psychological trait, or physical defect. There will come a time in our lifetime when it will be possible to adjust your child's genetic code in vitro, just as we make improvements to the design of automobiles. The goal: a more perfect human. Conversely, there will remain "less-perfect" humans out there, by choice or otherwise. Chances are, those who can afford it will create more perfect offspring, and those who cannot, will not. Will the world we create have room for them? With the population projected to grow to ten billion by 2050, can we afford to let "defective" people hang around, consuming the world's ever more limited resources? The idea that we are technically making this possible repulses me.

At the same time, by harnessing all of nature to serve human good, we are remaking nature after our blueprint for productivity: creating simple systems that operate on overdrive and produce a superabundance of goods for people to consume. Examples abound: corn and soybean agriculture, fast-growing hybrid trees for "new forestry," ocean-farmed salmon, sun-grown coffee, herbicide-resistant plants.

In short, we are replacing natural selection with human selection of genetic traits, species populations, and natural systems and processes. Beauty will now lie solely in the eye of the human beholder, and not in the spontaneous products of nature.

My grim imaginings to the contrary, the Earth remains a beautiful place. I have, after all, the Question Mark butterfly in my backyard, the call of nighthawks in the slightly steamed evening, a lazy pulsing egret flying back to its rookery, the whine of cicadas at mid-day, the pendent yellow-and-purple petals of coneflowers, and the scimitar moon hanging in the west after sunset. These beautiful forms, these ephemeral objects of natural origin, uncontrolled by me, inspire and placate my agitated modern sensibilities. Genetically inspired or otherwise may not matter; the fact is they are here, and the human-created equivalents cannot mimic them for elegance, complexity, and power. Power is another matter: the sum total of our planet's biology underpins our existence. The function resulting from billions of forms interacting with each other and their environment establishes the "ecosystem services" supporting human life. The silent environmental crisis is about disappearing species, an aesthetic and spiritual, as well as ecological loss. Biosphere II, that ill-fated experiment in human-created ecosystems, proves how difficult it is—impossible probably—to sustain human life in a human-created world. It is both too costly and complex to do.

Looking at Lad's etchings I return to the detail of them: how they draw us in, as the natural world does, by their complexity and mysterious forms. That's what makes field trips to the woods fun. Sometimes I wonder if my genetic make-up isn't a throw-back to the nomadic epoch of human culture, prompting in me an openness towards biological complexity in order to notice and make good on opportunity that nature presents. Yet I find that most everyone, given the chance to notice, will stop and wonder at the Question Mark butterfly, how its cipher came to be, and what it might signify. I was on a field trip recently and the leader, a twenty-three-year-old ecologist named Laura, who was taking field measurements at the prairie we visited, told me she didn't intend to get her master's degree or doctorate in ecology. "Why should I reduce all this to numbers? We don't need more numbers, we need more understanding. We need people to live in a place long enough so they don't need numbers, so they can tell everyone about what they see there. That's the only hope." I think Lad presents us with a challenge to stay put, slow down, and notice the detail, and in doing so, preserve ourselves and nature.

Jim

Perhaps there is a link between our desire to *find* God and our desire to *be* God—that is, our seemingly unquenchable need to see the universe as the product of a single unified intelligence might, when frustrated by the lack of corroborating evidence, induce us to fill the void with our own actions. In this respect, our replacement of nature with humanist nature, that odd hybrid of physics and desire, is always coming up short aesthetically because it is based on a false premise: that creativity is solely the province of the unchecked "I am"—which is to say that creativity is the conscious will of an, or *the*, ego. What if the definition of creativity were otherwise: order spontaneously erupting in a communal field, a synergy of competing and cooperating parts? And isn't this in fact the way creative leaps occur in science or in art?—the individuals who leap have absorbed the diverse nuances of their era to such a degree that their innovations often well up from the unconscious, or appear in dreams—or are the product of intuitions that grasp suddenly and at once the new shape of things—so it might be said, as the Romantics did indeed theorize, they are more the product of the Zeitgeist than of the individual credited with their origin. Just so, innovation in nature seems to come in peristaltic local leaps that could not be predicted but are everywhere adumbrated in existing forms. An engineering God would have given us a very different world than the one we inhabit—one much less beautiful and mysterious, one less cohesive as well. It is precisely the combination of nature's unity and nature's variety, its unexpectedness, that endears it to us. Innovation that is at once superfluous and supremely practical—because pruned by the strict demands of a universe that is—in spite of our joy in it—still grimly Darwinian. "Beauty that is always fresh, and always works." Humans seem to produce either beauty that doesn't work at all (the perennial jeer against *art pour l'art*) or work that has no beauty—and perhaps this is because we are obsessed with the notion of central planning—because we wish to be the products of a Divine Geometer.

If you look at objects from the pre-scientific era, you get a very different impression—the demand that things "work" was seemingly counterbalanced with the demand that they be beautiful—not because anyone thought they "should" be beautiful but because they could not help themselves. If they made a sword, it would be decorated with intricate engravings or given at the very least an extra flourish, a delicate curve to the hilt or elegant pommel. A jug or bucket would have an ornate handle—an ox yoke would sport a daub of paint limning a local flower. It was as if the hands that made these things could not help themselves—their instinct was toward embellishment. But once scientific principles of production became widely disseminated, and especially once machines began to make our things, the unconscious yearning of these hands was stifled: objects became truly utilitarian, and lost their naturalness. They became purely functional in a way objects had never been before.

So our problem is not that we are replacing the natural with the human: we are replacing the natural with the rational. We are acting like the God we keep hoping to find—a kind of eighteenth century watchmaker who has no time for frivolity. At our "natural" best, we are forces of nature too—the ancient landscapes around the world testify to a fruitful interrelationship between human business and the wider natural business. In fact, nowhere on earth—saving perhaps Antarctica—was "nature" devoid of man's shaping hand, even before the industrial age. To return to Lad's work: at first contact, the prairies and woods of southwest Michigan were full of the signs of human habitation, the bur oak savanna maintained by regular firing, the garden beds and ceremonial mounds for native agriculture, the pathways worn deep in the earth. We have always shaped nature to our ends. But our ends and our means have usually been in better balance—and our ends have included spiritual as well as physical goals.

I believe a city can be as beautiful as a field of wildflowers—Paris seems so to me. But a city built in a purely functional manner—the "radiant cities" of Le Corbusier, with their featureless grids and draconian divisions of function and their vast, inhuman scale—cities without nuance, ambiguity, or regard—cities of the impoverished and divorced ego, cities with neither history nor poetry—these seem truly "unnatural" to me. In fact, they remind me of those descriptions of the heavenly Jerusalem—a titanic cube entirely made of minerals, in which everybody is engaged in the same occupation. Our current metropolitan culture is out of whack precisely because it is so transcendent—as if our cities seek to levitate above the earth, to become orbital shopping malls, entirely self-sufficient. For example: what major American city is currently taking provisions to safeguard its local food supply? Wouldn't you be considered a crank if you asked such a thing at your city council meeting? Yet can the California's Central Valley supply us with shrink-wrapped vegetables in perpetuity? If petroleum got scarce (not if but *when*), would we suddenly miss our local truck farms, obliterated by suburban sprawl?

Perhaps this is what Lad aims at: those ears of corn, streaming towards us like a torpedo array—aren't they a warning? We are imbedded in nature, and there is no getting out—here is no transcendent economy, despite what you see on TV. Civilizations rise and fall on the viability of their soil, on the availability of fuel and drinking water. If you don't believe it go look at the abandoned Roman urbs in North Africa: once the breadbasket of Europe, now an arid boneyard. Lewis Mumford said long ago that the only future for our civilization is to learn how to build cities that will build soil, that will enhance the environment instead of degrading it as the cities of the past have always done. For all our "modernity," our civilization is just more efficient at using resources up. Entropic vortexes. How to marry the intellectual creativity of the city with the agricultural creativity of the Neolithic village—that would be the goal of the next millennium.

Kim

And with that flourish, Jim, you've hit on the idea of conservation rooted in local community concerns. In order to supply the needs of people who, for multiple generations, have lived in one location, a different view of living is required. Communities and individuals across America are experimenting with techniques based on principles of self-reliance and local control. Examples abound: buying fruits and vegetables in season from nearby growers, revitalizing brownfields made worthless and discarded in a previous fit of economic endeavor, preserving green space amid congestion, valuing and conserving the plants and animals that elevate a mere city or farm to an intriguing bastion of biodiversity, and so forth. Really, this is nothing more than a return to the "Neolithic village" of our origins, where everything you valued was of necessity found within traveling distance on foot—long-distance trading in exotic materials being a tiny fraction of the economy of the day. It doesn't matter that this village is located in the heart of New York City: it could and should operate to the benefit of the people living there, who control their own environment and destiny.

The dark side of local control is seen in such things as Jim Crow laws, the despoilation of Appalachia by Peabody Coal, and the Wise Use movement, which allies local users of natural resources with multi-national timber, mining, recreation, and other exploitative businesses. But I believe that an environmental consciousness will only get stronger in America, as more people receive more information about the natural world and the effects of people on it—and the Wise Use movement will fizzle in time.[1]

It's easy to set up the dichotomy: on one hand, "godless" functional bottom-liners use the global market to accelerate the exploitation of local nature and the people living there, on the other, "godly" inhabitants of a place fight to preserve its beauty and livability. The former become God themselves, while the latter continue to serve God as a more or less separate entity. Insert Lad's work here, a certain conceptual blueprint—and there are hundreds of other people like Lad telling the same story—and you give both camps a chance to do something that can only improve our situation with time. Facts are mutable only in the absence of integrity. I believe that, whether you are a supply-side auto-dealer or an aging hippie selling solar panels, when given a choice between beauty and ugliness, beauty wins hands-down. It may be that there are degrees of beauty, but people innately respond to some level of it and prefer to keep some of it around because it makes their lives more enjoyable. As we've discussed, a healthy environment may intrinsically exude beauty, although the more sophisticated a person's knowledge, the more subtly that beauty can be appreciated. Even my little girl, barely six, is more intrigued by a Comma Butterfly having seen the "comma" on its underwing.

And that is why education is so important. The ignorant man perhaps cannot be blamed for the bad around him. In time, messages like Lad's—and even our small contribution here—heard by enough people will leave no-one in doubt about the need to preserve nature and our proper place in it. Let's hope it's heard in time.

HERON

JIM

Up to his backward knees
in the silken wash,
the color of ash, he is two
characters at once:
the original,
upright, relentless,
god of spearmen,
and the blue messenger.
He wades in morning light, against the horizon
where the perfect clouds
are pushed by the wind. Gulls
wheel in the long shadows of the dunes.
Suddenly he unfolds
his cloak, and with exaggerated slowness
withdraws each leg
from the wave, doubles his neck,
suspends himself from the sun by wires,
and leaves without speaking.

WORKING FROM MEMORY: PRAIRIES, SAVANNAS, AND LAND RESTORATION

KIM

Dedication of the visitor entrance at St. John's Arboretum, Collegeville, Minnesota, September 26, 1998.

The thing we call prairie has been in existence in Minnesota for some 8,000 years. It may not have looked exactly as it does today, but many of the grasses and wildflowers were the same ones found in modern prairies. And there were people living here to admire the prairie. By admire I mean it in its old sense: to wonder at, from the Latin, *mirus*, meaning something wonderful, like a miracle. The words miracle and admire have the same root.

Whether these earliest of prairie admirers looked at it then as we do today, no-one can say. Their admiration was maybe of a more practical kind. Certainly they stood on a high point in the prairie, hands shading their eyes, and scanned the horizon for bison, elk, deer, grizzly bear, wolf, and pronghorn antelope, thinking about them as dinner, but also as something miraculous, given the important role animals have in Indian belief and legend. By that time, however, 6,000 years before Christ, the people living in the prairie had wiped out the giant grazers using a new technology—the flinty, razor-sharp spear tips called Clovis points, a technological edge these hunters manufactured by the hundreds of thousands.

If you had been alive in 6,000 B.C. and had use of an aircraft, on a flight around the world you would have seen scant evidence that people existed: a few settlements, small cities and their agricultural fields in the Middle East, herdsmen and their livestock here and there, and the rest of the planet simply in a state of nature. Still some few thousand years in the future were the ziggurats of Sumeria, the pyramids of Egypt, vast irrigation works in the Tigris-Euphrates valley, the

Big sagebrush and grass stretch to the horizon near Medicine Bow, Wyoming.

well-planned cities of northern India, the palaces at Knossos, and the temples of the Olmecs in Mexico. Meanwhile the prairie covered half the land in what would someday be Minnesota. It is still here 8,000 years later, long after the pyramid-builders abandoned their work and the cities in the cradles of civilization became buried rubble. Only the herdsmen continue as they did, enduring perhaps because the grass itself endures.

I give this brief history to impress on you one thing—prairie has longevity surpassing human endeavor. It's good to have something like that around. It puts our works in perspective. For thousands of years, prairie has survived blistering episodes of drought and at other times wet and cloudy weather. It has been hailed on, trampled to dust under millions of hooves, beaten by windstorms, frozen to a depth of a dozen feet, devoured by countless mouths. It has migrated hundreds of miles following a drier climate northward, then been pushed back by forest and woodland in wetter times. It has been burned, and burned, and burned, first by bolts of lightning then, beginning 10,000 years ago, by people. Through all the turmoil and violence of millennia prairie survived.

But all that changed. Most of you know about the prairie's demise after European settlers arrived in the Midwest. Of 160 million acres of tallgrass prairie in 1800, less than four percent remains. Of eighteen million acres in Minnesota, perhaps 150,000 acres remain. One hundred sixty years ago you could have set off from Albert Lea and ambled in a lazy arc northwesterly to Pembina, an early settlement where the Red River crosses into Canada, without stepping from the prairie except to cross rivers and streams. That journey would have taken you several months. By comparison, you could gather all the prairie left today in Minnesota and fit it in a square of ground that is fifteen miles on a side. You could walk across that in less than one day.

In the long lifespan of prairie here in Minnesota, the arrival of the plow was the most dramatic event since mile-high glaciers cut a swath across the state. It was profound in its outcome, but a recent event. Let me put it this way: picture walking a prairie mile, with 6,000 B.C. as your starting point and the year 1998 as your destination. At a leisurely pace it would take you twenty minutes. For almost your entire ramble you would see and smell just grass and wildflowers and wild animals. In the last fifteen seconds of your walk, just sixty-six feet from your destination, you would encounter a plow. And being a sensible pioneer wanting to feed your family and earn a little cash, you would plow up that prairie, leaving just tiny shards too wet, too sandy, or too steep to farm. A new technology—the moldboard plow—had enabled an immigrant people to wipe out the prairie in a few dozen years. The manufacturers of Clovis points might sympathize with our puzzlement and understand our surprise when we suddenly realized that the prairie was not limitless. And it might be with some regret that we view the remains, knowing the likes of it will never been seen again: neither the mastodon nor woolly mammoth nor endless prairie vista.

We are here today to dedicate a reminder of the prairie that once was. With this restoration we remind ourselves that towering seed-heads of big bluestem once stretched to the horizon. Here we have established a place-marker to recall the colorful and panoramic change through the season as wildflower after wildflower comes into bloom and fades, much as the seasons of our own lives blossom and pass. We are erecting a monument that helps us to cultivate a garden in our hearts, seeded down with prairie and big enough to yearn for ten thousand bison coming over a distant, hazy hill. In time we will understand better with our hearts and souls the words of those first white settlers who saw the prairie:

Beneath, about and beyond me, as far as the eye could reach, was spread out, in undulating elegance, an emerald carpet of nature's choicest fabric, inlaid profusely with flowers of every imaginable variety of name and tint—gorgeous and fascinating as the most brilliant hues of the rainbow.[1]

We also remember the oak savannas white settlers first saw and named "oak openings" as they traveled through western New York and Ohio. The oak savannas seemed like parks to the immigrants and they compared them to the grand estates of European aristocrats, wondering who tended them so carefully to keep out the underbrush and which gardener sprinkled their grassy floors with delicate wildflowers. Their admiration of the miraculous is best appreciated through their own sentiments:

I have not words sufficient to give you any adequate picture of them . . . the woods looked more like an old orchard than a forest. Roads wound at will among the trees, making the most graceful curves and pleasing turns. In early summer the grass was overtopped with wild flowers surpassing in beautiful effects the most skillful landscape gardening and city park scenery. . . . All these came on together in rapid succession, co-mingling in the wildest profusion, and stretching as far as the eye could reach under the delicate oak foliage. Why try to describe the earlier growths of violets, asters and all their sisters, their cousins, and their aunts. The now nearly exterminated fringed gentian then flourished in abundance.[2]

The wetlands too are here—sedge meadows and wet prairies, marshes and fens. We glimpse the original scenes the settlers saw in the words of Laura Ingalls Wilder, an exact and eloquent observer:

Millions of rustling grass-blades made one murmuring sound, and thousands of wild ducks and geese and herons and cranes and pelicans were talking sharply and brassily in the wind. All those birds were feeding among the grasses of the sloughs. They rose on flapping wings and settled again, crying news to each other and talking among themselves among the grasses, and eating busily of grass roots and tender water plants. . . . The lake melted into the slough, making small ponds surrounded by the harsh, rank slough grass that stood five and six feet tall. Little ponds glimmered between the grasses and on the water the wild birds were thick.[3]

A thousand bison may never again thunder over a Minnesota prairie, never again may a flock of whooping cranes rise on giant white wings over this wetland, and perhaps never again will a crowd of children skip and leap unhindered through miles of oak savanna gathering armfuls of wildflowers. But we can preserve these images in our memory, and in so doing raise our expectations of what we are capable of...what the human spirit guided by new information and skills can accomplish.

Simply put we are capable of taking care of the land. This restoration of prairie, savanna, and wetland is basic land care or land management. It is no different than painting your house or roofing the shed, changing the oil in your car, putting clean clothes on your children's back and making sure they learn their spelling words. It is an assignment, in a way, a duty and promise to ourselves, our children and their children, and to the land. By remembering, by keeping a place in our heart for prairie, savanna, and wetland, we are preserving it just as certainly as if we set aside forever inviolate a million acres a hundred years ago. That in fact is how land is saved—by first making a place for it in your heart.

We fall in love with many things. Our wives or husbands, our friends, our children even before they are born, our home, maybe our first car—the one with the immense engine and lousy traction. Many of us fall in love with a place. Maybe it's the farm you were raised on, or the town you grew up in, or your alma mater where you first tasted complete independence. Some of us fall in love with a waterfall, or a piece of scenery, or a particular white pine tree standing sentinel on a stretch of romantic lakeshore. A few of us fall in love with prairie, with savanna and with wetlands. You might think that's like falling in love with a passing cloud or the blazing sun at mid-day. No . . . it's more personal that that. Standing in this land restoration today you are in fact showing up at the dance. Now you've been introduced to your dance partner, and in a moment you will begin small talk and take a stroll. Along the way you might notice how the light shines on the leaves of the oaks, or how beautifully shaped is the lip of a fringed orchid at the edge of the wetland. The minty scent of bergamot may entice you to pluck a leaf, crush it and hold it under your nose to catch the aromatic tang. Perhaps the feeling of moist soil beneath your feet will encourage you to take off your shoes. With each step of growing familiarity, you are dancing, dancing, dancing . . . and falling in love.

Treating the land well is proof you are in love. Someone truly loves this land to be putting so much time and effort into bringing it back to its former utility, elegance and bounty as a delight to everyone coming after them. I think it's a lot like nursing a family member or friend back to health. At the worst of their sickness you are almost in despair at whether they will get better, but as you tend to them, nourish them not just with food, drink and medicine, but with your generous spirit and kindness, they improve. As you apply the medicines and treatments gently and with careful attention, they improve. And then one morning they rise from their bed and get on with life. In the middle of all that, in your heart, is a place that loved this person and caused you to demonstrate your love when hope was at low ebb. It's the same hope we have for our children before they are born. What good is a helpless infant? We know the good a child promises to give back to us and so we raise our hopes higher for its future than is reasonable.

This restoration is an infant. If the other unplowed, undrained and well-tended prairies, savannas, and wetlands had consciousness, they would recognize this new restoration as kin, but also they would know how many years it will take to bring these habitats to the peak of health—a century or more. Much has gone wrong with this land over the past hundred years, and undoing the damage will take effort, creativity, and resources. It is both miraculous and heartening—it is in fact to be admired—that the work has begun. It is miraculous because in each of your hearts is already a small place for the land, and it is heartening because so much has been accomplished in so little time.

As this land heals and fills again with variety and life, as God's bounty is restored on this patch of ground, we will be filled with wonder at the miracle of it all. Even if wild nature is constrained, our spirit and will to make things better remain limitless. That is the greatest force in land conservation. Today we not only dedicate a monument and reminder of what once was, we dedicate ourselves to the task of land restoration and management. It is an assignment with possibilities as romantic as the flight of sandhill cranes in spring and as limitless as the prairie vistas of yesterday. Don't stop. Keep on doing what you're doing because it is the one thing you do that will last for 8,000 years.

THE LANDSCAPE OF NOSTALGIA: MICHIGAN OAK OPENINGS IN THE SCIENTIFIC AND LITERARY IMAGINATION

KIM AND JIM

Presented at the Third Biennial Conference of the Association for the Study of Literature and the Environment, Kalamazoo, Michigan, June 2-5, 1999, this paper is a collaboration between science and literary scholarship.

The Setting (Kim)

White settlers to the American Midwest in the early 1800s encountered a type of landscape so surprising yet so utterly familiar that their descriptions of it revealed an immediate emotional bond springing from a resemblance to the civilized lands of the eastern states and Europe. They called this landscape "oak openings," a term that was both ecologically accurate and geographically based.[1] The oak openings were located in the Upper Midwest from western New York State to Minnesota. Southwest Michigan was roughly at the center of its distribution.

Modern descriptions of the oak openings, which scientists now call oak savannas and oak woodlands, provide the details but do not substantially change the general impressions written down by white settlers. Two main ideas emerge from the writings. Sun-loving plants—and the animals that depended on them—made up a large proportion of the organisms living in the oak openings landscape. Second, the oak openings required frequent fires to keep them open and full of sun-loving species.

Here are some excerpts from the diaries and letters of just a few individuals who left a record of their first encounters with the oak openings in Michigan:

I liked the land and bought 80 acres for £23 in a wild state. It is mixt soil partly timbered and part openings and look [sic] like a gentleman's park. I admire the providence of God in providing such a country for the rescue of the distressed of all Nations.[2]

In technical terms the oak openings were a "vegetation mosaic" or patchwork quilt of three habitats: grassland, savanna, and woodland. The "openings" were grasslands that varied in size from areas as big as this room to areas such as Prairie Ronde, thirteen thousand acres in extent. But it was the thousands of smaller anonymous grasslands that set the oak openings apart in the minds of visitors and settlers from the forested regions farther east.

Imagine yourself emerging from a New-Jersey swamp, and coming at one bound upon one of the English parks. Clumps of the noblest oaks, with not a twig of underwood, extending over a gently undulating grassy surface as far as the eye can reach: here clustered together in a grove of tall stems supporting one broad canopy of interlacing branches, and there rearing their gigantic trunks in solitary grandeur from the plain. I rode on for hours, unable without an effort to divest myself of the idea that I was in a cultivated country.[3]

The prairie wildflower, ox eye, escapes the cattle's hunger at a fenceline in a bur oak savanna.

The "grove" mentioned here an ecologist would call woodland. As many as sixty trees grew in an acre. From a distance it looked like a forest. Tree crowns touched in most places, but in the broken shade of the oak forest enough sunlight passed through to allow the sun-loving plants to flourish.

The solitary trees in a sea of grass mentioned by Hoffman made up the savanna patches. As few as four trees per acre grew in the savannas:

> The variety so essential in a landscape, of woodland, glade and sheets of water, are here combined in a manner which seems the result of art, but which is not less truly inimitable. It is difficult to resist the impression that we are surveying an old abode of civilization and of tasteful husbandry. It resembles those exquisite pictures of park scenery, where the vision roams at will among the clumps of lofty oaks and over open glades, gemmed with flowers, while the distant woodland bounds the horizon.[4]

> To-day, for the first time, I saw the meadows on fire. They are of vast extent, running far into the woods like the friths of a lake. . . . These fires, traveling far over the country, seize upon the largest prairies, and consuming every tree in the woods, except the hardiest, cause the often-mentioned oak openings, so characteristic of Michigan scenery.[5]

Many of the first white visitors reported that, without fire, the oak openings landscape grew up in twenty years to thickets and brushy forests:

> The annual fires burnt up the underwood, decayed trees, vegetation, and debris, in the oak openings, leaving them clear of obstructions. You could see through the trees in any direction.[6]

Studies by modern ecologists confirm this impression.

What Cooper Found in Michigan's Oak Openings (Jim)

The landscape of southern Michigan had the capacity to charm even after it had been settled for a decade—at least it acted powerfully on James Fenimore Cooper, who traveled to the Kalamazoo area in 1847 to inspect some city lots which he had received in partial settlement of a legal dispute involving his niece's husband, Horace Comstock (founder of the local village that still bears his name). On this first visit, Cooper was deeply impressed by the countryside, especially "Prairie Round," the island prairie south of Kalamazoo[7] where Cooper traveled to visit early settler Basil Harrison on his prosperous farm, and where Cooper viewed the operation of a Moore-Hascall harvesting machine, an early precursor of the McCormick reaper.[8] This was a significant excursion because, although Cooper had written an entire novel about the prairie, he had never actually seen one. It seems apparent that Cooper's exposure to this prairie island and to the oak savannas of the Kalamazoo area stimulated his imagination to such an extent that he began making plans for what would be his last "Indian novel."[9]

When he returned to Cooperstown a few days later, Cooper wrote to his publisher, Richard Bentley:

> I have a new work in hand, scene Michigan, time the commencement of the war of 1812, incidents those of the wilderness but in a somewhat new form. I shall call it either "The Oak Openings," or "The Bee Hunter." A Beehunter is the hero, mingled with Indians, Lake sailors and a little touch of war. I offer it on the terms of the "Crater."[10]

When the book was published the next year, it was substantially as Cooper described it, less the "Lake sailors." The plot involves Ben Boden, a bee hunter who has a shanty on the Kalamazoo River and who makes a living gathering wild honey, which he trades at the settlement in Detroit. Boden and three other whites—one of whom (Marjorie Waring) provides the novel's romantic interest—find themselves caught up in the intrigues of an Indian war-council called by "Scalping Peter," a charismatic warrior based on historical figures like the Prophet and Tecumseh. Emboldened by the recent massacre at Fort Dearborn and by the fall of Detroit and Fort Mackinac to the British, Peter is attempting to rally local tribes to present a united resistance to white invasion.

Ben Boden is clearly an analog to Natty Bumppo, the hero of Cooper's best known novels—he is a skilled woodsman described as having a "passion for dwelling alone" and enjoying the "strange but certainly most alluring pleasures of the woods."[11] He is contrasted with the other white male in the book, the drunken idler Gershom Waring, by his self-restraint and by his sense of honor and compassion. Moreover he is sympathetic to the Indians, and is well liked by them. There is even a Chingachgook parallel in Boden's friend Pigeonswing, a Chippewa who sides with the "Yanqui" in the burgeoning conflict. Yet the novel represents some very interesting departures from the Leatherstocking formula, departures that have a lot to do with the landscape of southern Michigan.

All of Cooper's novels are obsessed with finding a principle of individual restraint suitable to a democratic culture; the Leatherstocking tales in particular propose the figure of Natty Bumppo: someone whose long exposure to wilderness has produced in him a natural sense of religious humility and reverence, which gives him something beyond self-interest to base his actions on. In Cooper's formulation, Bumppo is the best wilderness has to offer, but the fact that wilderness is doomed to fall under the axe makes the Leatherstocking tales essentially admonitory. In the words of Donald Ringe, "Change is inevitable, Cooper seems to say . . . but. . . care must be taken that the fundamental system of values that Leatherstocking has lived by shall not be lost in the greedy exploitation of the wilderness."[12]

Many of Cooper's novels are deeply pessimistic about this possibility. When Cooper writes about the present, as in *Home as Found, The Pioneers,* or the Littlepage novels, he is writing a kind of social criticism that demonstrates his deep dissatisfaction with the way Americans are managing the transition from wilderness to civilization. They are commonly depicted as lacking all restraint: despoiling the land and democratic process as well. It is this pessimism which gives the Leatherstocking Tales such an elegiac tone.

What makes the *Oak Openings* different is that Cooper seems, at the end of his career, to have found in the prairie-savanna landscape a setting in which the act of settlement will not substantially alter nature. Unlike the forests, whose destruction Cooper's Leatherstocking novels are lamenting, the open grasslands and savannas, when put under cultivation, will not be that different spatially from their aboriginal configuration. In fact, the Michigan landscape is described as having the appearance of a landscape which has already been long settled, like the landscapes of the European countryside. As Cooper says, describing "Prairie Round," the "remarkable little prairie" is. . .

> . . . held in repute, even at the present hour, as a place that the traveler should see, though covered with farms, and the buildings that belong to husbandry. It is still visited as a picture of ancient civilization, placed in the setting of a new country. It is true that very little of this part of Michigan wears much, if any, of that aspect of a rough beginning, including stubs, stumps, and circled trees, that it has so often fallen to our share to describe. There are dense forests, and those of considerable extent; and wherever the axe is put to them, the progress of improvement is marked by the same steps as elsewhere; but the lovely openings form so many exceptions, as almost to compose the rule.[13]

Of the oak openings themselves Cooper remarks that "they stand with a regularity resembling that of an orchard; then, again, they are more scattered and less formal, while wide breadths of the land are occasionally seen in which they stand in copses, with vacant spaces, that bear no small affinity to artificial lawns, being covered with verdure."[14] The book returns continually to comparisons either to husbandry or to settled "parkland."

As Daniel Peck has remarked, the fact that the landscape almost immediately resembles a long-settled European province would have made it extremely appealing to Cooper, who was very critical of the chaos of American landscapes and praised the "air of neatness and order" in the European countryside.[15] As a result, Peck says, Cooper's forest landscapes "are defined as much by European parks and gardens as they are by the actual terrain of the American continent. Because of this they have very little regional identification: they are not particular woods but classic woods—a landscape of the mind."[16] Oddly enough, in stumbling upon a landscape that literally resembled that of his own pastoral imagination, Cooper was for once driven to specificity. His descriptions of the savanna and prairie in Oak Openings (drawn as much from notes and memories of the pioneers, whom Cooper spoke with, as from his own observations) are considered accurate enough to complement the scientific literature on the subject (as Kim has noted). Peck states that the novel can "fruitfully be seen as a celebration of discovery, a discovery of an edenic landscape which answered the writer's deepest sense of what nature *ought* to look like."[17] Because the oak openings so nearly resembled the kind of landscape Cooper was most attracted to—a landscape which Daniel Peck has described as "classical" in its park-like openness and pastoral commodiousness—it seemed physical evidence at last of the natural suitability of the American wilderness for inhabitation by the whites.

The landscape was not only satisfying aesthetically, however. To Cooper, it seemed to suggest that the violence and subjugation which followed settlement—the fall from natural restraint into civil and moral conflict—might be foregone in this particular geography. If the land *looked* already civilized, perhaps it would be easy for its settlers to become likewise—as witnessed by Ben Boden, who, at the end of Cooper's tale, is depicted as a successful farmer and a state senator, the epitome of a Jeffersonian citizen. It was a landscape whose picturesque qualities the transformations of agriculture would not substantially alter: there would be no violent deforestation. His solitary sojourn in the wilderness has naturally segued into a useful social life in a way unthinkable for Natty Bumppo, whose wilderness purity forces him to move ever westward, ahead of the ringing axes.

In fact, Ben Boden marries; this is an act proscribed for Bumppo (Cooper explicitly states in *The Pathfinder* that bachelorhood is Bumppo's natural state). Bumppo's religion relies upon the wilderness to support it—it cannot be domesticated. In Oak Openings, however, Cooper seems to have decided that the natural man can become the social and domestic man without penalty. This can only happen because the landscape of this novel is a version of the biblical Eden.

The explicitly edenic overtones of Cooper's description make it clear that this reconciliation between what has heretofore been irreconcilable should be seen in biblical terms. At one point Boden is explaining to Pigeonswing the biblical account of creation; he says that God made Adam and Eve and "put them both to live together, in a most beautiful garden, in which all things excellent and pleasant was to be found—some such place as these openings, I reckon."[18] In fact, Boden's marriage to Marjorie Waring takes place in the openings, under the "deep, fathomless vault of heaven," and at an altar of "nature's own erecting," implying that Boden and Waring might become a kind of new Adam and Eve and perhaps (as the novel implies) alleviate if not revoke the original curse. This is also apparent in the strongly apocalyptic tones of Cooper's "Preface" to the novel, in which he states that:

> . . . we firmly believe that the finger of Providence is pointing the way to all races, and colors, and nations, along the path that is to lead the east and the west alike to the great goal of human wants . . . and the day, in the sense of time, is not distant, when the whole earth is to be filled with the knowledge of the Lord, "as the waters cover the sea."[19]

Another way in which the novel seems edenic is in the way in which Scalping Peter is dealt with: unlike Cooper's other Indian characters, who remain outside the white ethical and religious systems, drawing their virtue from the same source as Bumppo's natural religion, Peter becomes a convert to the white religion (this occurs after he watches Parson Amen, the Methodist minister, die while blessing his tormentors). At the end of novel, Peter, who once attempted to unite his race in war, now denies that race even exists: "Tribe make no difference," he says, "All children of the same Great Spirit."[20] In fact, Peter has the last words in the novel; he says to the narrator, "Stranger, Love God . . . B'lieve his blessed Son, who pray for dem dat kill him."[21] Reflecting on his former inability to understand this concept, Peter insists

> It want de Holy Spirit to strengthen de heart, afore man can do so great t'ing. When he got de force of de Holy Spirit, de heart of stone is changed to de heart of woman, and we all be ready to bless our enemy and die. I have spoken. Let dem dat read your book understand.[22]

Thus, the fierce Indian warrior is pacified and feminized, just as the pioneer has become domesticated and civilized. It is as though the conflicts which drove Cooper's wilderness fiction for so long—conflicts between nature and civilization, between stasis and change, between native American and white claims to ownership of the land, between the promise of democracy and the dangers of unbridled mob behavior—could be resolved in the right landscape. The oak openings of southwestern Michigan provide Cooper with a kind of pastoral ending to the story of western expansion—pastoral both in the sense of the classical pastoral landscape, and in the sense of the Christian ethos. In the oak openings natural religion and Christianity merge, and nature and art become one and the same.

Finding the Modern Oak Openings (Kim)

Cooper did not see the oak openings. He saw their brush-filled successors created by the cessation of wildfires. Yet using notes by pioneers he met in Kalamazoo, he cobbled together a description that accurately portrayed both the settlers' impressions and foretold the scientific descriptions that were to follow. As Jim demonstrated, his attention clearly was stimulated by the image of the original oak openings evoked for him by those who had seen their well-tended state in the late 1820s and early 1830s. And from what he observed in the landscape of 1847, he could envision that pre-European condition without actually witnessing it.

My earliest experiences with oak openings were akin to Cooper's—largely abstract and based on other people's writings. In 1979 I began working on my master's degree with Richard Brewer at Western Michigan University, reading about oak savannas and prairies in scientific texts. Of these, John Curtis's *Vegetation of Wisconsin* summarized the oak openings habitat best.[23] He was well aware of Cooper's book and quoted from it, as well as from original accounts. But in concluding his scientific work on oak openings, Curtis selected the savanna portion of the landscape mosaic to focus on because the woodland portion had become dense forest, and the grassland portion had either been plowed or had grown up to forest as well. Thus I—and nearly all midwestern ecologists—were raised on the notion of oak openings as scattered trees in a sea of grass. It was wonderful, though, to imagine the African savanna home-grown in America, and try to picture its diverse plant life, deep beauty, and expansive vistas. I urgently wanted to see one for myself.

I got my first inkling of what oak openings might be like when studying the prairies of the St. Clair River Delta. While visiting Harsen's Island and the mainland around Algonac, I used the U.S. Geological Survey topographic map which happened to include a portion of Canada, namely Walpole and Squirrel Islands. These lands are home to the original inhabitants of the oak openings, the

Potawatomie, Huron, and Ottawa Indians, who maintained them by setting annual fires as they had for centuries. A cartographer at the USGS had created an abstraction on paper of the oak openings landscape, revealing the peninsulas and islands of forest, the interdigitation of prairie with woodlands and savannas. On paper I could see the commingling of the great Eastern Forest Biome with the grasslands of the Great Plains, just as I also "saw" what the oak openings were like through the words of the pioneers.

In 1980 I met Don Langendoen who was completing his master's degree on the prairies of Ontario. He confirmed that the Indians burned their reservation yearly and that it was the best location in Canada to see tallgrass prairie. I visited Walpole Island the next year. A boat ferried me across the St. Clair River, and, after checking through customs, I slowly drove through the reservation greeted by Indian children and dogs. I drove randomly and somehow ended up at a road bend overlooking what I'd not yet been able to accurately form in my imagination. The burned oak woodlands, the grassy openings, and scattered old oak trees appeared to be the authentic landscape of historical accounts to which I'd formed an attachment, as Cooper did, albeit without actually seeing it. I had stepped back in time, witnessed for myself what had existed in my home state of Michigan, and felt satisfied that a dreamlike image had become real.

Little of the original oak openings remains. By some accounts, less than one percent of its original thirty million acres retains a semblance of its former ecological constituents and beauty.[24] Because of this rarity and the picturesque vistas that oak openings conjure, many groups and individuals in the Midwest have taken on the task of re-creating examples of the oak openings. Their work has an aspect of longing. Longing for what is absent is at the heart of nostalgia. As Jim pointed out, Cooper sought to remake the American wilderness experience in the oak openings landscape, if only in his imagination. A modern ecological understanding demonstrates that Cooper's view of American history playing out in the oak openings at his career's end was flawed—settlement destroyed all but the scattered oaks, leaving the job of picking up the pieces to later generations. What does the modern "restorer" of oak openings expect while engaged in the re-creation of the oak openings landscape?

There is a large movement in the Chicago area to restore oak savanna over vast expanses of land in the Cook County Forest Reserve District. The impulse behind this painstaking labor is to make it possible for people to recover a more beautiful landscape while participating in its resurrection. The restorationists want to save and see the plants and animals of the oak openings and also be agents of husbandry, as the Indians were agents of husbandry before them.

One restorationist writes: "Our objective was clear. . . . It was to restore these tracts to their original, natural condition. . . . People responded quickly to the purity and grandeur of the vision. Right in the metropolis we would restore something of real cultural and ecological significance. . . . "[25]

His feelings are echoed by others: "We are attempting to heal past abuses, to make the ecosystem whole again," writes a participant in restoration activities. At the end of their lives some of the pioneers who settled and destroyed the oak openings understood their part in its demise, while accepting this as the inevitable consequence of progress. At an 1893 meeting of the Pioneer Society in Centerville, Michigan, settler Ruth Hoppin revealed feelings like those of the modern restorationists:

> Your secretary has requested me to describe the appearance of a Michigan oak openings in its primeval beauty. Such a description would require the eye of an artist and the pen of a poet. Much as I loved those forest scenes, I have not words sufficient to give you any adequate picture of them. . . . I see the day coming when there will not be a patch of forest where the child may see the flowers which charmed his parents eyes. Like buffalo, the deer, the wild pigeon, the Whip-poor-will and the prairie hen, these, too, will soon be things of the past. The last pioneer will soon be gone and with him many of the native plants and animals will soon disappear.[26]

The impulse to despair of a loss, or to rally against the loss of something valued, or merely to evoke in a reader sympathy for something beautiful but doomed, are reactions to the destruction of the oak openings exhibited by some white settlers and by modern restorationists. If in *The Oak Openings* Cooper allayed his own misgivings about the way the wilderness was being settled and elevated oak openings as the ideal wilderness landscape for western civilization, the restorers of oak openings seek to redefine their role in the American landscape and redefine the proper place of humans in nature. Restorationists are driven by a heightened understanding of what oak openings represent to people: "Similar to good parenting or coaching or teaching, the goal of restoration is to help some life go forward on its own—and in the process become more truly itself."[27] The early descriptions and first-hand accounts of oak openings, together with scientific information, have so captured the imagination of non-scientists, that they are leading the reclamation of the oak openings landscape.

As he or she works, the restorationist has in mind a time when people co-existed with oak openings in a mutually beneficial way. Actively manipulating nature to recreate the oak openings, just as the Indians created them originally, restores a type of relationship between people and nature which existed at different times and places around the globe: people as agents of beneficial change. Writes Packard, "The new view of nature (i.e., restoration) is admittedly poorer in romantic purity and mystic detachment. Yet it's richer in participation. . . . Throughout most of our species' history, we were a part of nature. Our challenge now is to rediscover that role and play it well."

"Restoration implies surrender," affirms a participant in the Chicago restoration effort. Surrender in her sense means a return to a kind of garden—the oak openings—which we lost because we could not tend it well. In his *Oak Openings* Cooper created a landscape that can reconcile this contradiction between the violent process of settlement and the enobling lessons of a wilderness landscape. The modern environmentalist essentially shares Cooper's own nostalgia for a landscape of primeval purity and wild beauty. Modern oak openings restorationists are recreating that landscape and in the process reclaiming people's place in an actual garden. In this image, the past and the future merge.

Prairie and
the Land of Imagination

Kim

*I was invited to speak at the Blue Mounds Writer's Series, Luverne,
Minnesota, July 28, 1999 after the publication of* Valley of Grass.

It's so pleasant to be here on a prairie evening, listening to wind caress the
grasses, smelling the earth, watching the sun lock the doors at the end of
its rounds. Fred Manfred, Jr., Dave Breifogle, and friends of Blue Mounds
State Park, thank you for inviting me to speak this evening. I wish my family
could be here, but they're in Sioux Falls where we'll be leaving from tomorrow
for the Black Hills. I'd mostly like to see my kids' surprise when they see their
daddy talk for more than five minutes without interruption.

Much of what this state park is about is prairie. Most likely during your visits
here some facts about prairie have seeped in to your general store of knowledge.
Better writers than I have explained, from a scientific and literary point of view,
the essence of prairie, the stuff it's made of, and its history in North America, so
I won't try to imitate them. Just to put us all on the same footing, let me give a
few pointers on understanding prairie here in the Upper Midwest—or if you are
a westward-looking type, here on the flanks of the Great Plains.

Prairie is easy to sum up. It is old, it is complex, and it is opportunistic. Some
kind of grassland has always been around the central part of the continent since
the Rocky Mountains pushed upwards between 135 and 65 million years ago and
turned off the water supply from the Pacific Ocean. Without getting into the
details, let's say that a few hundred thousand years ago the gigantic mammals of
the Great Plains—the mastodon, woolly mammoth, saber tooth tiger, horse, giant
bison, and ground sloth—had found a home in grassland about where the Great
Plains exist today, including the Blue Mounds area and the Inner Prairie Coteau.
Some 8,000 years ago, everyone pretty much agrees, this region was a vast grassy
landscape inhabited by the same range animals that white explorers found in the

The Sioux Quartzite at Blue Mounds, southwest Minnesota, formed some 1.7 billion years ago.

early 1800s. In short, when the ancient civilizations of the Middle East were in their infancy, prairie was already eons old.

Looking at a prairie you wouldn't expect much from it. We tend to associate trees with things of nature that are comfortable and helpful: shade, shelter, fuel, fruit, nuts, honey. Wasn't it a tree that dispensed knowledge in that famous Garden? As for the grass, that was what all things returned to. It was associated with death and decay. It also happened to be very good for feeding cows, though to some people's minds, not quite good enough, so improvements were made— interseeding with Asiatic and European forage grasses, herbiciding to get rid of the wildflowers and give more elbow room to the grasses, planting exotic shelter belts of foreign trees and shrubs to shield animals and people from the brunt of the elements. But in terms of what it could do for soil, the grass had it all over the trees. It is no coincidence that the corn belt, and the wheat belt, the nation's larder, the breadbasket of the world, our country's heartland—its vital, nourishing, replenishing center—are located squarely atop the lands that had been underneath grass for at least 8,000 years. And the forested regions? Well, some of them make good cropland too, except that in many of the best farming districts once forested—Ohio, Indiana, southern Michigan—grass was there before the trees. The point is that if you grow prairie grasses instead of trees, in time you will get a deep, fertile soil that surpasses in growing potential any other kind of soil.

Let's talk about complexity. If you think that 500 cable TV channels are confusing, imagine trying to tune into the myriad, indecipherable connections of the prairie ecosystem. There are usually some 300 to 500 plant species in a square mile of native midwestern prairie. Throw in a couple thousand species of insects, one-hundred-fifty types of birds, several dozen species of mammals, reptiles, and amphibians—and we haven't begun to list the strange cryptic aquatic insects and other life forms, the darters, madtoms, shiners, mussels, and the rest—put them all together and you have more than exhausted the human capacity for under-standing just what the heck is going on. In one simple example, there is a kind of weevil that lays its eggs inside the pods of false indigo, a robust legume with spires of white flowers. The larvae that hatch eat the seeds, which you might think is bad, but...ah, here's the mystery. In those wild indigo pods left alone by the weevil, the seeds fail to germinate. What is going on? Well, it is one of nature's truisms that you've got to give a little to get a little. As it turns out, the weevil carries a fungus on its body which infects and breaks down the seed coat of the legume, letting water and air in and the engine of germination to start. The prairie is an encyclopedia of individuals, habits, doings, and goings-on rooted in the processes of ebb and flow, give and take, death and rebirth.

And out of this complexity comes a kind of balance utterly foreign to our way of thinking. It is a balance of the whole based on harm and even disaster to the individual. How was it possible for prairie grassland to survive more or less in its current incarnation for 8,000 years? And for tens and hundreds of thousands of years before, how did it persist as a grassland we would recognize as very similar to the ones we enjoy today?

Let me paint you a scenario. Start with a clump of little bluestem grass. It is the early 1800s. We are standing on the Rock, this spot by the river Inyan Reakah, the Lakota words for River of the Rock. A small herd of two or three hundred bison have ambled towards us from the northwest all day, coming up from the creek where they drank this morning and now we see them eating steadily as they walk. They pass around us now, and a huge bull twists its head and bites deep into the clump of little blue, taking over half its top. Since the prairie had burned over early this spring, the grass tastes delicious, without any of last year's old tops to get in the way, and the fresh leaves are rich in nitrogen. They were stimulated to grow rapidly after the fire killed a portion of the root crown, and the prairie roots delivered whatever nitrogen they could spare to the fast-growing shoots.

Now the herd is beyond us, but not before several of the beasts have stepped on and crushed the remaining upright stems. The next day a pocket gopher pushes up from underground where it has been eating the roots of nearby purple coneflowers and prairie turnips. The black grains of earth spill over the little bluestem, burying it. (It gets worse. Like a soap opera, isn't it?) Winter comes and with it an early snow. Bison digging through the crust in December uncover the still-green spring-flowering prairie grasses, which grow on the drier ridge crests. The snow is trampled, scattered, piled, and when spring arrives the little bluestem finds itself in full sun before the snow has completely melted. The warming rays stimulate its growth, and a few sprigs press through the gopher mound. But this is a dry spring. The plants all around quickly use up the moisture in the soil's surface, and by mid-spring draw the life-giving element from their deepest roots. Since the little bluestem lost much of its top last year, it did not provide its roots with the sugars they needed to sustain life, and some of the roots died. As much as a third die naturally in any year, but the plant has no cushion. Its hold on subterranean territory wanes. Next door, clumps of muhly grass and western wheatgrass had a good year. By mid-spring they are growing better than they have in years, and their roots push into the territory once claimed by the little bluestem. With its waning reserves, our little bluestem pushes up a profusion of flowering stems that ripen into seed stalks that will be shattered by the winter winds.

The summer is dry, as is the fall and spring. Next year the bison spend more time in the river bottoms east of the Rock. We see the herd several miles away, like brown pebbles on a billiard table. Over half the calves died in the winter when the great white wolves came north to escape a rising drought. Now in mid-summer, catastrophe. A prairie wildfire ignited by a company of white explorers sweeps east on a dry, hot wind. The fuel is light—just two seasons worth—but a conflagration engulfs our ridgeline. In seconds it is over and streamers of flame pick up steam below the escarpment where wind-blown embers sparked the fire again. For the little bluestem, this is its last year. With scant root reserves, it will send up a few new shoots. Overtopped by other plants, outcompeted underground, it dies and becomes the beginning of another plant's success story.

And on that failed bluestem hinges, perhaps the fate of a butterfly that laid its eggs, and on the success of those eggs, perhaps a plant will not be pollinated. And without that pollination, a coneflower may not cast seeds one last time before it is killed by a foraging pocket gopher. And the pocket gopher? It could be food for a badger someday, and in their ceaseless cat-and-mouse game, the gophers and badgers dig in the soil, the pursued and pursuer, breaking up the roots of dead prairie grasses, combining them with the rock and bone and flesh of millions of individuals that have lived and died in this spot for millennia. But the whole endures, doesn't it? And who is to say what is failure, and what is success?

There is a mystery here. Once I name it, I will probably be corrected. In reading about this place, I learned two things. First that the original name for this spot was "The Rock." The Lakota Indians who mined pipestone inter-bedded in the Sioux Quartzite that crops out here and there in southwest Minnesota called the river running beneath the escarpment Inyan Reakah: River of the Rock. The Rock they referred to is the one we are standing on. Passing by here in 1843, Joseph Nicollet drew a map depicting the Rock and the River, which he translated as Rock River. The name stuck and became the county name. What is more interesting and mysterious is how the Rock itself disappeared from the language of the landscape.

I heard and read two stories of what came next. In one story, the Rock was renamed the Mound by white settlers. Why they chose this less definite description of the place, I don't know, since the river and county kept the original name. "Rock" is a little stark perhaps. Today Mound Township contains the Rock and the little creek flowing off the plateau named Rock Creek. The other story is more romantic and picturesque. In this version, the settlers called the Rock "Blue Mounds" because they fancied it gave off a bluish cast seen from a distance in a certain light. Today the two stories collide on maps and atlases.

Which is it? An unadorned, softened version of the original Indian word, or a gussied up name to attract tourists and conjure up a magical aura? We can talk about this later, if you want, but I think the three names served three different historical periods and levels of awareness—the Rock, the Mound and most recently, Blue Mounds. What did and do these names signify to people living and working here and in the Inner Prairie Coteau?

The Rock was created some 1.7 billion years ago, as life on the planet blossomed. Over a billion years away were the first dinosaurs, and 1.699 billion years away were the first humans. Now we're standing on it, transformed from its original composition of shifting sands and calcium-laden waters to a scintillating, warm-colored rock that shows up all over the state in schools, courthouses, libraries, and commercial buildings. The Lakota called it what it was—Rock—and laid claim to a lineage among the most ancient on Earth. Then came the settlers with a new name: the Mound. It sounds more civilized already. It is not feral rock, not rough and jagged, not uninviting, but rather broken in as an accoutrement of a settled landscape. It doesn't sound very hard to walk up. To the settlers it was truthfully a mound or high spot in the plains compared to the peaks and promontories of the Appalachians and Adirondacks back East.

By 1920 the automobile age was upon us. Promoters of the "Good Roads" movement inspired a massive government program to straighten and pave roads across the continent. The frontier ended just thirty years before, but tourism and attractive destinations already were important to the economies of rural America. "Blue Mounds" anyone? I actually like the name, Blue Mounds. But I wonder what the change means for our relationship to the land. Do we treat the land as we view it? As our kinship with land changes, do we change our behavior towards it? Rock: Mound: Blue Mounds. Lakota: white settler: economic booster. What does this evolving emphasis mean for the land itself?

I think it mostly means forgetting what the land is about and the bounty it can give if treated well. It seems to represent a fading faith in land as the prime source of wealth and prosperity. The land and what it produced—bison meat and hide, wild fruits and vegetables, ceremonial objects and medicines—were certainly enough for the Lakota, though they did engage in a little capital accumulation by mining the ruddy, easily worked catlinite and trading it for what they couldn't get hereabouts. The first settlers applied a different standard, for they wanted the land to give up more of itself. They needed a cash economy to build their towns and roads and import from the East the customary trappings of civilization. The plow and cow replaced fire and bison as major forces on the land. Still the hunting was good in the early days, and the streams mostly clear. But a clean break with the past was earnestly desired, and the Rock became the Mound. That ancient lineage was clipped and sutured to a different time line beginning in Europe. This was nothing less than a dramatic and radical shift in attitudes towards the land. The land was treated very differently as the settlers built here a facsimile of the civilized Eastern U.S. and Europe.

At this point some of you are secretly telling me to stop dwelling on the past, quit bemoaning the loss of the wilderness. And besides, you think, the speaker wouldn't even be here if this were still Indian territory. True, very true. Let me fast-forward then to the present day.

I won't dwell on this, but you all know we have the greatest system for mass agricultural production in the world. And we are exporting that model to the rest of the world. It is based on devising a way to make the land put out the maximum amount of biomass year after year without variation, despite hail, floods, pests, and other disasters. It isn't perfect yet, but we're working on making it perfect. We can feed the world, which is good in a way. But are we successful in other ways equally important?

It may be that people are increasingly putting less and less faith in the land itself, the cornerstone of life on the planet, and trusting more and more in the human-built world for survival. The human-built world is more predictable than nature, the logic goes. Perhaps the markets we build and grease with capital from around the globe will provide us with the investment power we need to grow ourselves out of any economic downturn or technological problem that comes up. Perhaps the businesses now creating new life forms and methods of using those life forms will build us a way of living on Earth freed from the bondage of nature's ups and downs, fulfilling an age-old dream of perpetual cornucopia, that old horn of plenty idea that's been around forever. It is what we want and need as a species—to feel secure in our individual lot, and to pass on a legacy to our inheritors, children, students, and beneficiaries. But how much of this may turn out to be just a dream, a fanciful concoction as we shift our gaze from the Rock to the imagined landscape of the Blue Mounds?

The book you invited me here to talk about, *Valley of Grass*, tells the stories of many who are turning their gaze back to the land. They are figuring out how to give back to the land its native strength, and live off that. They are finding that the land is not stingy, but bountiful. They are learning how to induce the land to give up just a little more than it might under wilderness conditions—a little more forage, a little more meat, a little more seed, a little more tourist dollars—and discovering that this breathes life into the entire landscape. Streams run cleaner, fishing is better, wildlife rebounds, the place seems more alive . . . not a black desert from horizon to horizon where everything except the people are a temporary fixture or just passing through. This is the way it was supposed to be if only our settler forebears had understood the land a little better and not been so hasty to cut themselves off from the past. The human future in this place will be, I am sure, a more secure partnership with the land, more ecologically blessed, happier, and more sustainable. People already are pointing the way in the Red River Valley.

What do you have here in this place to help that along? For one thing you've got several square miles of grass that couldn't be plowed because Sioux quartzite is underneath it. Most prairie counties in the state are lucky if there's enough native grass left to cobble a couple hundred acres of prairie together. All the ingredients are here: grass, bison, fire. Grass endures. Bison have done just fine for 100,000 years. Fire is a tool easily mastered. And beneath it all you've got the Rock that split the last glacier in half at a time when most of

Minnesota was buried under a half-mile of ice. There's something special about a place that can resist the irresistible.

The prairie is old, complex and opportunistic. It can teach us how to grow old and endure as a civilization. To exist side by side with meadowlarks and pocket gophers, to celebrate the dying roots of grasses and vibrant green of each prairie spring...that is something to work for. We already know how to do it, and it begins with a little shift in attitude. Whatever you build starts with that. And for good measure, when you build, build on the Rock. Inyan Reakah!

Orange Lichen

Jim

Here on the beach beside this barren lake,
I'm reading a book with my back to a stone ledge
which has been disinfected by a glacier.

Life cannot everywhere triumph
if we want to be alone.

But orange lichen is splashed
all over the boulders—
close up, the petalled structure
expands from the center
like suburbs or cancer, the optimism
of an organism,
bent on wringing the silence
from each stone.

You find it wherever you look—
the intrepid virus, the pioneering bacterium,
breeding in deep sea vents, in the viscous darkness
of oil wells, on the glaciers,
in the arid valleys of Antarctica.
Yet once raised to the level of mankind,
this cleverness turns suicidal, manic,
cutting the throats of children,
inventing the car bomb.

How peaceful
to be the only figure in a wilderness
as the wind rifles the pages of my book.
Here where the gulls cannot ask
for answers, where
I might retire
to translate death's blue sutras
into the vulgar language
of my era.

OLIGOTROPHIC

JIM

Dead. Cold. Clear
as air. Pure
as ice: it takes 180 years
for water to leave this basin,
which means—
says the limnologist on the radio—
if your nose were fine enough,
you could draw a cup and taste the musketry
of 1812, the ashes of Toronto.
The lake remembers more than we do:
blood rinsed from a tomahawk,
carbon from the Cloquet fire,
iron ore in the bowels of the *Edmund Fitzgerald*,
the smell of Norwegian pancakes
from a cabin on the shore of Isle Royale in 1927;
the acrid taste of taconite,
the stink of bloated lake trout, stench of burning
pyramids of sturgeon. Potato peels
from Louis Agassiz's Harvard expedition
in 1845. The heel of a moccasin
awash in Two Harbors
in the McKinley administration.
The webbed feet of a fish duck
at the mouth of the Big Two-Hearted
River, right now, paddling.

A beer bottle tossed
from a party barge last night
in Murray Bay. Sawdust
from the last great white pines
on Grand Island
logged in the 1960s
and ferried across, section by section
on this very lumber tug
tied to the dock
and leaking diesel.

Environmental Restoration in Society

Kim

"The state is neither a good doctor nor a good teacher."

—Vaclav Havel

In the spring of 1999 Vaclav Havel, president of the Czech Republic, spoke at Macalester College in St. Paul. I was there. His words, delivered in a deep, evenly paced voice, electrified me. He spoke of the need for a civil society and of the failure of government institutions to create such a society. I saw in his comments many parallels to the environmental movement. I understood that Havel's background as playwright, humanist, and civic leader was very different from the background of the scientists and activists who have, to date, shaped the environmental movement. I think of Henry David Thoreau, John Muir, Aldo Leopold, Rachel Carson, Arne Naess, and so many other scientists, academics, philosophers, and naturalists—none has the unique perspective of Havel. Inspired by his words, and borrowing heavily from his train of thought, I wrote this essay while listening to him speak in order to inspire other conservation-minded people like myself who believe America must fulfill its promise as the incubator of just human relations, not only among people, but between people and their environment. The resemblance between his words and the following will be strong, although I have never seen the text he delivered that day. I consider the following a transcription of Havel's thoughts, were he to speak on the subject of the environment.

We are all complicit in a conspiracy of silence about the environment. We are comfortable in our material wealth yet insecure about losing it. And so we remain silent and conforming.

Our wealth flows from the environment, though we are hardly conscious of that fact. The flow of wealth is slowing now under the burden of too much prosperity and too much growth. The flow of environmental goods could be restored quickly, and a new kind of prosperity engendered, if we stopped degrading the environment. It is like the restoration of free speech after a period of repression. If the censure is removed, the flow begins again.

The restoration of subtle structures and species will take longer. The breakdown is not easily reversed when species go extinct. The degradation of habitats by pollution and bulldozers heals slowly. But eventually they can be restored nearly completely. If the decision to stop the degradation is made, what can be done to alter the course of environmental trajectories?

Creativity must be the foundation of all change. The human imagination is the greatest capital and source of solutions we have. Beyond this it is a matter of institutions. First it is important to have a local institution that will lead the initiatives to restore the environment and provide the will-power to begin. The second institution is the government that can pass laws and enforce existing good laws to improve the environment. The government also has a responsibility to facilitate and enable the acts of others.

The last important group of institutions includes the non-profits the state grants the powers to do the work of society in restoring the environment.

Co-option by the state should be discouraged by all the powers of society. Individual groups and non-state institutions must remain independent of any influence by the state, or else the inertia and recalcitrance of the state begins to infect the prime agents of change in society. Elected officials likewise should be held at arms length as they too often support the aims of the status quo.

The electoral outcomes opposing the environment do not mean that loyal opposition should not exist. A parallel and alternative set of initiatives to those promoted by government should be welcomed, not marginalized, by political institutions and the majority of the electorate.

A mix of points of view inevitably will lead to better conservation ideas and environmental restoration work. Competition among ideas is important. When power is used to squash ideas, the effectiveness of conservation and restoration work will falter.

The existence of local power bases and institutions outside the state helps insure that the stability of the restoration initiative continues. Environmental restoration, if centered in a narrow range of consensus around the government's norms, is easily defused the moment a government changes.

Moreover, a government-based initiative is less efficient than smaller, more mobile institutions. The amount of resources used in maintaining an organization would better be spent on the restoration work itself.

People are creatures who yearn for cooperative participation in the group and community and want to influence things around them.

The subtle elements of restoration work are perhaps the most important—attention to detail in the place where we live, working closer with others, feeling empowered to change one's environment for the better.

Finally, the state's best interest is not vested in itself but in the empowerment of others to accomplish society's aims. Blind allegiance to the institutions that currently are charged with environmental improvement should be transformed to the acceptance of others as the prime motivators. The state then becomes simply a helpmate to the work of the private citizen and institution.

In these ways, environmental health would be restored in a brief time such that the next generation will enjoy the full benefits of it.

PRESERVING THE ETERNAL

KIM

Address at the annual meeting of the Minnesota Center for Environmental Advocacy, St. Croix River, Franconia Township, Minnesota, September 17, 2000.

We are here today to enjoy a prairie planted by human hands and a savanna that was not. As we walk this ground, we will be reminded that each generation must struggle to keep a portion of the landscape for itself. Without that struggle, this prairie would not exist, nor would the savanna.

It is a paradox that the parts of nature that seem so well outfitted for survival over eons would need the help of creatures whose lifespans are but several decades long. Yet that is where we are today as a culture in relation to nature. We have lost sight of the eternal and, consequently, the eternal is disappearing. We tend to focus on the annual balance sheet, the quarterly return, the new building or dot-com, and the other signs of progress we expect from society. Of less concern are the millions of years of development represented by a single species, including ourselves, and the thousands of years of coming-to-be in a single community of plants and animals living together in a particular place. That legacy of life is the future hope of this planet we must preserve.

When you see the seedheads of big bluestem and the arching limbs of the bur oak, ask yourself how long ago did these plants first spread out across the landscape. And living on and with these plants, picture not just the bison and elk, but a host of animals stretching back to before the last glaciers advanced over 100,000 years ago. Imagine that unbroken line of life here in this place. Call that progress. Call that a mark of high achievement. Stay focused on that your life long.

There are many ways to serve. For you here who work with and for an environmental group, you work on behalf of that longevity. Whether member and donor, volunteer or employee, you are protecting a living lineage reaching back eons. You are helping to preserve the eternal.

BLACKBERRIES

JIM

This August my family and I left Chicago for a three-week stay in my father-in-law's house. It is one of those modern houses with an open floor plan, a kitchen island and a wall of glass facing into forty acres of pine and oak. It has a woodstove and a dishwasher and thus combines the rural and the urban in a manner conducive to a slightly removed contemplation of the organic world. This was a great improvement over our urban environment in north Chicago. Despite the fact that we have an roomy apartment on a shady street—hardly a concrete wasteland, that is—I find my peace of mind steadily eroding from June on, when our windows must be open and the wail of sirens and randomly triggered car alarms, the shouts of bar patrons returning home at odd hours, and the constant tattoo of the neighbors' basketball game conspire to drive away sleep and peace of mind.

Thus it was with relief that we pulled up the steep driveway of our temporary home in the woods. After I shut off the car engine, all we heard was the wind soughing in the pines and the occasional bird-call. Instead of smelling ozone, fried potatoes, and bus exhaust, we had oxygen fresh from its arboreal manufacturers—tinged with pine resin and various meadowy smells.

This was, of course, a very cliché moment for a writer: nothing could be more predictable than that I should find the air fresher in the country. The image of Eddie Arnold beating his chest and inhaling at the opening credits of *Green Acres* came to mind. Yet life does imitate art, and some clichés are cliché simply because they are so true. And what was cliché for me was entirely original to my one-year-old daughter, who has had never known anything but the city.

Her reaction was instructive: she took to the woods immediately. There was so much to look at, to touch and feel and sometimes (when I was not looking) to taste. The sensual complexity of her environment underwent a major upgrade, you might say—there were Queen-Anne's lace to sniff, and cone flowers and Joe-Pye weeds and various mints; there were pine needles and stones and dead leaves to pick up; everywhere were butterflies, beetles, all the cast of the rural

113

woodlot—ruffed grouse, baby racoons. Daddy longlegs. Spindly-legged deer edging out of the shade. A screech owl at dusk.

But best of all: there were berries to pick. From the moment she tasted her first, my daughter became a keen berry-hound, able to spot the glossy droop of a dewberry among the grasses along the path. She would first point at them, then sit down deliberately and, with index finger and thumb extended, carefully pluck one from its stem with the deliberation of a hydraulic sampling arm of the Viking lander. Once she had plucked it, it went right to her mouth and she became a perfect icon of gastronomic pleasure, her round moon-face stained with berry juice and bearing a little abstract smile of joy.

Dewberries are low, shy members of the rose family; inhabitants of the sandy wastes, they have sparse but succulent droops. Blackberries, on the other hand, grow on tall bushes, and their fruits are full and densely packed. These I had to pick for her from a patch on a western slope recently carved out by a developer's bulldozer. She would wait in her stroller, bobbing up and down and *oohing* with anticipation until I arrived with a handful of fruit; she would cram these in her mouth—turning her *oohs* of delight to half-audible humming noises of appreciation. Her capacity was apparently endless: she would continue to point and *ooh* at berries she saw winking at her in the sun until it was time to go.

The common blackberry of the Midwest is Rubus allegheniensis—delicious but thorny.

It was hard to know who enjoyed this more, my daughter or me. Thinking about it later, I recalled Coleridge's wonderful lines to his infant son, Hartley:

My babe so beautiful! it thrills my heart
With tender gladness, thus to look at thee,

The quote was from "Frost at Midnight," the meaning of which was very apropos to my own situation. In the poem, Coleridge is contrasting his own childhood, spent "In the great city, pent 'mid cloisters dim" with the life he hopes to offer his own child:

But thou, my babe! shalt wander like a breeze
By lakes and sandy shores, beneath the crags
Of ancient mountain, and beneath the clouds
Which image in their bulk both lakes and shores
The lovely shapes and sounds intelligible
Of that eternal language, which thy God
Utters, who from eternity doth teach
Himself in all, and all things in himself.

The power of the poem rests in the pathos the speaker stirs in us: the contrast of his sad remembrances and his naive hopes for his own child's future. To have a child is to dream a better life: to erase mistakes and heal the damage dealt by a sometimes brutal world. Coleridge is sure he has identified the most vicious influence on his childhood: the great city, whose main deficiency was, first, that it contained "naught lovely"—his friend Wordsworth would say that it was full of "shapes of joyless daylight"—second, that it was lonely. Indeed, loneliness is the heart of Coleridge's memory. He gives us this image of himself as a young student in Christ's Hospital, sitting at his desk and trembling at the "stern preceptor's face" and hoping, every time the door opened, to see the face of "Townsman, or aunt, or sister more beloved" who might relieve his isolation.

What is strange about the poem is that, what he hopes for his young son is not company, but a different kind of solitude—he wishes to trade the solitude of the city for the solitude of the country. He hopes for his son this will be a kind of divine congress, for the sensuous images of nature are God's "eternal language." By drawing close to them, he says to his sleeping son, "Great Universal Teacher! he shall mold/Thy spirit, and by giving make it ask." This is more the solitude of Moses in the Negev than the loneliness of the ninteenth century's disenchanted intellectual; it is a solitude full of meaning and beauty:

Therefore all seasons shall be sweet to thee,
Whether the summer clothe the general earth
With greenness, or the redbreast sit and sing
Betwixt the tufts of snow on the bare branch
Of mossy apple tree, while the nigh thatch
Smokes in the sun-thaw; whether the eave-drops fall
Heard only in the trances of the blast,
Or if the secret ministry of frost
Shall hang them up in silent icicles,
Quietly shining to the quiet Moon.

Coleridge asserts that "all seasons shall be sweet," because they will not remind his son of sadness but of joy. The final images of the poem are so detailed and intimate: snow on a bare branch, the thatch smoking in sun-thaw, the dripping of eaves, and the final, incomparable line: "silent icicles/Quietly shining to the quiet Moon."

I have been resisting that poem, or the notions behind it, for many years, having come to feel the main enemy of the natural landscape in America is not so much industrial rapacity as pastoral longing. The inability of Americans to reconcile themselves to civic life fuels the rapid spread of the suburb, that bastard landscape neither rural nor civil: less than an urb, not nearly field enough for the wild and semi-wild to inhabit. Americans are all too susceptible to the myth of the "natural man" versus the corrupt urbanite. Everyone of course wants to give his or her child grass and a shade tree and fresh air; because in America land prices are so cheap most of us can provide some semblance of this edenic environment, and thus the suburbs continue to burgeon. I have long held the notion that the best thing one can do for the environment is to stay in the city, to fight to make urban life more pleasant and so slow down the centrifugal flight of the population to the periphery—a periphery on which animals and agriculture must increasingly make do with less. The more we flee to the suburbs, the more we destroy what we run toward—as the past forty years can attest.

On a more theoretical level, I have come to understand that by splitting "nature" into dichotomies like urban/rural, human/nonhuman, nature/culture, we are often perpetuating the arrogant Western assumption that there *is* such a duality. If we are to take Darwin seriously, a city is as much a natural production as a forest. Both obey all the laws of nature, both are collections of completely natural organisms, pursuing non-mystical economies—that is, metabolizing the sun's energy and using it to fuel complex behaviors, most of which involve defense and/or reproduction.

Therefore, I have been impatient with my Romantic forbearers (let's face it, anyone who claims to be an environmentalist is one way or another a descendent of the Romantic poets). I have learned to see the products of human culture—smart bombs, Corinthian pillars, Poussin's oil paintings, parking meters, a bottle of Rioja—as part of the continuum of natural events, and to see the wish to avoid modernity as naive, if not reactionary at times. I have refused to think that the only life worth living for a poet is in a farmhouse in New Hampshire.

But fatherhood has its humiliations, and this is one. I, too, want grass for my child, and by grass I do not mean the postage-stamp of green in front of our building, with its dogshit and burger wrappers. I would also like some distance between me and my neighbors' insatiable appetite for noise of all varieties: television, stereo, car mufflers. I am suddenly envious of Coleridge's silent icicles.

Certainly my daughter's reaction is a rebuke to my jaded sophistication— she is unabashed in her enthusiasm. There are dun sparrows to chase, and shaded gothic clerestories of red pine, fragrant with the tang of sap, whose floor is soft with years of russet needle-fall—and at dusk there are Whip-poor-wills to pipe her to sleep (certainly an improvement over the blare of our city landlady's television, or the kid in the apartment next door practicing "Good King Wenceslaus" on his saxophone, over and over!).

What is at issue is the senses: it is the quality of a sensorium, not just the coordinates of the location. Modern urban life cuts us off from the sense-world by either the paucity of its sensual offerings, or the surfeit of the stimuli it does offer. It lacks the "unity in diversity" the romantics thought good art—and nature—possessed: the subtle interplay of harmonies and discords. Perhaps our beef with modern industrial society is not that it is unnatural, but that it is unsubtle—therefore, unhealthy and ugly. This is an objection that has to do with our well-being rather than with the metaphysics of essence. There is no reason, in theory, why the human environment may not be as beautiful and healthful as a field. I have seen hints of it, in fact—in the compact cities of Europe, for example, which, as they have entered the post-industrial stage of capitalism, have grown greener and more pleasant every decade, scaled as they are to foot traffic, and populated as they are with green parks, and equipped as they are with public transport that conveys you to pleasant countryside—since the countryside has not been utterly ravaged by the metastasizing suburbs. (I think of sunlit afternoons in the Forêt de Soignes, on the outskirts of Brussels, or in the Black Forest, which begins at a Freiburg tram stop.)

Nor is the dream of suburbia utterly false. When I was twelve my family moved to the suburbs (we had previously lived in a turn-of-the-century neighborhood of brick bungalows and overarching trees), and my siblings and I were somewhat dubious of the new landscape. The identical aluminum-skinned houses with identically skinny maple trees planted in front seemed, even to our young eyes, to lack character—yet at the edge of my neighborhood there were woodlots and cornfields. The raw neighborhood had been hacked out of farm fields so recently the barbed wire and weathered outbuildings still remained—the fields still had visible furrows. On my way to school in the morning I would scare pheasants out of the frost-rimed weeds, or find rabbit tracks in the new snow, or watch the winter sun rising behind a fencerow of 100-year-old bur oaks. In summer we could ride our bikes through the overgrown fields full of knapweed and timothy; we could follow the sandy paths through the remnant woods and find wild geranium and violet blooming.

I believe, in a sense, this was a divine language—certainly to have seen the moon in the sky, to have felt clean rain falling on one's upturned face, to have lain in the humid maze of tall grasses at midsummer—these are the sources of poetry and affection, memorable tokens that, despite the indifference and frequent cruelty of natural processes, the earth is still our natural home, its exhaled breath our best incense. To want this for one's children was not in itself foolish, and America's vision of suburbia was typically generous and expansive at its outset. Many people will never appreciate the world's great artwork, but anyone might look up at the moon, or a rainbow, provided the sky is not too lit up or polluted. "How does nature deify us with a few and cheap elements" says American Romantic (and Coleridge fan) Ralph Waldo Emerson; "Give me health and a day and I will make the pomp of emperors ridiculous." Perhaps the most compelling reason not to let go of the Romantic valuation of nature is this democratic availability: it is precisely the ubiquity of the natural sublime that was once a great recommendation for going into the country.

But the larger the suburb, the less available these pleasures are. The wild gets purged with weed-killer and mower. The empty lot next door is soon built upon. In my own childhood neighborhood, the suburban expansion that gave me the freedom of semi-wild fields and woods soon replaced them with houses and sterile lawns; the inexorable slide toward a fully tamed landscape—pheasants, rabbits gone the way of the rural lifestyle that once coexisted with them. Then the suburb is revealed as the worst of compromises—the congestion of the city without its compensating vitality.

I have come full circle back to Coleridge's desire to give his son a closeness to nature that might console him, or instruct him because I have discovered a new personal relevance in that desire—but I find the circle closes in an age vastly changed from Coleridge's own. My logic still seems unassailable: given our population numbers and the consumptive way we live, most of us will live in urban surroundings all our lives. The problems of over-crowding and resource scarcity are likely to get worse, not better, as we enter the next century. How to reconcile this dilemma? How can I hope to give my child what I did have, without being party to its destruction?

I have no panacea, only a few guidelines. I have resolved to live in some kind of a city—though perhaps a smaller one than Chicago. I have resolved to live near my work. I will reduce my life to a human scale wherever I can, riding my bike and walking. I have resolved not to fight for my own private compound, but for common grounds, for free access to woods and fields—this means resisting the sprawl of the city and the threatened privatization of public lands. These are the ethical beliefs I'd like to give my child—but along with them must come the first-hand experience of nature that might give her the heart to live by such rules—it is the "lovely shapes and sounds intelligible" as Coleridge put it, that bind us to the earth and motivate our ethics.

Coleridge found hope in the thought that his child would learn "far other lore/And in far other scenes" than those of his own miserable childhood. My hope is more modest: I only desire that my child will experience the natural joys of my own youth. Yet I do hope she will learn a different lore—a lore of respect, and of restraint. Such learning is not grim or austere—it merely recognizes that riches must be husbanded, that abundance may be a gift of the earth, but it is a gift that may be squandered or spoiled. Looking at my child gathering berries in the August sunlight helps me to remember that all civilizations must have an aim or goal to which they are dedicating their enormous push and drive, and I'd nominate the conservation of the natural world, source of our physical happiness, as a pretty high mark to aim at. In the words of Poet Laureate Robert Hass:

> . . . There are moments when the body is as numinous
> as words, days that are the good flesh continuing.
> Such tenderness, those afternoons and evenings,
> saying blackberry, blackberry, blackberry.

Lost in Space

Jim

*In my room, the world is beyond my understanding; But when I walk I
see that it consists of three or four hills and a cloud.*
— Wallace Stevens, "Of the Surface of Things"

L ately I have been obsessed by car commercials—their romantic promise
of freedom, of a weightless mobility across the American landscape (or
even above it, in the case of a car called "Avalon," which appears to be
able to soar among the altocumulus). Every car commercial, with the exception
of one blatantly urban Toyota spot, depicts an automobile against the backdrop
of scenic grandeur, most often Monument Valley (which has become something
of a *locus classicus* for automobile advertising), but often in those other landscapes that are visual boilerplates for America the Beautiful: New England's
woods and fields, the Colorado peaks, the California coastal highway. One
would think the car was designed specifically to connect Americans with the
natural sublime, rather than to ferry suburban children to their soccer matches
or adults to the grocery store and marriage counselor.

Regardless of the car being advertised, the scenario is relentlessly similar:
the latest passenger vehicle speeds gracefully around a curve on some two-lane
back road, the children in the back seat smiling blissfully, their parents gazing
fondly ahead as if contemplating a future full of similarly satisfying motorized
jaunts. But I ask myself, is there really a romance of the road as Ford, Honda,
Chrysler, and BMW wish to convince me there is? Can that family really be so
happy, gliding past the fields of waving wheat in its new Taurus or Saturn? A child
of the automobile age, I remember nausea, boredom, and impatience as we clicked
away the miles in our Oldsmobile VistaCruiser on yet another foray into the
American hinterland. It wasn't the road that was romantic—the road was
unremittingly dull—it was the destination, and we couldn't wait to get there so
we could stop breathing stale air, eating bad food, listening to my brother's stupid
jokes, and watching the monotonous sameness of the interstate roll by.

Speed and noise in a backward glance.

Those inclined to take too seriously the car companies' invitation to the "Freedom of the American Road" would be advised to consult their own memories, or perhaps recall Edward Abbey's description of the average family vacation in *Desert Solitaire*:

> ... *the tedious traffic jams, the awful food of park cafeterias and roadside eateries, the nocturnal search for a place to sleep or camp...the endless lines of creeping traffic, the smell of exhaust fumes... the boiling radiator and the flat tire and the vapor lock, the surly retorts of room clerks and traffic cops...and the long drive home at night in a stream of racing cars against the lights of another stream racing in the opposite direction, passing now and then the obscure tangle, the shattered glass, the patrolman's lurid blinker light, of one more wreck.*

The quote comes from Abbey's essay "Industrial Tourism and the National Parks," a lyrical diatribe against road building and as strident an anti-motorist tract as you are likely to come across. Abbey fulminates against the "Wheelchair Explorers," those "indolent millions born on wheels and suckled on gasoline, who expect and demand paved highways to lead them in comfort, ease, and safety into every nook and corner of the national parks"—an attitude Abbey condemns as destructive and low minded. Harsh words—but his intention is really therapeutic. He would have these tourists put aside their mobile chaise-longues and walk, for it is his opinion that the primary victims of industrial tourism are the motorists themselves—for they will "never escape the stress and turmoil of the urban-suburban complexes that they had hoped, presumably, to leave behind for a while." This self-victimization of the mobile classes is tragic, not only for the tourists, but for the landscape they profess to want to visit. The more accessible the parks and monuments become, Abbey points out, the more they become like the cities everyone is trying to escape. Abbey's essay hints at a more general American problem—our preference for time-saving over space-saving measures. In the most haunting words of the essay, Abbey states: "We are preoccupied with time. If we could learn to love space as deeply as we are now obsessed with time, we might discover a new meaning in the phrase to live like men."

There is a lot to ponder in these words. The motive behind the nightmarish vacation Abbey describes is exactly this time-saving obsession; the average American, having only two weeks off every year, seeks to maximize that pittance of a vacation by seeing and doing as much as possible in it. This is in accordance with the nation's general fascination with increased productivity—the worker on vacation is merely applying the discipline of the workplace to unstructured time, and the automobile is the ultimate time-saver. Yet this savings in time is accomplished at the expense of space, which is necessarily compressed, squeezed of its experiential validity. The faster you go from point A to point B, the less you see between the two points. Abbey asks, what if our emphasis were not on time, but on space? Wouldn't we spend our time differently? If we truly loved space, wouldn't we, instead of rocketing across vast distances, slow down and creep over the intimate spaces of the landscape with loving attention? If experiencing space were our goal, we would not want to miss an inch or an ell! We would certainly get out of the car and walk. Such "non-motorized tourists," says Abbey, are "hungry for a taste of the difficult, the original, the real." Here Abbey simply means that we have evolved in a particular relationship to a kind of space that is traversable by our very useful arms and legs. To move in such space is thus to recover an existence at once "original," in the sense of originary, and "real," in the sense that it is most basic to our nature.

To recover a love for human-scale space is to recover our own nature. This message seems more pertinent now than when it was first penned because never have we been so space-poor. The urge to save time, uncoupled from the urge to preserve and enjoy space, has plunged us into a new regime, one that threatens to remake the world into a kind of Cartesian abstraction so vacuous as to resemble one of Jupiter's moons. I am referring to those manufactured spaces—the strip mall, the parking lot, the airport, the divided highway—spaces hostile to the very notion of space, because they exist only to save time, to remove the obstacles between human subjects and the efficient fulfillment of their desires. Who has not felt, at some time or other, stranded on the shoulder of a modern highway, that the landscape all around one is being drained of significance, made flat and valueless by the tremendous roar and hurry of the traffic? It is like standing at the edge of a floodtide of accelerated time, a floodtide that is fast eroding the banks.

Strapped to the arrow of velocity, the modern citizen has no time for the enjoyment of landscape. Our situation is reminiscent of Heidegger's statement that, in a world where everything is equally far and equally near (thanks to improvements in communications and transportation) nearness disappears as a meaningful concept. But nearness is not merely a function of proximity, it is a function of *attention:* what we attend to draws near to us, grows larger in significance and detail. "Attention by itself is an enlarging glass," says Gaston Bachelard, the great philosopher of space. Such attention can occur only in inverse proportion to the speed at which one travels, for one's pace determines one's capacity for intimacy, and, says Bachelard, "Grandeur progresses in the world in proportion to the deepening of intimacy." Intimacy implies vulnerability, openness, a willingness to put the body at risk, at least to risk its exposure in the gaze of another, to risk nakedness. True travel—travel in space, rather than in time—requires such vulnerability, or it is only conveyance from one sameness to the next.

The landscape seen from a passing car is, by contrast, like one of those long Chinese scroll paintings that obsequious servants would unroll panorama-fashion, giving the illusion to their seated lord that he was traveling down the Yangtze or some other famous river. But this has nothing to do with a love of space. It is rather what the car companies are selling—see the USA while the CD player tinkles and the car fax keeps your commodities broker near. As a result of such conveyance, American space grows ever more two dimensional. Suppose, however, that we exit the superhighway and begin to follow the primary roads to the secondary roads, moving like a metallic salmon swimming up ever-smaller tributaries (not to die, but perhaps to be reborn). At last we come to the place where we must turn off the engine and step out of the car. If the landscape was a flat projection before, now it looms, beckons, a moving labyrinth of shadows and speckled light. The wind brings the resinous tang of the pine trees that tower over us. A path leads crookedly into the green and breathing enclosure. Anything may happen now, for we are on foot. We are conscious of shapes moving overhead in the branches, or rustling in the undergrowth. Before, we observed the landscape; now the landscape observes us. We are aware—wary! This sudden awareness fills every sense—indeed, we have come back to our senses, from the anesthesis of the highway. We are no longer drowsy emperors—we are pedestrians, vulnerable, alert, and the experience conveys a mysterious richness.

What most of us seek when traveling on vacation is just this experience of richness, along with some sense of adventure, some meaning beyond the rim of the everyday. In fact, that was the original purpose of a holiday: holy day. It was to interrupt the routine of labor, not for what most package vacations are offering—bed rest with a view of a palm tree—but for the purpose of recreating oneself through contact with the sacred. A holy day was meant to provide spiritual reactivation, so that a person might resume everyday life with restored commitment to ideals that routine can tarnish and blur. We call our parks "recreation areas" and on our holidays we make secular pilgrimages to them in the vestigial hope of renewal. But renewals come only with sacrifice, which was why the ancient pilgrimages were made on foot. The willingness to submit to the humble pedestrian role makes one receptive to the kind of transformations the pilgrim sought on his plodding journey to Walsingham or Rome or Santiago. Thoreau points this out in his famous essay "Walking," where he identifies the walker as a "saunterer," one "going a la Sainte Terre, to the Holy Land. For every walk is a sort of crusade, preached by some Peter the Hermit in us, to go forth and reconquer this Holy Land from the hands of the Infidels." He is in earnest about this—for the walk he wishes to take is into a kind of radical openness, beyond the constraints of one's social roles and commitments:

> We should go forth on the shortest walk, perchance, in the spirit of undying adventure, never to return—prepared to send back our embalmed hearts only as relics to our desolate kingdoms. If you are ready to leave father and mother, and brother and sister, and wife and child and friends, and never see them again—if you have paid your debts, and made your will, and settled all your affairs, and are a free man, then you are ready for a walk.

For Thoreau, walking was not a means of transportation, nor was it a way of taking exercise or improving one's digestion: it was a means of reclaiming the value of space. Thoreau made a living as a surveyor, after all—he knew well the ways in which space could be carved up as commodity. His daily walks enabled him to shake off this human imposition on the landscape and recover something more primal.

New York writer Niccolo Tucci, a passionate pedestrian, once differentiated between what he humorously called "l'Amerique Roulante," and "l'Amerique Eternelle." Tucci said he saw these "two Americas, one on top of the other." The first was an America always in motion between home and work, an America that consisted of the interiors of sedans and station wagons and train carriages and the insides of the board rooms and living rooms that they connected. The other America, "l'Amerique Eternelle," belongs to:

> . . . *crossing deer, to freezing ponds, to the infinity of clouds far beyond all the infinity of plains, to over-powering sixteen-cylinder crickets, katydids and grubs, to crows, to barns, to the negative mountains carved out of the earth, to nature eating up abandoned towns as quickly as barracudas eat up cattle, and no efforts of man have yet mastered that country and left traces upon it that decay could only improve.*

Tucci penned this thought in his notebooks at about the same time Edward Abbey was writing *Desert Solitaire*. At this later, much more crowded end of the century, "l'Amerique Eternelle" looks much less like a sure thing, as the exurbs metastasize into "edge cities," squeezing the deer and crows and grubs into narrower and narrower corridors and islands, turning the fields to gated communities and turning the barns into computer stores. The most devastating environmental crisis of the turn of the millennium, second only to global warming, is the destruction of wild and rural habitat—and the automobile is the main culprit in that rout. The acceleration of time eats up the surplus spaces that used to guarantee some ecological counterweight to the city—and, more importantly, it destroys the healthy dialectic between city and country, which was above all an argument about the enduring and primal necessity of space over time. The countryside was a necessary anchor firmly lodged in a past both cultural and biological—that is why Tucci called it "eternal" (which is another word for timeless, or outside of temporal flux). The wild ruralities were a brake on the hectic lifestyles of metropolitan men and women: they provided the vital seedbed of values—the beginning of all stories that all people, urban and rural, hold close to their hearts. Thoreau understood this more than anyone:

I walk out into a nature such as the old prophets and poets, Manu, Moses, Homer, Chaucer, walked in. You may name it America, but it is not America; neither Americus Vespucius, nor Columbus, nor the rest were the discoverers of it. There is a truer account of it in mythology than in any history of America, so called, that I have seen.

Cut off from space, we are cut off from our foundational myths. We are trapped in the shallowness of the present. As suburban housing obliterates the once-rural outlands, the city itself begins to decay—not only from lack of revenue, but also from lack of spatial definition. In fact, our cities suffer the same spatial erosion as does our countryside—though in the city this is more specifically a cultural tragedy. I noticed last year, walking up Fifth Avenue in Manhattan, that the Christmas decorations on the various upscale stores were no longer comprehensible to the pedestrian—either they were too large to be understood, or they were placed too high up or at an angle that made them difficult to see from the sidewalk. I wondered for whom the decorations were intended. The answer came to me suddenly: their huge size and high position meant they were best glimpsed from the middle of the street; they were meant to be seen from a car moving in traffic! This is only one anecdote, but it is undeniable that our cities are being designed for automobiles and increasingly exist in a different time zone, or, more properly, at a different velocity. This accounts for the paucity of surface detail in both modern and postmodern architecture—one does not notice fancy brickwork or carved cornices from a moving limousine or Jeep Cherokee. Thus in our urban centers the destruction of human scale is directly proportional to the mechanical acceleration of time.

It has not always been this way. Walk once on Boston's Beacon Hill, for example, and you will experience a city framed with the human body and the observant walker in mind. The Federalist townhouses with their bay windows and iron doorknockers crowd the street. One can carry on a conversation with a person leaning out of a window. The architectural detailing is clearly visible: the Palladian fanlights and Doric pilasters, the dentils and scrollwork, the stone pediments and acanthus leaves. Sunlight filters down on window- and stoop-boxes to nourish ferns, geraniums, and basil plants. In the morning and evening the street fills with people, and one hears the click of heels on cobblestones, the low sound of voices in conversation. At dusk, house lights reveal the busy kitchens, the libraries lined with books, the high-ceilinged dining rooms. We return to a time-space appropriate to our physical selves. On these narrow eighteenth-century streets, the automobile must creep along, an unwelcome intruder, its tires reverberating on the cobblestones as if to announce its embarrassing presence to all. To feel the difference this restriction makes, one has only to walk downhill to Storrow Drive, the multi-laned artery that funnels traffic into the city's heart. Traffic noise—the ubiquitous roar of American urban culture—strikes one with redoubled force as cars, with their freight of harried and sometimes angry passengers, streak by in such numbers that one is terrified to cross to the park on the other side (in fact, a special pedestrian bridge has been built for this reason). We sense borders here: at the foot of Beacon Hill we leave a civic and pedestrian paradise and enter a modern auto-utopia (from *ou-topos*, "nowhere" in Greek).

Television car ads put a positive spin on this Utopia. They depict us whizzing toward glamorous destinations, passing gorgeous scenery en route as though aesthetics were at the heart of the driving experience. The truth is that every time we clamber into our Jeep Cherokee or Dodge Neon we are choosing to save time at the expense of space—a distinctly anesthetic choice. Never mind the economic and environmental issues: it is the speed and manner of our conveyance that determines our experience of space. We should remember Abbey's point that to prefer time over space is to become dispossessed from the landscape, to become lost in one's own country. To recover our love for space, on the other hand, is to relearn what it means to live like men and women.

Gaston Bachelard once said of the poet Baudelaire that, for him, "man's poetic fate is to be the mirror of immensity; or even more exactly, immensity becomes conscious of itself, through man." To love space is to have a similarly noble idea of human destiny. It is to believe, as Abbey did, that our human purpose lies not in getting from one place to another, but in staying in one place long enough to invest that place with meaning. Such an investment is easy to make, really: you only have to get out of your car and walk.

The rolling, forested side roads of southwest Michigan—this one in Kalamazoo Township.

Vanishing Act: Dreaming of a Place in Passing

Kim

On a visit to Kalamazoo around 2001, I drove the back roads I used to bike west of town and sensed something was missing.

Somewhere west of Kalamazoo, in a southern Michigan county of the same name, is a mysterious swimming hole. Some twenty years ago I rode my bike out of town and turned south on a crowned paved road I had never seen. Suddenly the road narrowed and dipped, then passed under an arch of oaks. The prospect invited me in, and I fell into an embrace of beauty and wonder.

I braked and rolled my bike to the shoulder, legs straddling the bike's frame: to the east, a small clear pond ringed with sand-bar willow and red osier, and near the road a patch of sand and delicate grasses fringing the water. In the heat after a hard ride I wanted to plunge in. Standing in the cave of dark oaks watching the wind stir the blue surface, I was baptized by the luscious vision of the place. Then I got back on my bike and pedaled away. There was a class to attend and dozens of miles to ride, but I promised to return.

Kalamazoo County crowds my memory. I feel its cooling patches of forest and damp river bottoms, see its delicately grassed shores, its prairies of changing blossoms, hear the gurgle of limy springs in its fens, and smell its aromatic sodden bogs. These habitats, these relicts of an unsettled distant past and of my youth buoy my imagination, charting a past and future freedom. Never was I as unfettered or exuberant in wasting time, nor convinced of how to live properly as a creature of nature. It is times like these that we reach back to for sustenance when convention and the rigor of bread-winning begin to span weeks, months, years. Times like these are the antidote to merely getting by.

Since my bike ride, our country added fifty million Americans to its national total and the Dow Jones Index grew from around 1,000 to 10,000. To most people's thinking Kalamazoo County benefited from this surge in human and economic energy. Dozens of new roads now pass through woods and fields, distances between places are shorter, and people can build homes in the county's remote corners. Other roads are wider to accelerate travel. Shopping malls, gas stations *cum* food marts (they used to be gas stations with candy racks at the check-out counter), and other places of commerce anchor the four corners of major intersections. Some people have gotten rich. Others find shopping and traveling more convenient and home life more relaxing. By one standard, our dream has come true: you can buy a forty-nine-cent-bag of Doritos within five minutes of any spot in Kalamazoo County.

That wasn't my dream, but because so many Kalamazoo citizens have a vision of unbridled, relentless, unending growth, it became my reality. A few shared my dream, but most—or the most influential—did not. Was it a good vision, and is it good in execution? Should we continue this path to the future?

It's been said that if a cell behaved as people in Kalamazoo County do, a doctor would diagnose the condition as a sickness. In that county the normal functions of the biological body are being compromised by growth, and the waste products of the unrestrained growth are poisoning the organs and tissues of the body. Hundreds of Kalamazoo County residents have noticed and wondered about this terrific human and economic growth. These are neighbors and tax-payers. They include housewives and truck drivers, high school teachers and college professors, members of clubs, students and bird-watchers. They get their information from newspapers and magazines, television and public radio. They see a problem and want to know why it isn't being fixed. But most of all, they notice what is happening in the county.

One of my first forays into the essential nature of Kalamazoo County, the original land that the surveyors of 1835 witnessed and demarcated, was to Portage Bog. This parcel of water-logged ground, which even the settlers agreed was not worth draining, is wedged between Portage and Westnedge Roads. It is undrainable because it is basically a three-hundred-acre bathtub filled with acidic brown water and half-decayed plants that have been growing and filling the basin for some ten thousand years. Of all the habitats in Kalamazoo County, bogs have survived the best. They are unreformed nature, inhospitable to economic ventures, and ignored by people because we have no cultural experiences that compel us to use them. Hunting proves the only regular use a man or woman puts a bog to, but hip boots or frozen ground are required if the experience is to be enjoyed.

I was there to study the pollinators of asters and goldenrods. Inspired by Bernd Heinrich's ground-breaking work in elucidating the energy budgets of bumblebees, I'd hoped to become his disciple, watching the floral visitors suck up the nectar and scrape pollen for their larvae, then racing after them when they flew to their nest or another patch of flowers. Alas, I was not very adept at tracking speeding bumblebees. I didn't have the hang of bog-walking and found myself plunging into deep pockets, the water over my boots, or tripping on tangled stems of leatherleaf. So I had to be content to watch the bees at the flowers, capture one of each kind so I could identify it (which is the scientific way), and take careful notes of what I saw.

It was a desultory time, bee-watching. They were not as lively as they could have been because it was a cloudy day. From time to time a sunny patch broke through and coasted over the landscape, passing the length of the bog before it reached me. The bees sped up when the sun hit them, and I busily scratched down a record of their bee ways. Mid-day I took a break and sat down on a high hummock of sphagnum moss covered with leatherleaf and sprigs of bog rosemary. There was even a backrest of several small tamaracks. I leaned and munched my cheese sandwich, letting my eyes rove over the bog. Nowhere is it more possible to feel a sense of isolation than in a Midwestern bog. The mounded topography of cushioning moss seems to absorb all sound, and the soughing wind glancing off the soft leaves of tamarack evokes times spent lazing beneath pines at a lake. The cars skimming along Portage and Westnedge sent up a hissing drone, but by the time it reached me it blended with the splendor of green silence and didn't perturb my mood the least.

Sinking deeper into this state of mind, I didn't notice the small birds arriving. As all flocks of little songbirds, this one arrived in dribbles and drabs, one and two at a time. The others, seeing their brethren flashing ahead and dipping into boughs and leaf shields, chased after them as if to fall behind were the greatest sin, until all clustered and twittered in the group of trees and shrubs inspecting and gleaning the tableau for lunch. Suddenly I woke up and noticed them. I caught a flash of white edging the tails of several birds and knew instantly I was seeing juncos. Then I heard the upward zip of a siskin's voice and the undulant *swit-swit-swit-swit-swit* of talking goldfinches. A chickadee plopped itself on a branch two feet from my face and scolded me. *Chicka-dee-dee-dee-dee.*

Perhaps it was my mental state, perhaps I was an impassioned young man or a too-sensitive soul, that caused these small birds to penetrate my heart. I felt compassion wash over me for the small lives there. I sensed their helpless fragility against the human enterprise, their utter vulnerability to our whims and passions. If there had been a way to make money with this bog, it would have been done. A pitiless desert, an ice-bound Antarctic, a frigid mountain top have little economic use to people, and so we leave it alone. Likewise this bog. Worthless. And yet so full of worth, because otherwise, I and others like me would have little worth ourselves for valuing them so. I identified with the birds, saw their lives and mine as commingled in some way, wished them no harm, hoped for them the best that life could offer, saw in their small activity and limited power a metaphor for all the ordinary people of this planet, myself included, who have no recourse when the richest, most powerful of us change our world for the worse without our assent, or constrain us by an economic philosophy that values the bottom line over all else.

I didn't consciously express any of that. I just felt what I felt, which was a kinship. And a tear ran down my cheek. I spoke out loud, "You are so small, so fragile." I thought of the road barely 100 yards away, and beyond that an entire county pressing in, an over-muscled economic engine that required all land, water, air, soil, animals, and plants be converted into dollars and cents for a final summation of their value. How powerful we are, how weak they are. In that moment it dawned on me that there is a holy obligation to preserve these lives, as we have a holy obligation to preserve the lives of our children, of our aging parents, our brothers and sisters who are sick, our friends and neighbors who are less fortunate than we. And I wept because I did not feel at the time that people were capable of that—that I was capable of that. Our relentless genes, our fierce desire for self-preservation and enlargement, prevent us from caring about other creatures. And why not? Those creatures do not care about us, nor would they mourn if we disappeared tomorrow. And so we have this in common with all life: the impulse to procreate, expand and fill the Earth as our shared and mighty eternal imperative.

Certainly I had this in common with those birds. We each try to fill the earth with ourselves individually, and with our kind communally. But unlike the other creatures of the planet, it is possible for us to harbor the sentiment that the Earth wants to receive us. Of course, the truth is that this planet is an often brutal, anxiety-producing place, where death and mayhem (or at least a financial or day-care crisis) arrive without warning. Whether you are a chickadee or a person, this is the struggle of living—coping with greater and lesser disasters. But the idea that humans can imagine themselves as welcomed or belonging on the earth sets us apart from the rest of our fellow voyageurs.

And it opens the door for feeling compassion, I believe, since we can see that we are the fortunate ones among the species. People also have an ace up their sleeve. We have for the most part now bent nature to our will, while the rest must accept what the world throws their way; and more recently what humans throw, too. The world is a doubly difficult place if you're not a person. Being a person, I am obligated by my enlightened point of view and powerful influence to show compassion to the rest of nature.

Over the next decades of work in the Midwest, as I plowed through brush, splashed across streams, clambered down wooded hillsides kicking leafmold ahead of me, I carried that moment like a talisman, a reminder of vulnerability, a guard against my hubris, a charm that rooted me in the fragile beauty of each place I visited. I stood in the small woodlots of the countryside, estimating the size of tree boles and the constitution of the forest canopy, while all the time thinking how the leaf of a beech tree captures the cell-driving sunlight with complete aplomb, held at an optimal angle the way a champion diver enters water. How standing in the shallow waters of sandy softwater lakes, their bottoms tapering to their centers as gradually as a carefully planed surface, I delineated with reverence the zones of immersion, documented the exquisite plants found here yet separated from their relatives on the East Coast by hundreds of miles—how I soaked up the feathered tops of sedges and the sight of the bands of plant life merging with the concentric circles of watery domains as if seeing the water lilies of Monet for the first time. How the last prairies gave up to me the secret woven in their vestments, intimated by their deep black soils of decomposed prairie roots from which the yearly crop of grass blades sprang. Where these once dried and were ignited to wild conflagration by the Potawatomi—whose name means "people of the place of the fire"—and where prairie flowertops were torn by elk and bison (whose saliva mingled with the soil and decaying roots) now lies some of the greatest farmland in the world.

Today even that rich soil is disappearing, paved over for development, entombed beneath short-sighted dreams of concrete and mini-malls. To the place of my dreams I say farewell. To the new Kalamazoo County I say, I hope your citizens realize soon what they are losing, which is not just the scientific discoveries, the timeless knowledge contained in the native habitats, nor even the places where young men and women can feel vigorous and alive exploring rarely trafficked realms, but the beauty of the land and water that sustains a wide-eyed wonder, a heartfelt gratitude, and a gentle soul. Look at it this way: if you want to feel better, you won't drive around Zug Island at the dirty mouth of the Rouge River. That is ground zero of the American automotive industry where no living thing survives. While it's a long way from Zug Island, Kalamazoo County is inexorably walking in that direction. Where it will stop is the question. I hope the people living there, my old neighbors, stop somewhere just this side of the end of paradise.

I still wonder about that mysterious swimming hole. The fact is I did go back later to swim but I couldn't find it. Strangely, I found a spot like it: a dip in the road and an arch of oaks, but no pond. Instead a small stream trickled under a culvert at the road. The pond eluded me. For the next ten years while finishing my bachelor's and master's degrees, I'd occasionally take a stab at finding that swimming hole. I drove the back roads by car and bike. I studied the county map. After a few years I got too busy to spend any time looking, and then a couple more years would go by and I'd find myself in the general area with an hour to kill and I'd look for that pond. Then my wife began to rib me about ever having been there at all. You must have dreamed it up, she said. Eventually I began to doubt it myself. But recently, even though it's been over twenty years, I started looking for the pond again. In the middle of the day, weighed down by care with no prospect for immediate relief, I close my eyes and stand still, legs straddling my bike. As I stand with eyes closed, I look around and my damp skin feels the chill pouring from the tree shade into a valley in the road. The sun's rays glint off water, coming at me in sheets of light. Birdsong fills the green around me and a great blue heron rises on slow wings and beats upward and over the scrim of trees and shrubs. That place lives still.

THE WISDOM
IN NATIVE LANDSCAPES

KIM

*Groundbreaking for the native landscaping at the Lutheran Church
of the Reformation, St. Louis Park, Minnesota, April 25, 2004.*

We are gathered here today to mark an event that has never happened
in the Twin Cities: a church congregation has deliberated and
decided to take a leap of faith in order to live more lightly on the
land they use for their parish.

With that decision, your congregation stands on a threshold. Behind you
lies the old view of land and how we should treat it, that ancient story of master
and the subjugated. Even if many believe that old story to be true, in fact
human history tells us that the land and all its life do not belong to us. With
this one decision—to recreate a facsimile of the plant life that existed here 150
years ago—you begin to doubt the outmoded wisdom of dominion. With this
decision, you begin to put that perspective behind you.

Before you waits the possibility of communion with all life. This is not an easy
path. You are undoing more than asphalt and lawn. You are undoing centuries of
notions. You are questioning whether the formality we see all around is necessary
for humans to thrive. You are testing our cultural view of what well-tended land
looks like. You are asking, "What kind of beauty comes by letting go?"

Here at this church you are creating prairie and savanna, not seen in these
parts for over a hundred years. As they return to the place they once occupied,
the plants growing here will remind you of another story that needs telling. In
their living fabric is a story of interdependence. Despite drought and deluge,
the prairie lives. Its strength is not in the numbers of a few, nor in the power
of powerful entities, but in its collective variety. If there were a single prairie
grass, big bluestem ... if it stood eight feet tall with roots reaching fifteen feet,
it would still be weak, just as lawns are weak because they lack complexity and
resiliency. Prairie's longevity against adversity rests in its many types of plants,

each contributing to the whole according to its individual talent. Lose that variety, and you give up possibility, you lose resiliency.

The new planting of this old landscape brings a world of meaning to this place. When we let go, when we trust that the wildness of other living creatures can frame our world, we become different people. We cease looking inward at our culture and ourselves, admiring the most visible and dominant there, as if that were all that should be considered. We open ourselves instead to the fragility and vulnerability of those among us, who, though seeming to not influence the larger course of human events, nevertheless shape our lives. The prairie does not cast out the least performers among its citizens. For its longevity it also needs those not able to produce the most vegetation each year, or command the most ground. Their role is subtle but entirely necessary. All are welcome in the prairie's tapestry of life.

By deciding in favor of the wild and native world, you show wisdom. By bringing back a part of that world, you display courage. In your wisdom and courage you will in time apply the ideas embodied here to the human realm also. More than anything, this is the significance and usefulness of the prairie and savanna restoration you begin today.

3

Now
(2000s to 2010s)

Granitic whaleback near Magnetic Rock, northern Minnesota, in a landscape burned by the 2007 Ham Lake Fire.

CONSIDER THE LILIES

JIM

Winona, June, 2012

T he day lilies in my front yard are in full bloom—a month early. That is in line with everything else that has been happening in my yard—from dandelions to rhubarb to milkweed, the plants are telling me what the meteorologists confirm: for the lower forty-eight states, this has been "the warmest spring, largest seasonal departure from average, warmest year-to-date, and warmest twelve-month period" in recorded history.[1]

"So what?" many of my friends and neighbors say—happy to get a head start on summer in normally cool Minnesota. They don't mind that the average temperature for January through May has been a startling 7.5 degrees above average. And you might agree a little heat is a good thing: perhaps you were following corn futures earlier in the year, when the price of corn plummeted because of early planting and predictions of good yields. The price was up again last week, though, because the market is predicting crop loss due to heat waves. Yes, corn does not like extreme heat—in fact, predictions for the future are for decreased crop yields for both corn and soy as the temperature climbs.

Heat is not so good for people, either. According to a recent study in the *American Meteorological Society Journal*, the Twin Cities could see 7,500 more heat-related deaths this century.[2] Down south it will be much worse. Under our current emissions of heat-trapping carbon dioxide, methane and so forth, we are pretty much guaranteeing that temperatures of up to 122 degrees F would be experienced in the central, southern and western parts of the U.S. Our nation's capital could have temperatures above ninety-eight degrees F for up to sixty days a year.

And then there are the storms: warm air contains more moisture, which leads to more violent weather. According to a recent report by the Rocky Mountain Climate Organization and Natural Resources Defense Council, "The frequency of extreme storms has increased so much in recent years that the first twelve years of this century included seven of the nine top years (since 1961) for the most extreme storms in the Midwest."[3] In southeastern Minnesota we understand this: we've had three "100-year storms" in the past decade, and one of them nearly wiped out Rushford.

Floods are in fact the most expensive form of natural disaster, and they are on the rise everywhere—except of course in the West, where droughts unprecedented in recent memory are threatening agriculture and forestry (consider the Whitewater-Baldy Fire Complex, the largest in New Mexico's history and the latest in a string of "mega-fires" eating up the Forest Service's firefighting budget).

So it is pretty clear that we are facing a dire threat to our future. And what are we doing about it? Kow-towing to the oil and gas industry, which would just as soon fry the world as reduce its profit margins. It is an established fact that the industry is spending millions to keep the average American uninformed or misinformed on this issue, using everything from creating fake grassroots

Everything in view was underwater in August, 2007, when seventeen inches of rain fell on Rushford and the hilly Driftless region of southeast Minnesota.

organizations claiming to speak for the working person ("astroturfing"), to churning out fake science (through "think tanks" like the Heartland Institute) to funneling enormous campaign donations to your elected officials. Nowhere is this more up close and personal than with hydraulic fracturing, touted as our route to "energy independence."

As has been asserted by other writers fracking is about as noxious as it gets. The nastiness of the process is summed up in the fact that Vice President Dick Cheney insisted that the 2005 energy bill exempt hydraulic fracking from EPA regulation—because if we had to frack safely and responsibly, we probably wouldn't do it at all. Instead we are allowing huge corporations to use and then inject millions of gallons of water with dangerous chemicals (in often water-scarce areas) which poisons the land and air and reduces vast sections of this country to "sacrifice zones" where no-one will want to live.

We would never do this if we weren't desperate. We have based our economy on a resource that has become so scarce we'll pay any price—either economically or morally—to keep it coming. We'll drill two miles deep in the Gulf, destroy vast sections of the boreal forest in Alberta (to get at the "tar sands"), and disrupt our own water tables to force recalcitrant pockets of oil and gas to the surface. And here in little Winona, we'll allow our farmland and scenic bluffs to be mined so that the companies that lie to us and endanger our future while corrupting our politics can use our sand and spread their poisons—all to keep their uninterrupted profit stream.

Make no mistake. The money you make from fracking is as tainted as the water in a fracking well. The oil and gas industry wants you to think otherwise, but consider the lilies of the field: they have a warning for you. The climate is changing because of carbon pollution, yet we are finding more ways to squeeze the last poisonous drop from the earth. People with vast unchecked power are destabilizing the climate for their short term gain, and we are letting it happen.

BIRD MIGRATION, BELIEF, AND SCIENCE

KIM

October 24, 2004. With a little time on my hands, I set down my thoughts on the fundamentalist strain in American life, its relationship to science, and what it means.

Part 1. Science and Belief

Yesterday I leafed through my notebooks and found this entry: "May 24, 2004. Spring Lake. Continued south wind associated with stationary front (low pressure over North Dakota); rain overnight ending early AM; mostly cloudy all day. Around 10:30 a.m., suddenly a flock of long-distance migrants fell out of the sky and fed on insects in the plum, rose bush, on the ground, and in other trees and shrubs."

With this entry another annual cycle, marked by similar notations over the past fifteen years, was underway. This way of marking the passage of time is ancient, rooted in careful and regular observation of nature and its predictable events. Stonehenge was built several thousand years ago by purposeful spiritual leaders who behaved as scientists in order to demonstrate to their skeptical community that both sun and moon could be trusted to mete out months and seasons like clockwork. Even more importantly, human society could be wrapped around the enigma of nature's cycles to increase culture's certainty and longevity. Sowing the crops, the harvest of salmon runs, first frost, peak summer rain—all were noted after years, perhaps generations of observation and codification, culminating in the construction of a stone colossus whose main intent was to signify society's control over the natural cycles it was designed to illuminate.

While I have no illusion about their broad application to society, from the beginning I'd intended to erect a conceptual Stonehenge using my fifteen years of notes on the arrivals, departures, and changes in non-human beings around me. Looking at these notebooks I see the increasing dedication of a man to an idea. In the first few years he reports scant information: a date, the names of bird species that appeared in his back yard on that date, perhaps a note regarding the general season (1989: Second year of big drought; hot, dry spring and summer). As his idea takes shape, the number of observations grows and precision improves. He adds location for observations from farther away, a description of the weather on that date, including wind direction and speed, because he suspects this is important. In this suspicion he hears a distant chord of memory striking, a moment as a very young man when, standing beside an accomplished naturalist, his eyes are opened to the miraculous migration of warblers, vireos, thrushes, flycatchers, and the other birds that traverse hundreds and even thousands of miles every spring from equatorial regions to North America's temperate zone. On low-hanging tree limbs, bushes, and the outer rinds of close-leafed tree canopies dart small patches of color: Blackburnian warbler with fiery orange throat, chestnut-sided warbler a motley of rust, yellow, and white, yellow-throated vireo singing briefly *ey-ay, three-eight!* Confusing movement, kaleidoscopic movement, together with whistles, trills, and chattering, surround us. The birds feed frantically on moths and insect larvae just emerging with the exploding buds of leaves and branchlets, starving for energy after their impossible journey. "It's a warbler wave," said my friend. "They were held back, then the weather cleared, and here they are."

Sandhill cranes today number in the hundreds of thousands after nearly disappearing around 1900.

This memory of beauty and excitement married to intellect permeates my notebooks. In later entries appear weather maps; also notes to anchor the sudden emergence of beauty to solid ground—"oak leaves now 1.5 inches long." Information accumulates year on year, supporting a theory about the exact moment when a specific bird, the Tennessee warbler, appears on my doorstep. Some time in the mid-1990s I begin to amuse my friends by calling them the day before I believed it would first arrive and saying, "Big warbler wave tomorrow." The Tennessee warbler—so-called because it was first shot, stuffed, and described for science by Alexander Wilson in Tennessee, despite its sojourn there of a scant two weeks in a fifty-two-week annual cycle—is a drab bird by comparison to other New World wood warblers. It inhabits thickets, cut-over forests, brushlands, and other ecosystems either in recovery from disturbance or permanently arrested in mid-succession, ranging from near the Canadian border in the eastern United States northward to the tundra, where the growing season is too short to raise a youngster to a size that will survive the journey to Mexico, Guatemala, Honduras, Costa Rica, and Venezuela in the fall. The bird's back is a pretty olive color, though rather dreary in poor light, and its chest and belly are white. The male sports a light gray cap that diffuses into olive in the neck and upper back. A narrow white streak shoots through the eye horizontally in both sexes. In the only reference to the bright colors of its relatives, females and young birds wear a patina of yellow on their breasts. During migration Tennessee warblers will alight in woodlands broken by crop fields and pastures, and also in the tops of the largest trees of suburbs, such as American elms that survived the 1970s blight and now stand as supercanopy sentinels above the younger forest of ginkgos, honey-locusts, green ashes, and other cultivars. When it arrives in the company of colorful warblers, red-eyed vireos, and the other long-distance migrants (to distinguish them from the short-distance migrants coming from the southern United States, and from resident birds who live year-round in the same place), its song makes up for its unimpressive appearance. The Tennessee shouts while flitting branchlet to branchlet in search of food: *ticka-ticka-ticka, swit-swit-swit, chew-chew-chew-chew.* Even if unaware that the long-distance migrants have arrived, anyone outside on such a morning cannot miss this stentorian voice. On that same morning, once again, I call my friends and announce, "Here they are, just as I predicted."

My friends are always a little amazed, as if I were a wizard. It must look a little like magic, and to be honest I make my prediction from conviction—belief even—because I do not have a cause-and-effect gun that I could raise to my lips, and with a breath clear the muzzle of its smoke trail. I believe that, given the right weather conditions at the right time of year, millions of winged creatures, each weighing mere ounces, will pour from the sky, tinting the shrubs and trees with bursts of color. My belief is no less a belief because it has the strength of accumulated observations behind it. Until the moment they arrive, I have nothing but a concocted theory, as ephemeral as the next observation that might cause it to crumble. Even as birds fall out of the sky and I am proven right once again, I do not have immutable natural law. What I do have is another observable fact in a host of facts which, each year, I gather to substantiate my claim. There is not an experimental theater large enough to accommodate the needs of this research. Studying migration across continents whose weather is spawned in ocean currents, funneled and diverted by ferocious winds high above, and charged with local character by mountains, plains, lakes, and cities is strictly a "found experiment," as dissimilar to those created in a laboratory as a farm windmill is to an internal combustion engine.

A controlled experiment of global life patterns is possible, but requires the utmost care to create and its cost exceeds the budgets of all but the largest NSF-funded project. Researchers studying global climate change have constructed outdoor laboratories, open to the wind and rain, where tubes exuding carbon dioxide supercharge the air around planting beds in order to simulate the Earth's climate twenty, fifty and 100 years from now, assuming trends in carbon dioxide accumulation continue unabated. It is predicted that, the more carbon dioxide in the artificially charged atmosphere around the planting beds, the more biomass—weight, in effect—the plants will put on. The experiment's set-up requires an appropriate number of planting beds combined with carbon dioxide levels to achieve a strength of statistical prediction such that a reasonable person would accept the outcome as very likely the truth, or as near to the truth as one can get given the difficulty of creating an atmosphere fifty years into the future. Of course, the cost of setting up and running this experiment in the out-of-doors runs into the millions of dollars. Setting up an equivalent experiment to study migration is out of the question because, regardless of what I may think about it, a human-induced change in migration patterns—numbers of birds and species, arrival and departure dates—is not of great interest to the future of the human enterprise, except for what it says about how we treat the rest of the life forms we share the planet with. That, however, is not in the realm of scientific debate, but rather belongs to the purview of ethics and philosophy.

Migration permeates life. So many migrations in human history are one-way. The Israelites carried their civilization on their backs out of Egypt and into the Sinai Desert where they wandered for forty years before entering the Holy Land.

Moses, the instigator of that migration, never arrived, being permitted by God only a distant view of the land his people would have to conquer before they could build their civilization. Europeans traversed the Atlantic and continued westward across the Americas, first by foot and horseback, then by train and highway, until an ocean became their front door again. Along the way they swept aside the disease-decimated remnants of people who had arrived from the opposite direction 18,000 years earlier. They, too, had been part of the great dispersal of the human race out of east Africa, with the settlement of Australia around 40,000 B.C., and the last outpost established in that spasm of colonization, Easter Island, reached by Polynesians in about 800 A.D. Europeans coming from the opposite direction met those early migrants here a few centuries later. My own backyard, the upper Midwest, had been settled, after Indians, first by the French seeking furs in the late 1600s, then by British and Dutch New Englanders seeking land in the early 1800s, then by Germans, Poles, Irish, Scandinavians, and Italians in the mid-1800s and early 1900s seeking refuge from starvation and war, by black sharecroppers and poor southern whites heeding the call of industry after World War I, and finally by Middle Easterners, Asians, and Latinos seeking opportunity in the second half of the twentieth century. Also in that last period, urban migration reversed itself, the cores of Midwestern cities emptying into the rings of suburbs thickening around them.

The place migration starts is less than hopeful, judging by the singular direction of human migrations. Abused Puritans, Pilgrims, and Anabaptists, Scottish clansmen butchered by British, British scions disinherited by elder brothers, French Huguenots pursued by Catholics, starving, grief-stricken Irish, all left somewhere imbued with less than hope, destined for a place (they hoped) where hope was guaranteed. But not always. Numbering more than their white owners, slaves taken from Africa's west coast rebelled in Barbados, South Carolina, and other New World settlements, killed many, sought the freedom they had once known, and were put down brutally and kept in their place by prohibitions against literacy, congregating in numbers, and acting in any way other than servile. Thus, their journey led to a long period of even worse enslavement that continued through the 1800s, and in a different form, into the mid-twentieth century.

For animals, the journey is on the whole quite fortuitous and famously self-gratifying. The many wonderful examples of one-way migrations assisted by humans teach the biological imperative to reproduce early and often. Some eighty European starlings were let loose in 1890 in Central Park, New York City, by the American Acclimatization Society—dedicated to bringing every bird mentioned by Shakespeare in his plays to North America so that we would be reminded of the bard's intent each time one flew by—and by 1950 European starlings had blanketed the continent. The English sparrow, or house sparrow, likewise brought here under a misguided idea, that it would rid urban areas of flying insects (it is by design a seed-eater), filled its portions of the Americas within fifty years. The zebra mussel, a recent immigrant, hitch-hiking in the ballast wells of ships delivering goods for the global economy, is well-known to people living in the Great Lakes region. Within a decade it has filled up a presumably empty niche in the Great Lakes ecosystem, in the process fouling intake valves on city water works and power plants, encrusting the shells of the world's most diverse native freshwater mussel fauna, extracting by way of its feeding filters nearly all particles of organic matter that form the base of the food chain, and giving a previously innocuous green alga, *Cladophora glomerata*, a nutrient windfall by which it also can reproduce madly and enrich the previously low-nutrient beaches of the Great Lakes shorelines, bringing about the slow demise of one the most diverse shoreline plant communities in the world. Migrations like these in the main allow a species to magnify itself many fold beyond what would otherwise be possible on its home turf.

Where animals have been in place for a while, migration often becomes part of their life repertoire. It is movement timed to an external force. It comes about, it seems, because a great mass of individuals living in one location cannot cope with that external force: drought, change in food availability, severe winter weather, and so on. When the force is fairly regular—the emergence of leaves on oak trees, for example—the great mass of individuals move as if a trigger were pulled when that force takes effect. Alexander Wilson, the unknown but equally talented contemporary of John James Audubon, reported in his notebooks from the early 1800s a great squirrel migration across the Ohio River. Millions upon millions of the animals attempted the crossing, and tens of thousands were swept away and drowned. He wrote that the river appeared alive with the dark backs of squirrels, wet, shining, bank to bank, flowing steadily into the forest beyond. North America sang with these migrations prior to and in the early years of European settlement. Every spring, bison and passenger pigeons flowed north with the seasonal changes, the former in vast clouds of brown hide from the southern to northern Great Plains, the latter in vast clouds of gray feathers from the Gulf and southern Atlantic states to forests of the northern United States and Canada. Cloud is the right metaphor, because they were like the passage of weather fronts, seemingly unstoppable, immutable, and eternal in their steadfast year-upon-year return.

To us, time is another tool, rather than a fluid medium to be immersed in. We use time as we would a mallet or screwdriver, scheduling work and play, production deadlines, marriages and funerals, anniversaries and remembrances of tragedy. We walk into a meeting at 8:29 a.m., or slip into our seats five minutes before the curtain rises on *The Merchant of Venice*. Once it was not so. Time flowed around us as if we lay in a warm stream among the smooth rocks. Time carried us downstream in the life rafts of our individual selves, and collectively in the larger vessels of our communities. We woke, we lay down to sleep, we ate as the sun reached different positions in its daily arc across the sky. Women grew aware that their menses and the full cycle of the changing moon were of similar length. The planting of the large-seeded wild grasses that became the world's cereal crops was linked to the match-up of the sun's or moon's position in the sky at a certain time of day, and codified by spiritual leaders who, at that time, had as much power, or more, as the community's warrior leaders. Those who had harnessed time to their use gained authority; after all, they alone claimed to hear the barely audible words of God, "It is time." The dates of Easter, Halloween, and Christmas are rooted in ancient observations of time's passage, and the Christian spiritual leaders of the early first millennium, rather than sever the new religion from these ancient observations, pasted the Christian holidays on top of those dates.

What did the annual migration of birds mean to them? They must have noticed it. First no swallows in Capistrano, then, around March 19th, the swallows fill the skies overhead. Making a connection between biological events, even those inside our bodies, and the movement of sun, moon, planets, and other immense forces entirely beyond our control, must have been a supreme achievement, culture-shaping in its implications. A person able to predict the spring arrival date of those Capistrano swallows, or any biological event—the first warm weather and gentle spring rain after planting, for example—would have seemed in direct communication with God, or the gods, and been given the respect required for someone so familiar with the awesome divine.

The professional clan I belong to, comprised of scientists, ecologists, and other observers of nature, has sought to predict the future since Aristotle first wrote down his conclusions regarding migrating cranes.[1] The idea is simple: pay attention to something you are curious about, record your observations, propose a theory to explain what you see (your hypothesis), collect additional information on actual conditions or conditions you create (an experiment), examine the information for patterns, test whether those patterns are real, re-state your hypothesis as a theory, then compare your theory to new observations . . . just to be sure. If what the scientist observes in the future is consistent with the theory, it eventually is thought of as truth, though not immutable. Immutability only belongs to God, while all particulate matter and invisible ether alter as they go. The one exception, in Shakespeare's opinion, is love: *Love is not love which alters when it alteration finds.* If love between lovers were true, he thinks, it would not fade despite years slipping by, hair graying, wrinkles deepening. If, however, the husband or wife take a lover in mid-life crisis, one would assume that the husband-wife pairing never truly loved, because—here it is—the observation is inconsistent with the theory. Just the same, the scientist who finds that the swallows of Capistrano fail to return on March 19 one year, then a second year and a third, would have to reject his or her theory and move the celebration forward a week. Theory only stands when future observations fit it.

My own observations of the spring arrival of long-distance migrants tell me as much about how science is made, and how I make science, as the birds that plunge into my yard tell me about their reaction to the weather and their urge to move with it. Here we have my observations of the arrival of the first wave of Tennessee warblers, that signature yearly event of long-distance achievement, in shorthand:

Year	Date	Pattern	Wind	Note
1989	12-May			Great drought
1990	11-May			
1991	11-May			
1992	—			6th warmest winter on record
1993	9-May	high-high	S	Storms
1994	11-May	low-high	SW	Storms
1995	11-May	low-high	S	Rain
1996	14-May	low-high	S	Overcast
1997	18-May	high-low	NW	Very cold spring
1998	9-May	low-high	SE	Rain; 3rd warmest winter on record
1999	7-May	low-high	S/SE	Rain
2000	5-May	high	S	Hot dry spring; 9th warmest winter
2001	7-May	low-high	S/SE	Rain
2002	5-May	low-high	SE	Thunderstorms; 2nd warmest winter
2003	16-May	low-high	SE	Clear
2004	8-May	low-high	SE	Partly sunny

What to make of it? Having watched this event for sixteen years, I can sum it up by saying that, sometime in the first two weeks of May, when a low pressure system is giving way to a high, and helped by a tailwind from a southerly quadrant, the birds will arrive. That's my theory, and armed with it I amaze my friends by watching the weather, calling them up, and casually saying, oh, by the way, the warblers will be here tomorrow. And they are.

If you look closely, though, you see inconsistencies. No data for 1992 (I lost it moving from one house to another); a high pressure to a high pressure system in 1993 (a tiny low pressure trough between highs wasn't shown on the weather map); a high-to-low pressure migration, with a northwest wind, in 1997; a high pressure system in 2000, and so on. I used to say that the migration took place during rainstorms, but that's not always right because some low pressure systems don't have enough moisture in them to produce rain. So now I leave mention of rain out of my general theory of migration.

Of all my observations, the very late migration in 1997 against a northwest wind, troubles me. Like any scientist, I try to explain the anomaly. That year was a very cold spring, one of the coldest in twenty years. Large, back-to-back high pressure systems sweeping out of Canada in April and May delayed the emergence of the oak leaves which feed the emerging insects, which in turn feed the energy-depleted insect-eating long-distance migrants. When at last the oak leaves emerged, small as mouse ears, the birds were desperate to move north, build nests, lay eggs, and raise the next generation of migrants. A lot was at risk. They moved despite a headwind. The morning after they took their leap of faith, I found an ovenbird, exhausted and crouching against the garage door in the alley. We took it into the kitchen, put it in a shoebox for safety against cats, and left it there all day. The next morning was slightly warmer and sunny. My daughter and I drove the bird to the Mississippi River—a navigation pathway northwards—and set the box on a west-facing slope (for afternoon warmth). We went back that evening and the bird had flown.

Other strange observations keep me from believing my theory one-hundred percent. After the first big arrival, other waves follow on similar weather days. In most springs, there will be two or three more deliveries of migrants on the back end of a low pressure system. The migrants landing in my yard—perching or passerine birds, they are called—nearly always fly at night, at an altitude of 500 to 7,000 feet. But simultaneously, the ones that arrive earlier keep moving tree-top to tree-top steadily northward during the day. I once followed an American redstart, yellow warbler, and Tennessee warbler cross-country bearing northeast by dashing across busy streets, cutting through yards and alleys, watching what they were doing as they moved. The birds called out as they danced among the fresh green leaves, practicing the territorial song that would keep rivals at bay, and I saw them shoot from a large elm to a 150-year-old bur oak by the Super America store. The ground-migration during the day confuses my theory—are these birds that just dropped out of the sky, or did they hoof it here from the Mall of America several miles to the south?

Despite all my misgivings, the numbers stand up to scrutiny. Throwing away all the extraneous factors, distilling the essence of the phenomenon from the welter of other details, is a consummate scientific act. It is as if Michelangelo were at work scraping away the detritus that cloaked from view his *David*. Standing back, then, you finally see it—the bare truth. For the migratory birds, what is that truth? They are a procreation machine, first and foremost, bringing forth each year the future's abundance of their kind. They are influenced by forces beyond their control—weather, oak leaves. They are also ephemeral beauty, light as a breath of wind, voices sibilant as running water over rocks. And they are numbers in a table that can be parsed and analyzed, as below:

Year	Date	Year	Date
1989	12	1999	7
1990	11	2000	5
1991	11	2001	7
1993	9	2002	5
1994	11	2003	16
1995	11	2004	8
1996	14		
1997	18		
1998	9		
Mean 1989-1998	11.8	Mean 1999-2004	7.7

These fifteen numbers represent some kind of truth about the migrants. Prior to 1999 they arrived, on average, 11.8 days into May. From 1999 on, they arrived 7.7 days into May. Is this pattern real? Are those means, and the swarm of inaccuracy surrounding those means, able to speak a kind of truth? The scientist takes those numbers, averages them and organizes the range of numbers comprising the mean into a bell-shaped curve, or standard deviation, then tests whether the means are different and whether the inaccuracy (or variance) clouds the picture by making you think the means are just blips in a cloud of similar numbers. You can take those numbers, average them, and compare the averages using what is called a t-test. The result is a probability, or "p-value" equal in the warbler's instance to 0.04, meaning there were only four chances in a hundred that the arrival dates before 1999 were the same as those after 1999.

It seems incongruous to hang an entire theory on a number, but it is how science is done. I once stood behind a colleague—working on the carbon enrichment experiment—as he punched a key on his laptop and said, "There it is." A table with half a dozen lines and a few columns appeared—means, variances, and p-values—the culmination of a several-million-dollar, several-year experiment to understand how plants respond to rising carbon dioxide and nitrogen levels. But that is what science is about, and has been about in the few centuries since it wrested itself out of the discipline of philosophy to create its own practice and methods. Chief among those methods is to test a theory by summarizing repetitive observations and draw a conclusion about the validity of the theory. The functioning of the stomach's digestive juices, the speed of light and sound, the power of gravitational attraction, and now the arrival date of Tennessee warblers . . . all are amenable to theory and testing. In the last century the social sciences and semi-sciences—sociology, economics, psychology—have adopted mathematical theory testing to answer their urgent questions, while philosophy, that ancient wellspring of these disciplines, my own included, continues using thought experiments and reason to delve into the largest questions of all.

Why hasn't philosophy jumped on the scientific method bandwagon? Can't it test theories about society's ethical preferences by observing people in action and testing the means of their choices? The philosophers I have known seem hardly the type of people who want to use statistics to prove a point. Rather they demonstrate truth by argument, the laying of self-evident truth upon self-evident truth, until they have a structure as solid as a coursed brick wall. Should we do unto others as we would have them do unto us? Should we know ourselves? What is the nature of deity? The proofs of these lie outside the numerical realm, in language and intellect. It is much like religious belief, except that the guiding light for philosophy is attaining wisdom through reason, instead of knowing one's God.

Part 2. Faith and Reason

I am writing this after a family reunion where religion was the centerpiece. After a church service, a potluck lunch was served, accompanied by saying grace, then followed by a two-and-a-half-hour program of singing, music, and sermons. Because they are family, I sat genially through the program, enjoying the old hymns, laughing at the jokes in sermons—there were two sermons! As I have known since I was a child, sermon topics would be chosen from: our mortal sin and divine redemption, the necessity of a strong military and the honor in military service, the righteousness of our country's cause, the lack of a moral compass in secular society today, and sometimes the godlessness of evolution.

Evolution. It has for decades been an earnestly debated subject in my family. My parents were neutral on the topic, but my other kin still work to overturn the Scopes decision of 1925, if not Darwin's *Origin of the Species by Means of Natural Selection*. I recall two uncles, both with doctorates in their fields—sociology and physics—discussing the red shift that occurs in light traveling through space. At the time, around 1970, astronomers had detected that the wavelength of the red portion of the spectrum was slightly different in light observed on earth versus light observed in distant galaxies. The light from those had shifted position on the electromagnetic spectrum due to something like the Doppler effect on sound—a horn pitches lower as it passes then moves away from us. So too in the case of light from celestial bodies moving away from us—their light is farther toward the red end of the electromagnetic spectrum than it should be. My uncles were quite excited by this. We were on a back-packing trip in the Sierra Nevadas, and while we hiked to our destination—a rocky cirque where the cutthroat trout were said to be eager to take a fly—they discussed its ramifications. In essence they viewed the red shift as a way to argue for the literal six-day creation. The momentous events of early Earth history—magma flows, rifts, shifts in atmospheric gas composition, the rise and fall of entire orders of animals and plants, meteor strikes serving as continental erasers of life forms—all this took place, the argument went, in six literal days, but our *perception* of those days is that they lasted for millions of years. The red shift, in other words, alters time, giving the impression that days in the distant past are longer than they actually were.

My uncles, being highly educated people, encountered in their universities the weight of evidence that cataclysmic (volcano) and pedestrian (erosion) events created the shining granitic landscape they saw around them as we trudged ever upward to that trout-brimmed lake. When on other trips they viewed the mile-deep layering of different rock types in the Grand Canyon, they understood the geological processes at work and the necessity of time in its formation. Even fossils and creature impressions in rock that spoke of a multitude of life forms no longer existing must have left them wondering about six days of work, and one of rest. My physicist uncle, especially, must have understood carbon-14 decay rates and other methods of pinning a likely period of years on the creation of a rock stratum. Yet despite all that, they spoke animatedly on the trail, pausing to catch breath from time to time while presenting an acute observation or agreeing on a critical point before hiking on. I was not a scientist then, but a wild teenager full of dreams, and their conversation struck me as strange and wonderful. I didn't comprehend the details, but the general idea led me to understand that there were people like my uncles who believed in a literal six-day creation and also in a scientific foundation to our understanding of the world. They held that a miraculous process was at work in the scientific facts of the earth's creation, and believed in the literal presentation of the Bible, yet they were also men of science and reason.

There were, in fact, many people like my uncles striving to find evidence of the Creator in the act of creating. In 1963, a decade before our Sierra Nevada fishing expedition, scientists and proponents of a union of science and faith, including Frank Marsh, author of the first scientifically argued case for Creationism, *Evolution, Creation and Science*, established the Creation Research Society. This society published a journal for the express purpose of proving that the Earth was brought to its current state intentionally, by an intellectual force; that Earth was the product of recent events; and that a worldwide flood did indeed take place, wiping out all life. If one visits the CRS *Journal*'s home on the web, one can read past issues with titles like "Helium diffusion age of 6,000 years supports accelerated nuclear decay." This article, published in the June 2004 issue, argues that because nuclear isotopes were observed by the researchers to decay faster than previously reported, their existence demonstrates that a billion-year-age estimate for rock strata is more likely 6,000 years.

Why 6,000 years?

Despite evidence that the Earth has existed for a long time, 6,000 years has become a benchmark to those with a belief in the biblical six-day creation. What happened exactly 6,000 years ago to the day as I write this sentence, was that God created the heavens and the earth, separated land from water, brought forth animals and plants of all kinds, and placed Adam and Eve in the Garden of Eden, launching humankind on its special journey upon this planet. In the early 1600s James Usher, Bishop of Armagh, Ireland, was inspired to discover the Monday of Creation Week, and so he sequenced the birth years of first born sons whose lives were chronicled in the Bible, much as modern scientists create chronosequences from bristlecone pines. When he had finished, his human chronosequence pointed to October 22, 4004 B.C., the moment that time and everything it touches began.

At the time of Bishop Usher, nearly everyone in the western world believed in the six-day creation. Those who pondered it would have known what God did on a Monday, then Tuesday, and so on to Sunday, when He rested and his children met in churches and chapels throughout Europe to consider his great works. But in 1859 Charles Darwin published his *Origin of Species* and established the biological basis for a competing view that has been warring with the literal six-day creation for 150 years. Darwin was influenced by the geologist Charles Lyell, who proposed that earth's geological processes are slow and continue to this day. Already in 1875 it had become clear to Charles Draper, an American scholar who'd earned fame with his treatise on the Civil War, that the ancient lineage of religious ideas was competing with those of a modern scientific upstart, when he wrote *History of Conflict Between Science and Religion*. He documented from ancient times the suppression of scientific ideas by religious authorities, including the early Christian suppression of the classical Greek and Roman texts and the Inquisition's violence against Protestant rationalism and science. That suppressive impulse found expression in America during the 1920s with the passage of laws prohibiting the teaching of evolution. In July 1925 Clarence Darrow was sent by the American Civil Liberties Union to Dayton, Tennessee, to defend the teacher, John Scopes, against charges that he had taught evolution to his students, violating the Butler Act which prohibited it. John Scopes admired his prosecutor, William Jennings Bryan, who was a popular orator and former presidential candidate. During the Scopes "monkey" trial, as newspapers dubbed it, the defenders of the law, including Jennings Bryan, came off to the nation as close-minded, anti-scientific religious extremists. Scopes was found guilty anyway, paid his $200 fine, and later remarked, "I will continue in the future, as I have in the past, to oppose this law in any way I can. Any other action would be in violation of my ideal of academic freedom—that is, to teach the truth as guaranteed in our Constitution of personal and religious freedom." Indeed, in 1968 laws prohibiting the teaching of evolution were found to be unconstitutional by the U.S. Supreme Court.

With about forty-five percent of Americans believing that God created people as they are today during the last several thousand years, resistance to teaching evolution will continue. No less than a presidential candidate stated in 1980 that "If evolution is taught in the public schools, then the biblical story of creation should also be taught." That was Ronald Reagan, responding to the Supreme Court's 1975 decision that "equal time" for Creationism, as this idea was beginning to be called, violated principles of church-state separation. The last equal time law was repealed in Louisiana in 1987. The intellectual heavy-lifting for writing these laws had come from the Creation Research Society, already mentioned, to which my uncles probably subscribed. The first international conference on creationism was held in 1986, and shortly afterwards, a new concept emerged: intelligent design. A first conference on the topic was held at Southern Methodist University in 1992. In 1999, this idea that the creative force behind life on Earth was not evolution, but rather a higher intelligence, was formalized in the book *Intelligent Design* by Baylor University assistant professor of mathematics and philosophy, William Dembski.

One would think that, with an organization, intellectually based concepts, and exponentially growing publications, creationism and its recent offshoot, intelligent design, would engage in the same dispassionate conversation about its theory that evolutionary biologists use when talking about theirs. Rather, current critics of evolution descend from and use the language of the centuries-old tradition of suppression of science. The great document of North American fundamentalist belief, *The Fundamentals: A Testimony to the Truth*, edited by R.A. Torrey and published in 1909, consolidates the myriad expressions of faith and opposition in the *fin-de-cicle* religious community, which resonate today with so many of my fellow citizens. In Chapter 68, "The Decadence of Darwinism," for instance, Henry H. Beach of Grand Junction, Colorado, wrote: "The actual origination of man, brutes, and plants, from one simplest and lowest form of organic life, by natural and Godless selections and variations, is the essence of Darwinism." How is this different from the statement by the chief proponent of intelligent design, William Dembski: "… more and more students are informing themselves about intelligent design and learning to ask the right questions that deflate Darwinism and its atheistic pretensions"? This is from his recently web-posted "Ten Questions to Ask Your Biology Teacher about Evolution."

Equally strange, but consistent with the belief that biblical literalism is the foundation for understanding life on Earth, is the fact that creationism and intelligent design both hew to the recent formation of life. Yet, if one wishes, one can match the growth rings in the sliced trunks of dead and live bristlecone pine trees (*Pinus artistosa* and *P. longaeva*) from the White Mountains of California and establish without doubt a climatic record that goes back 8,700 years. A single living tree in the White Mountains, 4,600 years old, began its life a thousand years before the exodus of Israel from Egypt. While carbon 14-dating is hotly contested in creation science publications, it is a simple physical fact that, due to its rarity in nature and the observable fixed rate of its loss from bodies following death, after about fifty thousand years carbon 14 cannot be detected in bones, teeth, and other remains of once-living creatures. New techniques of taking ice cores from Siberia, the Greenland Ice Sheet, and Kilimanjaro establish year-by-year snow accumulations that stream backwards 350 to 450 thousand years. Each year's snowfall and melting produce a layer, like a tree's annual growth ring, which can be counted backwards through time. Pollen cores from lake bottoms, foraminiferan deposits on ocean floors, and annual growth rings of coral—all these provide precise and repeatable measurements of the fact that years have piled up on years, centuries on centuries, and millennia on millennia over the course of time that reaches far beyond the 6,000-year touchstone of biblical creation.

Lest it be thought that all is confusion in the ranks of religious people, no less a defender of conforming religious thought than Pope John-Paul II felt that evolution is not something to discredit and replace. Addressing the Pontifical Academy of the Sciences in 1996 he called "... 'evolutionism' a serious hypothesis, worthy of investigation and in-depth study." Charles Darwin, writing in *The Origin of Species*, expressed what I think is increased devotion to life, not a negation of its significance.

> *When I view all beings not as special creations, but as lineal descendents of some few beings which have lived long before the first bed of the Cambrian system was deposited, they seem to me to become ennobled.*

My uncles might be uncomfortable with this, opening the door to theological slippage as it does. I will never know, since both have since passed away. I would have enjoyed the discussion, though. I would admit that Darwin got some things wrong, especially the details of speciation itself, and the speed with and mechanisms by which it may happen. But, all in all, he expresses a sentiment felt by many of the biologists I know—that deep spirituality and evolution are not mutually exclusive. In fact, for some, their admiration for God or a God-like force only grows as they ponder life grappling with the vagaries and obstacles to survival that existence on Earth presents. Elsewhere in *The Fundamentals* of 1909 writers say much the same thing. James Orr, Doctor of Divinity and a professor at United Free Church College in Glasgow, wrote that, rather than discredit the biblical account of Earth's creation, "Geology is only felt to have expanded ideas of the vastness and marvel of the Creator's operations. . . " and ". . . science and the Biblical view of God, man, and the world, do not stand in any real relation of conflict."

There is a Christian scientific organization, the American Scientific Affiliation, which was established in 1941, over twenty years before the Creation Research Society, and which holds the Bible as the final arbiter of matters of faith and conduct, but simultaneously seeks to use science and technology for good, especially in order to be better stewards of the Earth. The ASA does not dismiss evolution out of hand, but does posit that the universe is founded on "contingent order and intelligibility, the basis of scientific investigation."

This is all good news, making me believe that on both sides of the issue there are moderate voices striving for accommodation and resolution. But the bad news comes daily: a southern Florida community requiring that stickers be pasted on science textbooks emphasizing that evolution is only a theory; the Kansas State Board of Education now debating the merits of evolution versus intelligent design. The suppression of science is alive and well, but thankfully now plays itself out in a democratic society.

Poor Galileo. Called before the Inquisition to prostrate himself and beg forgiveness for the heresy of stating the earth and planets revolved around the sun: he escaped with his life and spent his remaining years under house arrest at his residence near Florence. It is popularly held that, as Galileo left the Holy Office, he murmured, "*Eppur si muove*"—"It moves nonetheless." Whether he actually said it or not is irrelevant. What matters is that he needed to assert a claim to observed truth, despite the opposition of authority or majority. Galileo wanted, above all, freedom of personal action and belief in the intellectual realm. He was seventy years old at his trial, and although he was ambitious, at that point in his life more important to him, I suspect, was his freedom to pursue truth through the scientific method: observation, theory, testing, restatement of theory when in error. It's that simple, although pride in solving nature's riddles is also a reward. For many scientists, their work also draws them closer to the awe-inspiring origins of the universe, whether God or some other purposeful energy.

Some think that the religious fundamentalist's rejection of evolution is part of a rejection of modernity. Certainly Galileo's discovery threatened to upset the apple cart of the day, the idea that there was a great chain of being, with God at the top, people below him, animals farther down, and so on. Within the human part of the chain were finer distinctions: king, nobleman, vassal, tradesman, laborer; or husband, wife, child. The rise of states and early democratic institutions, like trade guilds, had already begun to erode that view. Martin Luther, the founder of my family's church, chopped hunks out of the chain with his claim that each man or woman should enjoy a direct relationship with God, unmediated by monks, bishops, and the pope. The use of reason in science sprang from this Protestant inquiry into the nature of divine involvement in human affairs, starting with the data themselves . . . namely, the words of the Bible in the local vernacular. In the mind of these theologians and scientists, seeking God and striving to live a God-like life was equated with free thought and free will. The religious fundamentalists in America owe much to these people. They are free to believe that America should properly become a theocracy, for example. They are free to believe that God demands a specific belief about the world's origins, for another thing.

My sympathies are with them, and with my relatives, one of whom took me aside at the reunion—she must have sensed my scientist's discomfort with dogma—to say, "It's our tradition, after all. Yours too. You have to accept that."

I do. The fundamentalist in me rebels against pure science in the service of nothing. Science in an ethical vacuum will not serve either the scientist or mankind. The original questions we ask about the world need a context that is worth thinking about. Nazi doctors experimenting on people, for example, lacked all this. I reject whatever findings came from their research, preferring not to know rather than violate human dignity. If anything about the evolution debate, the scientific method, and my own studies of migration and Tennessee warblers, gives me pause, it is this: what is lost when mystery is lost? As much as scientists may believe they are drawing closer to God—those who feel this way at least—the truth is that when you find out what you are trying to find out, you have reduced a mystery to bald fact. That piece of the world is stripped of a particular relationship . . . no longer will a person wonder about that fact in a way that might be called contemplation. It becomes a datum for inclusion in a vast data set that will, someday, be distilled to an even more rarified essence by the push of a computer key. Do our own souls become the less for it? When everything is known, what will that do to us? For one thing, our place in the world relative to the mystery will be changed. Call it what you will—mystery, the sacred, God—our relationship to that object of contemplation and awe will no longer sustain us as it does. This would be properly called piety in an older time: accepting one's place in the world relative to the sacred.

One of Shakespeare's sonnets contains the line, "Art tongue-tied by authority." I love that sentiment because it conjures up the dynamic relationship between finding things out, and believing things are so. Authority can be many things: Catholic dogma, the Bible, a dictator, a police force, the wealthy and powerful among us. It can also be scientific findings that sharpen our understanding of the minutiae of the world, but dull our perception of it. There is no scientific inquiry into the nature of God, thank God, because that is a matter of belief. I want my God and my art to remain outside scientific authority. For the spirit to thrive, there has to remain something not known. As my daughter said during one of our nature walks, "I don't want to know more. It's not as interesting when I understand it. I like it when there's still a mystery about it."

WHAT LAURA SAW:
MAKING A LITTLE HOME
ON THE EXTREME GREAT PLAINS

JIM AND KIM

*In 2009 we presented the idea that the beloved books written by
Laura Ingalls Wilder, while unparalleled in expressing the American
mythology of the frontier, got the ecology wrong. This was published
in 2010 in the Proceedings of the Twenty-first North American
Prairie Conference, Winona, Minnesota.*

The Little House books are often read in schools, where they serve a variety
of curricular purposes: as examples of moral character, documentation
of pioneer lifeways, or investigation of family dynamics. Beyond these
issues—and permeating the entire series—there is a complex ecological story
interwoven with economic reality and misplaced cultural behavior which students
rarely encounter in works of literature.

In this alternate approach a teacher would look at this complexity directly
and draw students into an understanding of the way the books present the reader
with a conflict between a national ideology of westward expansion and the often
sobering degradation in the quality of the environment that resulted. It would
contrast the national ideal of individualism and progress with a specific story which
often shows us the real difficulty people had in trying to farm the Great Plains
using eastern farming methods. The story of Laura's experience is properly framed
by the broadly defined historical Great Plains, rather than the narrow modern
interpretation. (For details, see the Notes section.)

By focusing on the contradictions in what the character of Laura claims
to see in the books, students would be encouraged to think critically about the
way in which we interact with the environment, and about the way in which
our cultural stories, or narratives, influence our understanding of that

People have been abandoning their Midwestern farms for nearly 100 years.

interaction in subtle and complicated ways. Finally, the books show us that good literature preserves these rich contradictions and complications rather than resolving them or rendering them in an overly simple manner.

What Laura saw was a highly evolved environment, where several thousand years and more of drought, fire, grazing by ungulates and locusts, hail, and harsh winters shaped a responsiveness in plant and animal life that enabled the whole of the environment to persist even as individuals and species disappeared or shifted in abundance and location. That environment was beautiful and hostile by turns and she described this in memorable detail. She saw her parents struggle mightily to make a living in that environment, only to be rebuffed time and time again. She saw a wilderness, rich with game and a profusion of prairie flora; she saw this wilderness disappear before her eyes. Much later in her life, when she came to write the Little House books, she set out to write an instructive tale for young people which would reaffirm certain ideological beliefs; but because she was a good writer, she instinctively included much that is dissonant with those beliefs. The argument threaded through all the books was that an independent-minded family, pulling together and with a little help from neighbors, could make a living on the Great Plains by their enterprise and hard labor. As the books progress, however, the reader understands that Pa was not able to realize that dream for his family. This tension is what makes the books so readable today.

A Pioneer Epic

Little House books have long been acknowledged by scholars to be a fictional creation, rather than a pure work of autobiography: that is, although Laura Ingalls Wilder is factual in many specifics, she shapes her material to fit a preconceived narrative purpose. Facts are changed, experiences are deleted; characters are combined and chronologies altered. She conceived the books from the beginning not as simply autobiographical. Wilder claimed she wrote because "I wanted the children now to understand more about the beginning of things, to know what is behind the things they see—what it is that made America as they know it."[1] The books are not simply "things as they happened," but representative moments to educate children about the values and attitudes Wilder believed "made" their nation. She listed those in a public lecture around the time she was writing *On the Banks of Plum Creek*. John Miller recounts "She noted that running 'like a golden thread' through all of her stories were certain basic values: 'courage, self-reliance, independence, integrity, and helpfulness. Cheerfulness and humor were handmaids to courage.'"[2]

Wilder came to see her own family's past as being representative of the national experience of the settling of the Great Plains in the latter nineteenth century, following the Homestead Act of 1862. The Little House series functions as a midwestern epic, one which reinforces a notion of Americans as individualistic, self-reliant, resourceful farmers who found the land a wilderness of grass and, against difficult odds, converted it to productive farmland. This was the way Wilder was taught to frame her experience, as it was the way most people did interpret the western migration. Despite the extreme difficulties faced by settlers, forcing periodic rescue responses from government, and a rather high failure rate of the enterprise over time, Americans saw in the settlement of the Great Plains something akin to a re-enactment of the national drama of discovery and colonization. As Spaeth has put it, "They invested the West with a metaphorical dimension that fit their dreams and in turn shaped the very dreams that had created it."[3] This quality of mythology remains in place, as most of us continue to be moved by that interpretation of the past. The ongoing popularity of the Little House books is in part explained by the perfect fit between the story they tell and the beliefs we hold dear as a nation.

Anita Claire Fellman has said in an insightful article on "The Little House Books in American Culture," "the Little House books are one of those means by which people in the U.S. learn their political individualism: they are the mother's milk through which Americans ingest their deeply felt individualism."[4] In this effort Laura was aided by her daughter, Rose Wilder Lane, who edited her books, sometimes quite heavily, and she was inspired by political currents of the 1930s. Both Wilder and Lane were concerned that the Roosevelt administration with its "New Deal" was straying from the values of self-sufficiency and individualism and wanted to remind young people especially of the frontier values of the nineteenth century as embodied in her parents' character traits.[5] "Their old fashioned character values are worth as much today as they ever were to help us over the rough place," she claimed.[6]

Whatever did not suit the larger purpose of an educative mythology was deleted or altered. The chronology of the family's wandering was altered to clarify the story line—for example, most of the details in *Little House in the Big Woods* actually occur in 1871 to 1874, after the Ingalls returned from Kansas (1869 to 1871) and moved in with their extended family near Pepin, Wisconsin. The two years the family spent in Burr Oak, Iowa (1876 to 1878), after the failure of the farm in Walnut Grove, is completely eliminated, perhaps because during this time the family was running a hotel, which did not fit her ideal of the Jeffersonian farmer. Fans of *The Long Winter*, for example, would be astonished to learn that during those months when the Ingalls family is housebound in De Smet, grinding wheat in a coffee mill and twisting hay for fuel, they were sharing their quarters with another family whom they had taken in; to have mentioned this would have been to complicate the idea of the brave nuclear family, facing the world alone.

As Fellman says, Wilder and her daughter deleted:

> . . . the numerous times in which the family lived communally with other people, relatives and nonrelatives, rather than simply on their own, the better to emphasize the family's isolation and independence. The distance from towns of their various homesteads is also exaggerated and the degree to which the girls routinely played with other children is minimized. Because one of the goals of the series is to focus on Ma and Pa's ingenuity in wresting a living from natural resources and from the land, the books downplay the number of times Pa worked for wages.[7]

So far, we are summarizing what literary scholars have deliberated. What this talk adds to the mix is that there is another conflict between the myth that inspires Laura Ingalls Wilder and the facts of the settlement of the west. If you look past the mythologizing of the Little House books, what you find is actually a story of a sequence of financial failures. The Little House books present in literary form the ideal of Jeffersonian agrarianism—the notion, as old as the Republic, that the farmer is the representative American, because he is most free and independent. The ecological reality of the Great Plains, with its greatly stochastic environment, prone to drought, fire, severe winters, destructive storms and plagues of locusts, challenged the notion that the individual farmer could survive and prosper. This ecological reality plays out with Pa and Ma Ingalls losing their crops to locusts, being threatened by fire, disease, and drought, and living in real poverty throughout the series. The financial failure of their time in Kansas happened because Pa accepted the common belief among those on the frontier that the Osage Indians would be removed by the government from their established reservation just west of Independence, Missouri, as Indians had always been removed once whites began settling a region. The Osage were not moved away, and the family's efforts to settle there were in vain, a fact brought up in later books as the fault of the government.

In fact, Wilder had to end her family saga when she did, because to continue the chronicle of the Ingalls family (and the new Almanzo Wilder family) would have been to admit that not long after *The First Four Years*, Ma and Pa grew so discouraged by frequent drought, they moved off their claim and into De Smet, where Pa worked as a carpenter, a grocer, and public official until he died prematurely of heart disease. Like many western immigrants, Ma and Pa found the extreme climate on the Great Plains too much for them. Almanzo and Laura are similarly driven off the land by extremes of weather, bouts of disease, and plain bad luck. They end up moving to Mansfield, Missouri, in the Ozarks, which is typical of the forested eastern United States in its climate. The monthly temperature in Mansfield varies from an average of 34 F in winter to 76 F in summer, and the yearly rainfall is forty-four inches. By contrast De Smet receives just twenty-four inches of rain annually and varies in average monthly temperature from 15 F in winter to 70 F in summer. The larger historical truth is that Laura Ingalls Wilder could only live out her dream of being a farm wife by moving to a different climate.

Stochastic Frontier, Little House Economics

When the eastern method of farming, which underlies the myth of frontier independence, is set down in a catastrophe-driven landscape, it fails without subsidies of free or cheap land, fossil fuel, Eastern capital (in the form of both railroads and investment entities, such as banks), imported building supplies, processed provisions and the kind of machinery that will enable the farmer to efficiently work larger parcels of prairie land. Initially, also, the wild game was natural capital that subsidized Pa and other settlers on the Great Plains. The soil itself represented another source of natural capital, its deep, highly organic topsoil created by centuries of grass growth.

Even with these subsidies, farmers who practiced dryland farming techniques risked either failure or a hardscrabble life. This is evident in the Little House narrative when we compare the richness of life in upstate New York (the setting for *Farmer Boy*) and even in the Big Woods of Wisconsin (*Little House in the Big Woods*) to the prairie settings of Walnut Grove and De Smet. As the family moved out of the temperate east and onto the plains, their life became more risky, and they increasingly relied on outside sources of income to keep them on the farm. Whereas Almanzo's father viewed the farmer as the paragon of democratic America, in the climax of the series, when Alamanzo proposes to Laura, she hesitates: despite her allegiance to the enterprise that has so obsessed her father and mother, she doesn't want to be a farmer's wife.

> Because a farm is such a hard place for a woman. There are so many chores for her to do, and harvest help and threshers to cook for. Besides a farmer never has any money. He can never make any because the people in towns tell him what they will pay for what he has to sell and then they charge him what they please for what he has to buy. It is not fair. . . . I don't always want to be poor and work hard while the people in town take it easy and make money off us." "But you've got it all wrong," Manly told her seriously. "Farmers are the only ones who are independent. How long would a merchant last if farmers didn't trade with him? There is a strife between them to please the farmer. They have to take trade away from each other in order to make more money, while all a farmer has to do is to sow another field if he wants to make a little extra. . . . You see, on a farm it all depends on what a man is willing to do. If he is willing to work and give attention to his farm, he can make more money than the men in town and all the time be his own boss. (The First Four Years, p. 4-5)

Almanzo makes a promise to her that if after three years of trying to farm he did not succeed, he would try something else. When Almanzo asks if she will mind living in a little house, she replies that she is used to little houses. In light of this it becomes clear why the title of the Little House series resonates so: the little house is all a farmer can expect on the Great Plains. Compare this to the house Laura and Almanzo later built in Mansfield. According to Miller, "Her design included ten rooms, four porches, a native stone fireplace, large windows in the parlor looking out on the countryside, and a library."[8] This was made possible by the orchards, chickens, and livestock they kept in the moist climate of the Ozarks. Laura's parents' two-story frame house in De Smet, on the other hand, is so small tour groups are limited to ten people at a time.

So the narrative of continual war with the elements—which provides so much of the drama of the Little House books—really does highlight a central feature of the great western migration. To quote William Parton, "In the Great Plains—unlike regions farther east, where woodlands yielded to the axe and underwent a near-complete conversion to plowed fields—low precipitation and regional soil characteristics prevented farmers from cropping more than 70 percent of land in the east and 25 percent in the west, an average of 50 percent overall."[9]

This implies that it was always doubtful that the great westward migration would produce wealth for most of the settlers. Economic success from a moist-climate farming system depended on stability; environmental stochasticity—unpredictable outcomes due to randomly interacting variables—in the Great Plains undermined such an economic system. Unpredictable variables included prairie fire, periodic severe multi-year droughts, flooding from torrential rains in other years as well as severe weather events such as hail and tornadoes, locust plagues, bison herds, and severe winters.[10] The bison were eradicated by the time the Little House books begin, but the locust plagues, fire, drought and severe weather are major forces in the series—none were as problematic farther east.

If one contrasts the story of the settling of North Dakota with the settling of Wisconsin or Michigan occurring a few decades before, the narrative would involve a steady rise in wealth and productivity in the latter but rarely the former. For instance, the farms of lower Michigan became so prosperous within twenty years of settlement that it was not unusual for farmers to build elaborate Italianate farmhouses, as ornate and large as those in town, to showcase their wealth. The farther west settlers went, the harder it was to duplicate that success with eastern farming methods. It would not be until after World War II that the land would begin to be dramatically productive due to further subsidies in the form of irrigation, ammonium fertilizer, and pesticides.[11]

What drew the settlers to the Great Plains was free land and famously fertile soil. It was expected that an investment in a plow, seed, and two draft animals would produce a good wheat crop in the second year after breaking the sod, after the prairie roots had rotted sufficiently to allow the wheat to be sown efficiently. Cutting and threshing the wheat was part of a neighborly effort, or paid for with credit from a farmer who owned the more expensive machinery for this work. Yet wheat was a cash crop; it could be shipped to the grain mills of Minneapolis via the railroads, which were in place in Minnesota by the end of the 1870s, and milled using a recently invented method that turned hard red winter wheat into quality flour. The link to markets to sell the fruits of Pa's labor is one of the big differences between *Little House on the Prairie*, which details the family's early experience in Kansas, and the prairie books that follow. Whereas much of the early book focuses on Pa's ability to build and furnish his house from local materials using simple hand tools, the later books show Pa leveraging the commodity value of his harvest to purchase more of the materials he needs. In *On the Banks of Plum Creek* Pa calculates that a good harvest would net him cash enough to buy a house, carriage and horses, farm equipment, clothing and furniture, and he borrows against that prospect (as Almanzo will do in *The First Four Years*). In fact, the experience of many settlers was that although the land was free, the capital required to turn it into a farm was daunting, as prairie farming required a new level of technological investment that increased over time. As Spaeth says, "The land was, in fact, free, but the machinery was not: new farms required approximately seven hundred dollars worth of machinery for optimum operation."[12]

This need for capital investment was made more difficult because of the "capricious Midwestern seasons" as well as the dangers of fire, pest and drought.[13] This is exemplified by the set piece of *On the Banks of Plum Creek*, the locust invasion that destroys their wheat.

> "It's no use, Caroline," he said. "Smoke won't stop them [the Rocky Mountain locusts] . . . The wheat is falling now. They're cutting if off like a scythe. And eating it, straw and all."... Then Laura remembered that the new house was not paid for. Pa had said he would pay for it when he harvested the wheat. (On the Banks of Plum Creek, p. 202-203)

This was one of several episodes where the Rocky Mountain locust (*Melanoplus spretus*), as Laura's "grasshoppers" turned out to be, devastated portions of the Great Plains in the 1870s and 1880s. These swarms were among the great biological migrations of the planet, which included the north to south migration of the bison and passenger pigeon.[14] In High Mountain News, Jeffrey Lockwood describes the 1875 swarm—the same year that the Ingalls's wheat was devoured—documented by witnesses at the time:

> A swarm of Rocky Mountain locusts streams overhead for five days, creating a living eclipse of the sun. It is a superorganism composed of 10 billion individuals, devouring as much vegetation as a massive herd of bison—a metabolic wildfire that races across the Great Plains. Before the year is up, a vast region of pioneer agriculture will be decimated and U.S.

troops will be mobilized to distribute food, blankets and clothing to devastated farm families. . . . By clocking the insects' speed as they streamed overhead, and by telegraphing to surrounding towns, Dr. A.L. Child of the U.S. Signal Corps estimated that the swarm was 1,800 miles long and at least 110 miles wide. This suffocating mass of insects was almost large enough to cover the entire states of Wyoming and Colorado.[15]

Lockwood's own research on the locust revealed that swarming had been a regular feature of life on the Great Plains for thousands of years, as evidenced by the layers of frozen locust carcasses in glacial ice of the Rocky Mountains. The plagues in the 1870s were a major cause of settlement failure. As Charles Bomar writes, "Devastated by the volume and intensity of the locust swarms, many homesteaders moved back to the city or elsewhere. Farming was over for many and their fortunes were lost."[16] Recounting one pioneer's statement that the bugs "ate everything but the mortgage," Bomar continues:

Many homesteaders were held hostage. Some left, but many were unable to . . . in 1874, the federal government exempted the grasshopper sufferers from "residency requirements." This act allowed homesteaders to briefly leave their land to work elsewhere. In 1875, the federal government released $30,000 to distribute seeds to farmers in the Great Plains affected by the locust plagues.

This exemption allowed Pa to go and work the harvests in fields east of the plague—another example of the governmental help Wilder omits from her narrative.

The locusts went the way of the bison; by 1902 they were extinct. Ironically, it is thought that the cause of their demise was the settlement of the Rocky Mountain river valleys that were their native breeding grounds. Agricultural plowing and grazing destroyed the eggs of future swarms.[17]

Railroad Economics

Meanwhile, the Ingalls family continued west, following the logic that things were "always better further along," though in this case things tended only to get more extreme.

Pa did not like a country so old and worn out that the hunting was poor. He wanted to go west. For two years he had wanted to go west and take a homestead, but Ma did not want to leave the settled country. And there was no money. Pa had made only two poor wheat crops since the grasshoppers came. . . . "Listen to reason, Caroline," Pa pleaded. "We

can get a hundred and sixty acres out west, just by living on it, and the land's as good as this is, or better. If Uncle Sam's willing to give us a farm in place of the one he drove us off of, in Indian Territory, I say let's take it. The hunting's good in the west, a man can get all the meat he wants."
(By the Shores of Silver Lake, p. 3-4)

Even if the bison and the locust ceased to be problems for farming—and once the fields and roads established fire breaks against the prairie fires that periodically swept through—there was still the extreme climate. It was especially severe in the 1880s, a decade which began with the coldest winter on record, with many areas in the state receiving as much as eleven feet of snow. As Wilder recounts in *The Long Winter*, families in the little railroad towns were in dire straits, forced to eat their wheat seed and burn hay for fuel because the trains could not get through.

Here we encounter another contradiction in the narrative of individualism and independence. Whereas, in *Little House in the Big Woods*, all the elements necessary for self-sufficiency are near at hand, thanks to the prevalence of wood for fuel and building materials, the rich soil and the plentiful rainfall as well as the good supply of game and fish nearby, on the Great Plains the Ingalls family is much more dependent on supplies that had to be shipped for them to purchase. Their house must be heated with coal brought in by train; their structures are built with nails and milled lumber; and their diet supplemented with bought flour and salt pork. On the Dakota prairie they were enmeshed in the market system, selling their wheat crop or their labor in order to afford both heat and sustenance. There is a marked difference in the vulnerability of the Ingalls family in *Little House on the Prairie*, where Pa and Ma are shown to be truly self-sufficient in their isolated Kansas homestead, and *On the Banks of Plum Creek*, where Pa speculates on his harvest to pay for the lumber needed to build his house. The vulnerability of the farmer supplies much of the drama in *The Long Winter*: the story is about the stoic strength of the pioneer family:

The blizzard was loud and furious. "It can't beat us!" Pa said. "Can't it, Pa?" Laura asked stupidly. "No," said Pa. "It's got to quit sometime and we don't. It can't lick us. We won't give up." Then Laura felt a warmth inside her. It was very small but it was strong. (The Long Winter, p. 310)

"Well, girls," he said gaily. "We beat old Winter at last! Here it is spring, and none of us lost or starved or frozen! Anyway, not much frozen. . . ."
(The Long Winter, p. 311)

Yet that stoicism might have been less necessary had they been more self-sufficient in the first place.

In actuality, the towns had always depended on the railroad. The migration into Dakota Territory and the rest of the Great Plains, including Minnesota and Iowa, was determined largely by railroads, which went in advance of the large waves of settlement and platted the towns that became centers for shipment of the harvest on railroad freight cars. Lacking adequate river transport, and located far from eastern markets, the situation was, as Miller describes: "Until the railroads arrived, agriculture necessarily remained predominately self-sufficient, limited to a relatively small number of farm families ranged around the few towns that managed to get started in the 1860s in the southeastern part of the territory."[18] Large-scale Dakota settlement, as with settlement of western Minnesota and other places in the Great Plains, was the direct result of railroad expansion.[19] Charles Ingalls gets the capital he needs to homestead by working for the Chicago and North Western Railroad as a timekeeper in the Silver Lake camp. He also benefits from the land rush caused by railroad construction in that he speculates in a building he erects in De Smet, on the main line between Minneapolis and southern Dakota Territory, and he also makes money as a carpenter erecting other buildings during the frenzied first few years in town. Each volume of the Little House books takes us farther and farther west, but also farther away from the self-sufficient possibility at the log cabin in the Big Woods.

> *"Never mind, Caroline," Pa said. "We'll have a good house next year." His eyes shone and his voice was like singing. "And good horses, and a buggy to boot! I'll take you riding, dressed up in silks! Think, Caroline—this level, rich land, not a stone or stump to contend with, and only three miles from a railroad! We can sell every grain of wheat we raise!" (On the Banks of Plum Creek, p. 82)*

They also take us into an economy increasingly dependent on factory-made goods. As Ann Romines notes, it may come as a surprise to us that, when we search our memories of the Little House series, some of the more poignant scenes involve shopping.[20] Time and again, Pa or Ma are seen to purchase something they can't quite afford, but the getting of which causes supreme pleasure in the family: think of Ma's cookstove, or the fabrics for Mary's dress, or the Christmas candy that Pa must eat to survive. These purchases are in counterpoint to the moments in the earlier books when Pa or Ma are seen to produce their own goods—moments that stand out because they are so different from our own experience. Romines states:

*One of the great and mostly unacknowledged appeals of the Little House
books, especially for young readers, is that they frankly acknowledge what
all children know: that buying occasions, like Laura's ecstatic moments
choosing her new dress, are not trivial.*

In Wilder's posthumously published book, *The First Four Years*, we get a view
of the financial side of farming life that is much closer to the reality of the Dakota
frontier boom. Farmers in the 1870s and 1880s were dependent on credit to help
them purchase the wherewithal to cultivate the prairie. Whereas Pa used to
harvest with a cradle scythe, we see that Almanzo continually borrows against
future harvests in order to invest in the latest farming technology—the sulky
breaking plough for $500, the McCormick binder for $200, the mowing machine
and the hay rake, the seeder and the new wagon. "Credit constituted the lifeblood
of the agricultural economy. Lacking it, many—if not most—farmers could not
have gotten started. Even with it, they often were forced out of business anyway,
unable to pay their creditors."[21] This recognizes an essential reality of the Great
Plains: dryland farming in a semi-arid land could only pay if the farmer could apply
the amplified power of technology.

But Almanzo also bought things of intense interest to Laura: the bread plate
and the clock, for example. While it is hard to claim that the prairie environment
is responsible for this increasing consumerism, it is certainly true that the material
poverty of the South Dakota environment and the dependence on the railroad
for most essential supplies, combined with the technical requirements of dryland
farming, would tend to lead individuals away from the self-sufficiency implicit in
the Jeffersonian ideal. Moreover, the stochasticity of the environment would leave
them economically vulnerable to buying on credit against an uncertain outcome.
At the last, when Almanzo loses his crops to hail and then drought, "the arithmetic
of farming" forces him to sell his claim and move away.

Ecological Decline, Civilizing Life

There is a poignant contrapoise in the Little House books between Pa,
who has "itchy feet" and a constant urge move west where he can hunt and
trap, and Ma, who wants to stay put and enjoy the pleasures of a developing
civilization with its institutions, primarily church and school, and its access to
sociability and store goods.

*One evening at supper Pa said he had found a beaver meadow. But he
did not set traps there because so few beavers were left. He had seen a
fox and shot at it, but missed.*

"I am all out of practice hunting," he said. "It's a fine place we have here, but there isn't much game. Makes a fellow think of places out west where—" "Where there are no schools for the children, Charles," said Ma. "You're right Caroline. You usually are," Pa said. (On the Banks of Plum Creek, *p. 82*)

In the conflict between these two opposing interests, Laura often sides with Pa. Unlike her sister Mary, she chafes under the restrictions Ma places on them and longs to be outside, free to explore the new world they find themselves in. As a result of Laura's preference for Pa's world over the confining spaces of Ma's domain, we get to "see" along with her many of the things that Pa values—the natural features of the wilderness prairie, which settlement will soon destroy. Much of the enduring appeal of the Little House series comes from Wilder's skillful descriptions of natural settings from Laura's point of view. These descriptions include wolves, Indians, wildflowers, birds and insects, the expansive vistas, and the weather.

Millions of rustling grass-blades made one murmuring sound, and thousands of wild ducks and geese and herons and cranes and pelicans were talking sharply and brassily in the wind. All those birds were feeding among the grasses of the sloughs. They rose on flapping wings and settled again, crying news to each other and talking among themselves, among the grasses, and eating busily of grass roots and tender water plants and little fishes. (By the Shores of Silver Lake, *p. 77*)

Such vivid, sensuous passages provide the most memorable notes of dissonance in the Little House books—the reader can't help but sympathize with Laura's memories, and, therefore, on some level question whether the settlement of the Great Plains is entirely a good thing. Like Pa, Laura seems uneasy with the pace of settlement. She sees the freedom of life on the plains being constricted by the plowing up of the grasslands. She finds De Smet ugly, and is wary of the large crowds of people. Yet how are we to square this with the triumphant narrative of westward expansion?

"Not a goose within gunshot," he said. "The whole flock rose when it came to Silver Lake and kept on going north. They must have seen the new buildings and heard the noise. Looks like hunting's going to be slim around here from now on. . . ." (By the Shores of Silver Lake, *p. 245*)

They did not gather thickly any more on Silver Lake. Only a few very tired flocks settled late after sunset in the sloughs and rose to the sky again before the sun rose. Wild birds did not like the town full of people, and neither did Laura. (By the Shores of Silver Lake, p. 253)

And in this passage, after escaping a cattle stampede near Plum Creek, Laura reflects with her father at bedtime:

After a while she said, "Pa." "What, little half-pint?" Pa's voice asked against her hair. "I think I like wolves better than cattle," she said. "Cattle are more useful, Laura," Pa said. She thought about that a while. Then she said, "Anyway, I like wolves better." (On the Banks of Plum Creek, p. 79)

From our twenty-first-century perspective, we can clearly see that settlement brought over-hunting, habitat fragmentation, overgrazing and erosion, diminishing the ecosystem's diversity and sustainability and converting a distinctive community of plants and animals into a degraded mixture of native species tolerant of the new disturbance regime brought by settlement, and new-comer plants from Europe and Asia. Laura can't help but notice some of the damaging effects of settlement—and she can't quite reconcile it with the family's—and society's—heroic interpretation of events.

Charles Ingalls can in many ways be seen as a tragic figure—a man who was destined to destroy the very thing he loved, since what he loved most was the unfettered freedom of the frontier (defined as the boundary of interchange between civilization and the native environment). His "itchy foot" was really his uneasiness with the success of migration; he was capable of appreciating the beauty and integrity of the natural world, but could not quite bring himself to criticize the ideology that would compromise it. Yet he was close enough to that perspective to be sympathetic to the Native Americans he interacted with in *Little House on the Prairie* and *The Long Winter*. He also was willing to practice restraint in his own usage of resources (witness his sparing of the beavers, his refusal to hunt in springtime, and his resolve to never take more fish from Plum Creek than his family needs to eat [*On the Banks of Plum Creek*, p. 139]). His keen observation of plants, animals and weather make him almost a harbinger of a future understanding: a time when people would begin to understand the prairie on its own terms and learn to work with it, rather than against it, to wrest a living from it.

"Pa, could it really be a fairy ring? It is perfectly round. The bottom is perfectly flat. The bank around it is the same height all the way. . . . It is very large,

and the whole bottom of it is covered solidly thick with violets. A place like that couldn't just happen, Pa. Something made it. . . ." "You are right, Laura; human hands didn't make that place," Pa said. "But your fairies were big, ugly brutes, with horns on their head and humps on their backs. That place is an old buffalo wallow. You know buffaloes are wild cattle. They paw up the ground and wallow in the dust, just as cattle do. For ages the buffalo herds had these wallowing places. They pawed up the ground and the wind blew the dust away. Then another herd came along and pawed up more dust in the same place. They went always to the same places. . . ." (By the Shores of *Silver Lake*, p. 281-282)

Despite his keen understanding, which included naming many wild animals and knowing some of the natural processes of the prairie ecosystem, neither Pa nor Laura could assemble these details into an ecological whole. Given that he'd learned his farming technology in the moist deciduous forest biome, Pa was not able to conceive of the whole ecosystem in a way that would aid in achieving his economic goals—except for one reference in the last book to the idea that grazing animals might do well in Great Plains farming. It is interesting that, after failing to grow wheat in De Smet, Almanzo and Laura raised sheep, which, as was learned through trail and error, are a poor choice for livestock ranching in the Great Plains from both ecological and economic standpoints.

Ultimately, Laura's descriptions of the beauty, variety, strangeness, and scariness of the Great Plains environment, while evocative and entertaining, are a case of missing the forest for the trees. The science of ecology in North America would just begin in the Midwest in the 1890s, at the denouement of the Little House narrative. It is interesting to speculate that, had ecological theory and practice been available to pioneer settlers, the story of Great Plains settlement might have played out differently.

Laura Ingalls Wilder left the Great Plains for the East in the early 1890s. Population continued to grow, but since 1920 the rural Great Plains have lost a third of their people; the decline continues, with many counties losing ten to eighty percent of their population between 2000 and 2006, leading some to call for a partial abandonment of the Great Plains.[22] Several hundred thousand square miles of the Great Plains have fewer than six persons per square mile—the density standard that Frederick Turner used to declare the frontier "closed" at an 1893 gathering of historians. Many counties now have fewer than two persons per square mile.

Today we see trends in population associated with different modes of living on the Great Plains.[23] Today there are regional centers, such as Fargo, Bismarck,

Pierre, Rapid City, Sioux Falls, Omaha, Lincoln, Des Moines, Wichita, Kansas City. Here the economy is mixed, tied to national businesses and markets, and the population is growing at national rates. In some counties the population is growing slowly—but at least growing—due to irrigation agriculture. Lastly, population has diminished for decades in places where dryland farming and ranching are practiced. Here the population and the economy predictably shrinks, although recently it may have stabilized.[24] In the Little House books we come to understand that the Ingalls family, in trying to make a living by dryland farming in a drought-prone land, were on a cultural and economic path leading to the diminution experienced today in dryland farming counties. Charles's last act in farming was to sell his farm at the edge of De Smet and move to town where he kept a store on a railroad line, tethered securely to the desires and needs of surrounding farmers and the markets and sources of investment back East. Yet even small Great Plains towns like De Smet continue to lose population each decade, strongly suggesting that the fabric of a civilization created from the perspective of an eastern model is still unraveling.

Despite the trying birth of the Little House books and difficult post-settlement century, suggested by the Poppers' and similar points of view, the use and economy of the Great Plains appears to be converging on a sustainable solution. This story can also be woven into an understanding of the Little House books. Locusts, prairie fire, and bison herds—as well as dangers of wolves and cougars—are long gone. Drought, winter blizzards, and extreme cold experienced by the Ingalls family—and more recently the diseases and insect pests associated with large-scale monocultural cropping—remain challenges. Some of the modern solutions were perhaps dimly perceived by Pa and his pioneer cohorts, but clearly couldn't be implemented: bison ranching on native prairie, dryland crop plants, farmer cooperatives that add value to crops with additional processing. Genetic engineering and pesticides, of course, enable farmers to stay one step ahead of wheat rust infestations and other disastrous pestilence. Lastly, the windswept Great Plains are experiencing a bonanza in energy development—not just traditional oil and gas drilling, but now windfarm development and ethanol production, and perhaps eventually cellulosic biofuels. What Laura saw represented the beginning of this unfolding story; if she had lived in the twentieth century in an adventurous, entrepreneurial family, what mythology might she have used to tell the story of the events unfolding around her? It would have made for some great reading, without a doubt.

SHAKESPEARE'S BIRTHDAY
AND THE PASQUE FLOWER

JIM

Today is April 23, Shakespeare's birthday. My wife left early to pick up cupcakes for her high school English class. I biked to school with my daughter and her friend, following the shore of Lake Winona, which was tossing in an east wind. The cottonwood trees were full of cedar waxwings, making their high-pitched calls—*tsee tssee*. They are impatient to be heading north. On the way back from dropping the bikers off I stopped at the bottom of the river bluff that towers above my town and, locking my bike to a sign post, continued on foot up the park path, climbing through oak woods just barely beginning to bud. The steeply sloping forest floor was littered with last year's leaves and a few thin green tendrils were just emerging. About half way up I left the official path and began following a gully crowded with buckthorn and birch saplings, climbing more steeply toward the prow of exposed sandstone nearly 600 feet up—the forest fell back at the edge of a "goat prairie"—a slope so steep and sun-drenched that only prairie plants will thrive on it. There, on an exposed slope, I saw them: pasque flowers, with their purple-and-white blooms, shyly nodding in the dry grasses. I sat down to catch my breath and to look into those little cups with their saffron stamens, strange hairy flowers of the dry heights.

I went to college at Northwestern University in the 1970s. The campus was the usual academic jumble of classrooms, dorms, auditoriums and administrative buildings, sprawling along the shore of Lake Michigan north of Chicago —but between the engineering building and the seminary was a narrow little garden maintained by the Evanston Women's Garden Club. In it were all the plants mentioned in Shakespeare's plays and poems, or as many as they could get to grow: pansies, columbines, daisies and violets, plenty of roses and eglantine, herbs like rosemary and fennel, all enclosed in Elizabethan style boxwood hedges. There was a little fountain at the shady north end of the garden, with a bronze bas relief of the Bard looking suitably meditative.

This sort of garden was common in wealthy towns in the early part of the twentieth century, as it combined two predilections equally suitable to the upper middle class: the ostentatious display of learning and the cultivation of decorative annuals. The desire to propagate species mentioned in Shakespeare demonstrates Shakespeare's pole position as literary lion—but it also represents an unusual twist in the story of invasive species: unlike the medicinal and food plants like plantain, chickory, the dandelion, which European settlers brought with them as practical means of survival, these imports were ideological. These flowery tributes to the Bard of Avon were also tributes of the supremacy of Old World arts and letters—the botanical equivalent of the Queen Anne and Tudor style buildings so prevalent in the college quads and the wealthy suburbs from the Gilded Age to the Jazz Age.

A literary tradition creates a taste for, even an expectant desire for, the landscape and the creatures of one's native land. That is part of the function of the poet, to enable us to inhabit the landscape. An English person sees the English countryside, and the English city, in large part through the rich language of the poets and novelists. Thus we speak of Thomas Hardy's Dorset, or

The purple-tinted pasque flower is among the first to bloom in Midwestern prairies and savannas.

Wordsworth's Lake District, or even Robin Hood's Sherwood Forest. This is magnified across all aspects of culture, of course: music and art in particular can help bind us to the landscape. In an era when paintings were full of classical allusions and historical tableaux, the Impressionist habit of painting *en pleine air* connected the French to their seasides, riverbanks, and farm fields in a way that virtually defined what it meant to be French. Who cared much for haystacks before Monet? Who has ever looked at water lilies the same way since?

But what happens when you are imbibing culture from outside your environ-ment? Literature and art can devalue the local and create a lust for the foreign. Shakespeare is so full of mention of the green English countryside around him, his adoring and belated fans in America seemed ashamed not to have the very flowers he mentioned. Nor was it flowers only: the European starling, first released into Central Park in 1890 by a New York druggist who wanted to bring to the New World all the birds the Bard mentioned in his verse, is a species that has done billions of dollars of agricultural damage. It was as if Shakespeare made us see these plants and animals of old England so lyrically and intensely we could not appreciate our own native species—so much so that we wished to replace our own biome with the one we had left. And indeed it took some centuries before the American environment could fully enter into our national literature. Early American works seem vapid and placeless imitators of English fashion. Not until the mid-nineteenth century did the mockingbird and the dogwood begin to replace the nightingale and the myrtle in our literature. In 1844 Emerson writes, in "The Poet," that, "We have yet had no genius in America, with tyrannous eye, which knew the value of our incomparable materials," and then set about to remedy the problem himself, writing poems about blackberries and pine trees, using place names like Monadnoc and Musketaquid. He was surpassed in the next decade by his disciple, Thoreau, who immersed himself so deeply and specifically in a particular place that he invented a new type of literature—the hybrid of poetry, ethology, memoir, and philosophy that is *Walden*.

American writers have been playing catch-up ever since—seeking, like Thoreau, to live out Emerson's challenge that "Nothing walks, or creeps, or grows, or exists, which must not in turn arise and walk before him as exponent of his meaning." A long list of writers, from John Muir to John Hay, from Walt Whitman to Mary Oliver, have made the diverse American environment available to the imagination. Yet distressingly few Americans read this body of literature. In fact fewer and fewer read anything at all, distracted as they are at the myriad portals of wired media. Young people today are capable of identifying up to one thousand corporate logos, but fewer than ten local plants or animals.

Paradoxically, even as American literature grows ever more specific, American readers of literature are vanishing. If the old literary classes in American paid more attention to the flowers in Shakespeare than to the wildflowers out their back door, it was still true that most Americans then were farmers or children of farmers and were well acquainted with the flora and fauna in their native fields. Today, when less than two percent of the population is growing the food for the rest of us, and when that vast majority lives in urban or suburban enclaves, few people come in contact with their local environment. As we drive from generic suburb to generic shopping mall, purchasing identical products from identical businesses, it seems we are less adapted than ever to the native landscape. If Thoreau claimed that most men lived lives of quiet desperation, it would seem our current problem is more that we live lives of abiotic sameness, navigating through a placeless slurry of goods and services not connected to anything remotely original or local.

But that too is part fantasy. Everyone actually lives somewhere. The poorly-built retail outlet, the asphalt service road that takes us to it, and the billboard advertising its wares, are ephemera on the landscape, and they begin to crumble as soon as they are installed. Google may imagine our amazon.com shopping cart is our identity, but the air we breathe and the weather we suffer under are always real. Above my town, the bluffs carved over millennia by the force of the Mississippi are going to outlast this heedless generation of men, as will the delicate pasque flower, whose purple bloom advertises an older and more primal economy.

We do not need to have English peaseblossom or mustard seed to know that fairies live in the local flora: literature preserves an attitude of enchantment toward the sensual world that can motivate the reader to seek his or her own version of what Shakespeare had. What Shakespeare really means to us is what to *make* of the materials of the world. The Shakespearean gardeners of Evanston suffered not from insufficient patriotism but from a lack of imagination, for they could have had an original relation to their countryside every bit as vital as Shakespeare had to his. How much more powerful is my morning encounter with a pasque flower that did not have to be summoned or maintained in an elaborate floral zoo but rather appears on its own, its meaning as yet unplumbed. How much superior that is to any encounter I might have with the essentially second-hand briar rose, or eglantine, of the Anglophile. If our encounter with the objects around us is mediated in language, then new objects require fresh language, and fresh language gives us new worlds of thought and feeling. As Keats put it in his preface to "Endymion," "A thing of beauty is a joy for ever"—a joy that comes to us in language—the result will be "An endless fountain of immortal drink":

Therefore, on every morrow, are we wreathing
A flowery band to bind us to the earth,
Spite of despondence, of the inhuman dearth
Of noble natures, of the gloomy days,
Of all the unhealthy and o'er-darkened ways
Made for our searching: yes, in spite of all,
Some shape of beauty moves away the pall
From our dark spirits.

The specific representatives of beauty change, with both space and time. But we must re-weave our connection to them, or the fountain goes dry.

This is especially important in an age of accelerating environmental change. It is hard not to fear the cognitive disruption as the rhythms of the seasons—the familiar choreography of weather, with its attendant changes in leaf and blossom and animal life—are rendered unpredictable and strange. As beloved local species dwindle or move northward, we who have learned to love the land fear we will soon not recognize it, and that our culture (even our attenuated, still-unfolding culture) will no longer fit it. The English might ask, what will England be, without English weather and English fields? Will an England altered by climate change make Shakespeare unimaginable? And we might wonder, what will America be when the golden valleys of California turn to dust, when Wisconsin is as steamy as Florida and Florida is a drowned memory?

To the Dakota people of the prairies, the pasque flower is the first to emerge from the harsh snows of winter, and her appearance foretold the return of life to the prairie, the return of the buffalo to their grazing grounds. In Dakota legend, the flower speaks as an aged grandmother and tells her grandchildren that when all the other animals and plants have emerged from their winter sleep, she, the pasque flower, must fade away. Her message was that of mutability, of the eternal cycle of life and death. That story comes back to me now as I sit on an April morning, watching a bumblebee nuzzle the pasque flowers. I think of Shakespeare's sonnet 65—a fitting accompaniment to the Dakota tale:

Since brass, nor stone, nor earth, nor boundless sea,
But sad mortality o'ersways their power,
How with this rage shall beauty hold a plea
Whose action is no stronger than a flower?

In the near future, the pasque flower may be gone, fleeing northward with winter itself. It is not only the individual who is mutable—a species, too, is subject to change. Yet the pasque flower tells me life will always begin again in this valley. The powers that brought the flower into existence will still be operant. New beings will come with the new weather, and if those new beings have language they will have to weave new songs and stories to bind them to their surroundings. Perhaps they will be better at listening than we have been.

Now Winter Nights Enlarge, as We Grow Snug in Houses

Jim

Winona, December, 2008.

My favorite image of a Minnesota subzero night is the view from the trash cans in the alley. I like the look of my own roof gleaming in the moonlight, chimney smoke rising in a ghostly column like the breath of a hibernating animal. I remember the old poem by the Renaissance poet Thomas Campion:

Now winter nights enlarge
The number of their hours;
And clouds their storms discharge
Upon the airy towers.
Let now the chimneys blaze
And cups o'erflow with wine,
Let well-tuned words amaze
With harmony divine.
Now yellow waxen lights
Shall wait on honey love
While youthful revels, masques, and courtly sights
Sleep's leaden spells remove.

It's clear the poet feels the old communal joys—of winter-feasting and music-making and love-making—create an environment all that more pleasurable for the harshness surrounding it. The exterior landscape is dead, still, glittering like polished mineral, but life, banked and guarded beneath the snowy eaves, still smolders, and at that thought a kind of Nordic cheerfulness rises in us.

In good weather, my neighbors mostly annoy me—revving their motors, talking loudly at midnight, playing their music too loudly. But let the landscape

Ice-rimed bur oak on the shores of McMann Lake, Spring Lake Township, Minnesota.

turn cold, dark and inhospitable and our shared humanity is recalled. Walking down the street on these nights when the stars blaze in the zenith and the snow crunches underfoot like pulverized glass, the neighborhood, with its small modest houses, seems poignant and mysterious. The interiors of rooms are illuminated like great aquariums. Caught in the act of setting the table, or talking on the phone, or even watching television, my neighbors seem vulnerable, poignant characters in some vast operatic narrative.

In the ice of the frozen sidewalk, whose surface rings like an anvil when struck, I see the ultimate fate of energy in the cosmos: the universe will not end with either a bang or a whimper, but in the silence of freeze-up, which means life is a feebly guttering flame that must be carefully guarded.

In the early winter darkness, many of us recover the vestiges of communal and ceremonial life—the winter feast, the glimmer of candles, even communal singing. When else in American life do people actually sit down and eat together, much less sing together?

All year we work like indentured servants, coming home late to overscheduled and hectic lives—yet in December we caper a little, like Scrooge at old Fezziwig's party. We find we can stand one another. Yet winter is also a time when we withdraw into ourselves—a time of inwardness and reflection, when mental pleasures are paramount.

To be driven inside by inclement weather is to be thrust in among one's fellow inhabitants—hence the conviviality of the season. But when no one else is home, winter drives us inside ourselves. Minnesotans are not only snug in their houses while the winter winds howl, they are snug inside their heads—they have to be. A violence within, as the poet Wallace Stevens said, must counteract a violence without—a passionate mind is required to match the ferocity of one's environment.

In winter,
Some knotted riddles tell,
Some poems smoothly read . . .

. . . says Campion. The mind becomes our confidant and refuge. What's better than looking out into the silence of a wintry afternoon from the vantage point of the couch, book in hand?

Hannah Arendt has said that the finest effect of civil society is to guarantee a certain distance between individuals; in that discrete space, individuality may flourish. This gives social life its piquancy and its moral tone. The reflective mind is not inimical to society—it is the basis of a lasting social bond. But this only happens where solitude and reflection are granted some status. Disneyworld is no place to be alone and think; Boca Raton is not famous for its libraries or philosophers. It's nice to walk on the beach and to play tennis in January, but if that's all you do, how interesting will you ever get? Will you think of anything besides where the next margarita will come from?

The solitude of a Minnesota winter is unlike the solitude of the gated community, which the privileged are now disappearing into. There is no true sociality where one's needs can all be subcontracted. Minnesota winter reminds us that we need each other—we need our neighbor to help jump our car or pull it out of a ditch. Shoveling the sidewalk is a profoundly social act: you are aiding those who walk across your property. It is in those cold countries of Scandinavia that the ideal of socialism remains firm—those countries where people actually read books.

At 5:30 this morning, I was shoveling the snow from my front walk. The half-moon shone on three inches of glittering powder, in which I could make out the tracks of the rabbit that lives in the shrubbery next door and makes her nocturnal forays in search of what thin sustenance she can find.

In summer I never think of her, but in winter she leaves her haiku-like prints on the foolscap of my lawn. The world means more than its surfaces: there are signs which, when interpreted, will unlock secrets, reveal unknown mysteries. This is a poet's hope, of course, in the universal efficacy of reading. In the enlarged possibilities of a long winter's night

LAND CERTIFICATION:
A PATH TO SUSTAINABLE USE
OF LAND AND WATER

KIM

Prepared for a conference of landowners and regulators in the Driftless Area in 2005, this paper was never delivered. Instead, I gave a powerpoint presentation, now forgotten, on a completely different topic. How that happened is a mystery to me, but I like this essay better, so all is well.

In the United States there is a certification program to promote sustainable forestry practices and another one to ensure that buildings are designed and constructed in an environmentally friendly fashion. But where is the program that certifies the condition of an ordinary parcel of land or the uses landowners make of their land? Certification, as it is practiced, is a voluntary initiative by owners to incrementally progress towards environmental sustainability. Since the majority of land in the United States is privately held, certification of private land represents a holy grail for conservation.

If you ask developers, there already is a dizzying host of regulatory programs limiting their use of land. If you ask farmers, the government regulates how they grow their crops and use their back forty, and they had better comply if they want crop insurance and other subsidies. The truth is, however, that these programs developers, farmers, and other landowners love to hate consist primarily of prohibitions, with little reward for being a good landowner, whatever that is. As a result, a lot of energy is spent meeting the letter of the law in order to avoid the spirit of the law—good land use and the promotion of healthy land and water resources. The result of our nation's several-decades long efforts to improve the condition of land and water represents a series of running skirmishes between landowners and regulatory agencies, with a periodic Supreme Court decision to

186

Harvesting corn at the edge of a new neighborhood.

establish ground rules. Willing partnerships are rare and highly touted, and for every highly visible positive land protection deal, there are thousands of small decisions made daily which, taken together continually erode the productive potential of land and water by simplifying and damaging biological systems.

That is the rub. What does it mean to be a good landowner? What are the widely acknowledged practices on the land or in and around water that produce healthy ecosystems and improved environmental conditions? Ecologists, wildlife and fisheries biologists, land stewards, and others engaged in research or the actual work of land and water management believe they know the answer to this question, and their ideas are trotted out from time to time in newspaper and magazine articles, or radio interviews, but for the most part their audience is the faithful. For the most part they talk to themselves through their professional organizations and publications, they talk to their funders and supporters, and they talk to the regulators and government policy people who make the rules of the game. Less frequently do they talk to landowners, developers, city and county administrators, and the others who make daily decisions about the future of land and water in their neighborhoods. Unless this changes, in fifty years, with the U.S. population projected to increase by at least fifty percent, perhaps fifteen percent of our nation's land surface will consist of wonderful nature reserves and parks that brim with ecological health, while the rest of the landscape will experience deteriorating ecological integrity, lost diversity of species, and eroded natural beauty.

To counter that trend, a certification process is needed for ordinary parcels of land that you or I might own, or that a developer might be considering developing, or a corporation might be using as its world head-quarters. Farmers might use such a program, as might cities and counties ... even state and federal governments. At its core, a certification process for land would recognize the incremental steps landowners are taking, or could be encouraged to take, towards optimizing the ecological health and sustainable land use practices on a parcel of land. This process will target key indicators of ecological health and identify land use practices known to be benign—or even beneficial—for the land. When a landowner achieves the gold standard in such a certification process, the land would be noticeably different from land not on the path to ecological health and sustainability. Pictures would speak a thou-sand words about the details of what this looks like—before and after the landowner took a leap of faith into environmental stewardship.

What might this process look like? A landowner will begin by getting to know his or her land. It's a simple beginning, but for many people it's the most exciting part—getting to know their land intimately, exploring its possibilities, discovering its intrinsic worth and beauty. Nature writers, from Henry David Thoreau and his Walden Pond, to Rick Bass and his Yak Valley, always begin their histories of place by chronicling the beauty and variation in the land they are falling in love with. For the landowner on a certification path, it will be no different. With the help of people who know the details, the science of land ecology and use, a landowner would discover what makes his or her place unique, what parts of it need no repair, and what parts require intervention to secure and improve its ecological health. In short, a landowner in this first step will complete an ecological assessment.

With an ecological assessment, a landowner then will develop and implement an ecological management plan designed to address shortfalls. An example might help here. An eroding streambank represents a negative on the assets balance sheet. The eroding streambank is a lost opportunity to provide quality wildlife and fish habitat. It is less beautiful than a streambank clothed in natural plant life. It also harms one's downstream neighbors by sending dirt their way to cloud their water and bury fish spawning areas. The ecological management plan addresses those issues and directs a parcel of land towards ecological health and sustainability.

Depending on who designs it, an ecological assessment could take an environmental-lite approach to certification standards, or an ecological-purist approach. Where the balance is will need to be worked out. In the meantime, if an ecologist designed it, it would probably ask for answers to the following questions:

- Is the land a net exporter of ecological bounty, or of environmental problems?
- What is the land contribution to the ecological fabric of its surroundings?
- Does the land optimize ecological processes, such as water purification and soil formation and does it promote a variety of species, otherwise known as biodiversity?
- Are human operations on the land supporting ecological processes or detracting from them, and in what ways?

One noticeable thing about these questions is that the first two deal with the impact of the land on the lands around it. Landowners will balk at being responsible for lands and waters they don't own, but in fact, laws already on the books require this as a matter of course. The Clean Water Act, for instance, is designed to stop people from polluting their reach of river because it harms others using that river downstream. A foundation of ecological thinking is that land, water, and species are interconnected across small distances and very large distances—different scales, in other words. For a land certification process to have a real effect on the land and water, it must incorporate this essential truth about land—what you do to your own property affects land and water on someone else's property. Let's take these questions one at a time.

Is the land a net exporter of ecological bounty, or of environmental problems?

To tackle this question, the landowner completing an ecological assets worksheet might be asked to document the extent of polluting or sediment-laden water on his or her land. Are there areas where soil is eroding? What invasive species live on the land that have the potential to alter habitats and ecosystem functions? There are well known and not so well known species, depending on where you live and how problematic the species is—zebra mussel, common buckthorn, cheat grass, melaleuca, are just a few of the several hundred species in this category across the United States.

What is the land contribution to the ecological fabric of its surroundings?

Here a landowner might be asked whether the open space on the property adds to open space on the neighbor's land. (A fair amount of suspended disbelief is going to be required for a landowner to care about this, while thinking that the neighbors will have no regard for this issue on their own property—but for a certification process to take hold, someone has to begin it.) For the certification-minded landowner, again, does wildlife habitat on his or her land contribute to the quality of wildlife habitat on adjacent properties? One of the most important issues in conservation today revolves around this issue and another—connectivity. In brief, habitats around the globe are broken up by human land use, such that the resulting small pieces of habitat cannot ensure that populations of some types of animals and plants will survive another hundred years. The conditions inside those remnant habitat patches are too poor to allow some species living there to survive. As long as there are people, there will always be habitat for crows, house mice, and raccoons, but for something like twenty to thirty percent of North America's species, without high quality core habitat, they will slowly wink out here and there, until there are only a few places big enough and buffered enough against the inhospitable enveloping landscape where they will survive. Think of prairie chickens and sharp-tailed grouse, moose and lynx, even many types of songbirds . . . these go away when core habitat shrinks. At some point a species in decline because of shrinking habitat becomes a threatened or endangered species, with economic ramifications all the way down the line to landowners everywhere. Extinction may be in the future of these species unless landowners begin paying attention. So in addition to looking at the size of core habitat on and next to their parcel of land, landowners will also investigate whether they are part of a regional roadway for species to move around, find new places to raise young, feed and grow old—the term for these connecting habitats is ecological or wildlife corridors.

Does the land optimize ecological processes, such as water purification and soil formation, and does it promote a variety of species, otherwise known as biodiversity?

Optimize is the key word. It is simply impossible to return the Great Plains to the Kevin Costner-esque landscape of *Dances with Wolves*, as beautiful and romantic as that seems. Instead, a balance between use of the land and preservation of the land's capacity to absorb the slings and arrows of change will be needed. In a forest being cut, or a pasture being grazed, or in open space rimmed by nature trails, is the landowner providing high quality wildlife and plant habitat? Have all the wetlands, lakes, and streams been girdled with a protective strip of plant life truly wide enough to capture and filter pollutants and absorb excess water leaving the land? Are species provisions being made—nesting boxes for birds, ephemeral ponds for amphibians, leaf litter and fallen logs for insects and salamanders, dead trees for woodpeckers—so that wildlife finds all its needs met on the property? Is the fate of rare species positive or negative on this land—have their futures been secured or ignored? Finally, what proportion of the land consists of native plant life—a grouping of species natural for that land—versus the land where non-native species predominate in a species-poor mix or the land covered with a hardened surface—pavement, rooftops and the like?

Are human operations on the land supporting ecological processes or detracting from them, and in what ways?

More than anything, every parcel on a path to ecological health requires a strategic plan for operations. Plans exist for many American enterprises, why not for American landowners? This plan lays out the key activities required to bring a property back to better ecological health and ensure that land use practices can continue for centuries. This gives long-term thinking an ecological underpinning. For those land uses scheduled to continue, what adjustments need to be made? Should mowing be stopped, for example, in some areas of open space in order to provide better buffers to key habitats? Restoration activities are those that take degraded land and quickly elevate its status from critical to stable. Prairie seeding in cropland is an example of this. For other areas, what management is needed? Remove invasive plants to make room for an endangered plant? Introduce frogs to a pond so that herons, egrets and bitterns enjoy a nice buffet at dinner time? Cut fewer old trees and more young trees to create stands of timber with a mix of old, mid-aged and young trees? Plug a ditch in a wetland and let it fill up with water? This plan is called an ecological management plan.

Other fine points to put this in motion include a stewardship fund that ensures a landowner has the capital to pay for improvements and ongoing operations. Just as in Monopoly you need reserve cash to improve your property, so the land being improved and certified needs its reserve fund. In some cases, a percent of income is diverted into an account dedicated solely to the purpose of implementing the ecological management plan. Another fine point is a feedback loop. While implementing the plan, a landowner will want to check whether the activities for restoration and management are succeeding. Each year, then, the landowner will complete an audit of conditions—not as intensive as the initial assessment—but paying attention to the same issues first raised and fine-tuning the program to make it more effective.

There are no easy paths to ecological health. Repairing past environmental harms takes time and money. Support for certification exists in forestry and some construction industries (e.g., LEED, or Leadership in Energy and Environmental Design), but certification of the vast majority of the nation's land surface is decades away. The regulatory framework created over the past sixty years was a stop-gap measure because our culture's ethical framework did not consider ecological issues related to land use to be important. A certification process for land, if put in motion, has the potential to complement, and perhaps eventually render obsolete, the regulatory framework in promoting the ecological health of our nation's land and water. It may be the best hope we have in the long run, given current trends and the inevitabilities of the path we are presently on.

MOWING THE AMERICAN LAWN

JIM

When I came to Minnesota around 1999 I bought a reel mower to trim my lawn and from that came this essay.

Midway through the novel that bears his name, elusive millionaire Jay Gatsby asks the narrator, Nick Carraway, to let him use Nick's bungalow as a trysting spot so Gatsby can reintroduce himself to Daisy, the object of his obsessive desire. When Nick agrees, the next thing Gatsby says is "I want to get the grass cut." As Nick tells it:

We both looked at the grass—there was a sharp line where my ragged lawn ended and the darker, well-kept expanse of his began. I suspected he meant my grass.

I was thinking of this passage as I surveyed my lawn the day before my daughter's high school graduation party. It had been a very rainy spring in southern Minnesota and I had let the grass get out of hand—it now stood nearly shin high and had begun to develop flower heads. My lawn looked, to use Nick's words, "irregular." Scores of people were dropping by the next day to eat scones and egg bake and to congratulate my daughter, and I was in the embarrassing position of needing my grass to conform to expectations. Maybe not Gatsby's expectations, but I felt my little corner of the American dream should at least not look *feral*.

Gatsby and I are not alone in thinking that a neatly mowed lawn is intrinsic to our image of success. Lawn-anxiety is as American as eating with a fork in your right hand or asking for ice in your drink. Eighty percent of American homes have a lawn, and a well-maintained one contributes up to eleven percent of a home's value—which is the reason why we collectively spend thirty billion dollars a year on lawn care. That great suburban expanse of turf, shaved weekly, watered daily in climates desert and semi-tropical, edged carefully, fed lovingly and dosed regularly with herbicides and pesticides, takes up nearly 50,000 square miles—more than any cash crop. Yet it isn't a crop: it is sterile, inedible, it doesn't provide shade or color (beyond emerald). Children do romp across it, but since these days they are more inclined to stay inside and play computer games than venture out under the sun it seems obvious that the lawn exists primarily for self-display. The lawn would not be such an obsession except for the fact that, for the past century or more, a tidy, green swath of bluegrass, sculpted to resemble the baize of a pool table, has meant middle-class respectability, just as a weedy, shaggy lawn has indicated slatternly mores. Our lawns are ourselves, apparently.

And I have struggled hard to avoid that attitude. A child of the 1970s suburbs, I have little love for those sterile blocks of aluminum-sided Cape Cod houses and I especially hate the way people obsess over their meticulous lawns. When I started my own family, I turned my back on my station-wagon and lawn-mower heritage and purchased an 1880 two-story frame house on a narrow city lot near the center of a little Minnesota town. The neighborhood was of course pre-car. I was reminded of this every day as I walked the four blocks to work, passing the cement carriage steps in front of my neighbor's

Blades of a reel mower.

house (these were to aid ladies in stepping in and out of their horse-drawn buggies) and glimpsing, in the alley behind, the second-story haylofts on the older garages (stables, then). The lots themselves are small—fifty feet wide by 150 feet deep. Lacking the empowering joules of combustible petroleum, a nineteenth-century homeowner could not afford a lawn larger than what he might curate with the heat of his own muscles. Front lawns are shallow, bringing the house close to the sidewalk, because it was expected that householders should be able to address passersby from the front porch. Back yards are deep to accommodate the detached garages that face the alley; one of the ways you can tell an old neighborhood is that the car is kept out back, like a horse, in sharp contrast to the way the modern garage overwhelms the face of the suburban house, presenting to the street its giant rectangle, faceless and forbidding, throwing off all architectural balance and seeming to announce that the care and feeding of an automobile is the main concern of the house. The suburban front porch has become vestigial, and many suburbanites never bother to use their front doors, coming in the garage entrance instead. By contrast, the short walk I take between my little garage and my back door at least gives me a moment to shake off the effects of the road, to transition to a human being with legs. In doing so I pass my vegetable garden, which takes about a quarter of the yard—whose square footage, added to our front-yard flower garden—or wildflower preserve, depending on how often we weed— further reduces the portion of my lot dedicated to grass. My attempts to avoid indentured servitude to a lawnmower have thus been largely successful. What's left is barely large enough for a game of badminton.

The small size of their city lots doesn't prevent my neighbors from being lawn-obsessed. Though the fad for planting islands of native prairie flowers and grasses has caught on with some, and though others have a penchant for elaborate water features or displays of lawn sculpture, most of my working- to middle-class neighbors maintain the traditional rectangles of green, which many groom like putting greens. There is something appealingly Platonic about these barbered and edged rectangles. They speak of orderly habits, of a predominating will all the more affecting for the modest houses they surround. The most orderly lawns usually have a flagpole, and the pole often sports a Marine Corps flag. "Salute as you pass!" they seem to say—for here is a homeowner who has held entropy at bay.

Objectively viewed, this seems like a lot of importance to place on a patch of grass. But the social meaning of the suburban yard has deep historical precedent. The first usage of the word "lawn" dates back to the 1540s. Back then, a lawn was just a cleared space in the forest—its linguistic root goes back to either Gaulic or German, the same root as our word "land," but it comes to modern English from the old French *lande*, a moor or barren clearing. By the late eighteenth century, however, "lawn" had come to mean exclusively a mowed expanse of grass, and this had social implications. For English manorial estates of that time, a vast expanse of treeless pasture was essential to showcasing the expensive porticoes and gables of the country house—and conversely, once a visitor entered the house, the open lawn afforded great views of the estate through the tall and costly plate glass windows, which were a feature of neoclassical architecture. Open land that did not produce anything either edible or medicinal was a costly luxury. The grass had to be hand-mown with scythes, or cropped by herds of sheep, an expense only the wealthy few could undertake; hence wealthy people in Jane Austen novels have lawns, but everyone else has cottage gardens.

The extension of lawn mania to the middle classes, which occurred in the next century, was made possible by the invention of the lawn mower—not the gas-powered rotary mower of your youth, belching smoke and noise, but rather the hand-powered reel mower you may have seen in old movies. The reel mower was invented in the 1830s in England by Edward Budding, who got the idea by looking at machines that trimmed the wool nap on carpets by means of a spinning helix of blades that struck a cutting bar. Budding and an engineer friend put this machine on wheels and employed it with some success, such that by the end of the century middle-class homes all could aspire to a neatly mowed lawn. This is an excellent example of the bilateral nature of analogy: Budding saw a carpet trimmer and thought of cutting a lawn—and soon everyone was trying to get his or her lawn to look as uniformly trimmed as a carpet. As an unintended consequence, the game of golf went from a sport for hardy Scotsmen, scrambling among the gorse and sheep droppings, to a movable fresh-air chat for the businessman, a billion-dollar leisure activity, and the most boring television imaginable. The toxic combination of industrial monotony and class anxiety are welded insuperably into the modern lawn.

The reel mower may be blamed for the spread of carpet-lawns among the bourgeoisie, but it is in itself an elegant machine. Like the bicycle and the telescope, it belongs to a class of objects that can be readily understood at a glance and serve their purpose elegantly. Compact and low-entropy, the reel mower has only three moving parts. Basically you push the main wheels so they turn the pinion gear that spins the blade reel which incisively strokes the cutter bar. A reel mower works on the same principle as a pair of scissors: two sharp pieces of steel come into contact and sheer off whatever is between them. The main technical problem is keeping the reel blade and the cutter blade correctly aligned and spaced, which you do by tightening and loosening adjustment screws. When working correctly, the reel mower neatly snips the grass at a uniform height, unlike its successor, the rotary mower, which simply tears the tops of the grass off with brute force (you can see the trauma if you look closely: the white tips of the grass are scar tissue). The reel mower does its work with a quiet, nickering whir, a pre-petroleum sonata of precision gears and whetted blades. Anything thicker than a toothpick can stop the blades mid-spin—there is no danger of amputations or flying shrapnel.

As a result, the action of the reel mower is soothing, rather than enervating. In his novel *Dandelion Wine*, Ray Bradbury devotes a whole chapter to describing pleasant memories of the reel mower at work. The book takes place in a small town in Illinois during the summer of 1928: Grandfather Spaulding awakens to the sound of "a clatter of rotating metal through the sweet summer grass." There follows a lyrical description:

> *Clover blossoms, the few unharvested dandelion fires, ants, sticks, pebbles, remnants of last year's July Fourth squibs and punks, but predominantly clear green, a fount leaped up from the chattering mower. A cool soft fount; Grandfather imagined it tickling his legs, spraying his warm face, filling his nostrils with the timeless scent of a new season begun, with the promise that, yes, we'll all live another twelve months.*
>
> *God bless the lawn mower, he thought.*

One might compare the gas lawnmower to a lot of things, but not a cool soft fount, and God's name is usually invoked for completely opposite purposes when one is using it. I should know. In my youth I spent two summers as a "landscape worker" in a posh subdivision. My main job was operating a three-blade self-propelled deck mower, which I learned to spin on a dime and with which I could mow a boulevard of fescue to within a hair's width of a pachysandra bed. I can still feel the mind-scrambling roar and the wrist-numbing vibration of the thing as I steered it across the greensward under the insistent hammering of the July sun. It was a sweaty, repetitive and occasionally unnerving job. Why unnerving? With a power mower there is always the prospect of mayhem—loss of toes or fingers, if you get them anywhere near the blades, but also the danger that your powerful machine might strike discarded toys, sprinkler heads, gravel, or old croquet wickets. The peculiar WHACK of the blade hitting metal or stone, the stunned chortling hesitation of an engine, slowed or stalled by the concussion, then the triumphant throat-clearing of the cylinder resuming its cycle and mounting again to a full roar, was one of the inexpugnable sounds of summer. And was, at least for me, a chief note in the sound track of modern anxiety. This was before iPods and earbuds, or even Walkmans, so the roar of the mower was the loudest noise I was likely to experience all summer. My ears rang for an hour after work, and my head ached from the vibration. And if that weren't enough, the smell of inefficiently combusted petroleum hung over the yard like a miasma. There was nothing I liked about the act of mowing, except for the thrill of mastery a power mower gave—the ability to behead any vegetable foolish enough to oppose your onslaught. If you compare the aggressive roar and destructive force of the modern mower to the low chatter and "green fount" of the reel mower, you can trace the pathology of an entire civilization to the abandonment of a simple tool for a powerful one.

I bought a Scotts Classic reel mower at the local Menards the week we moved into our house. After reading the manual, and after viewing several how-to YouTube clips put up by reel mower enthusiasts, I pushed the metal carriage into the summer verdure and, sure enough, with a purr of blades, it cut the grass. As I walked my yard in diminishing rectangles—the geometric perambulation I remembered from my youth—rather than smoke, vibration and numbing roar, I experienced the song of birds and the smell of fresh flowers and felt the pleasant sheen of perspiration. This was nothing like the lawn mowing I was accustomed to. All the experts agree that the cut with the reel mower is superior because it does less harm to the grass, which remains more disease free and more aesthetically appealing as a result. When you add the other benefits—no carbon effluent to wreck the climate, no expensive repairs to thin the wallet, and, instead of a toxic annoyance, the chance for healthy aerobic exercise—one wonders why we abandoned it.

Before my reel mower, mowing the lawn was a chore to be gotten through. Now mowing was more like gardening, in that I found myself inventorying with approval the variety of crops that make up my yard. One immediate advantage to using a tool fit for its task is that you can pay attention to the task, instead of rushing through it for the sake of some imagined better pursuit. I had time to notice that my lawn is not a monoculture, but rather a jostling, motley crowd of species—clover, plantain, dandelion, wood sorrel, violets, galinsoga, creeping Charlie, pepper grass. It isn't so much a lawn as it is a kind of outdoor salad—literally, for the rabbits that feed peacefully in the evenings, placidly munching in courses as they gaze distractedly into the distance. I even discovered I have several distinct kinds of grass, from a wiry, drought-resistant fescue, which has the consistency of an Amish boy's first beard and which I hardly ever have to water or cut, to the more conventional commercial bluegrass, bland and green as a plastic bucket, to the clumpy and many-veined rye grass, to the varicose and lurid crab grass which springs up between pavers and next to the foundation.

The growing tendency since the Second World War has been toward limiting diversity in the lawn—raising the ante, that is, for the homeowner, who now must exterminate everything that isn't grass, using a broad variety of chemical agents against what are now thought of as "broadleaf weeds." Whereas the Grandfather Spauldings of the prewar America thought of clover and dandelion as part of the lawn, the fledgling herbicide industry, eager to use up chemical stocks built up during the war, began using aggressive marketing to brand anything not strictly grass as a weed.

Nothing exposes the cultural underpinnings of disgust like our hatred of what is undeniably attractive. I have grown to love my lawn's variety and its seasonal rhythms—unlike grass, the congeries of broad-leafed plants in my yard are allowed to bloom and seed (grass, because it is mown, is kept perpetually sexless). I have even come to love that most controversial weed, the dandelion. No flower conjures more shame in the American homeowner: I see men and women in my neighborhood with pump-tanks of poison, vindictively spraying the yellow blooms with the same expression they use for cleaning the cat box or scrubbing mildew. Yet in Germany's Black Forest I have walked through whole fields of *Löwenzähne*, or Lion's Teeth; to Germans they were not weeds, but glorious wildflowers. Admittedly it takes work to overcome "dandelion shame"— the feeling that the neighbors are judging you for your weeds—but once you get to know the resourceful little flower you can gain a European appreciation for it. The dandelion in early spring unfurls its nutritive spades of early green, then fills the yard with little yellow buttons the color of those mindlessly and irresistibly cheerful smiley faces from the seventies—then goes to puffballs, ethereal spheres of mathematically perfect fluff which drift off, allowing the exhausted mother plant to fade back into the carpet. When not in bloom, the dandelion is an unassuming part of the general greenery, and its gaudy social phase lasts only a couple of weeks. What justifies our hysterical hatred of it?

Especially when the plant has so many benefits. It was brought to this country as part of the traditional pharmacopeia: dandelion greens were an important dietary supplement in March, when few greens existed; their roots, dried and roasted, were important as a liver tonic and made a rather fragrant tea. The blossoms were used to make a cheery cordial, full of vitamin C (the very cordial which gives *Dandelion Wine* its title). In fact, many of the "weeds" in my lawn are originally medicinal: especially plantain, which was brought to America by the Plymouth colonists because of the curative properties of its leaves, which were applied as a poultice to deep cuts, snake bites, and sore feet. Plantain is still regarded as an effective treatment for wounds and abrasions and its young leaves can be eaten like spinach. Plantain leaf tea is also said to be good as a decongestant and blood purifier (in fact the list of things that plantain is said to cure is so long that it is called a "true panacea" by herbalists).

In addition to their health benefits, plants like dandelion and clover are important food sources for pollinating insects—and plantain seeds are a plentiful source of forage for sparrows. Why would we want to eliminate from the lawn plants that have human and ecological benefits? Certainly I don't. The reel mower has made me a much more relaxed homeowner. While I do maintain respectability by weeding leggy interlopers like knotweed, tickseed sunflowers, maple and hackberry seedlings, blackberry runners and of course, the occasional tendrils of poison ivy, I am in general content with the mélange. I am happy if the lawn is green. I don't care who contributes.

But there is one thing the modern gas mower can do that the reel mower can't: chop high weeds. As is true in all other areas of life, the way of virtue is the way of discipline. To own a reel mower is to be committed to weekly cutting, because once grass grows past a certain height the reels cannot get hold of the grass blades. You are left with two choices: scythe, or power mower. The power mower works because 1) it is so overpowered for its task, it will handle anything shy of a full-grown maple or power pole, and 2) because it uses the vacuum created by its rotating blade to suck anything into its maw, it will pull in tall grass.

Necessity and social conformity dictated my actions. I called a friend and begged to borrow her Toro self-propelled mower. She dropped the mower off one afternoon and gave a lesson on how to start it and how to deploy its horsepower: "Don't hold it back with the gears engaged or it will dig a trench," she said. The jump between my old Scotts Classic and this 149-cc engine with its 6.75 pounds of gross torque was like a Kittyhawk fighter to a G-6 jet. It had the power of four horses. It was certainly a step above the old second-hand mower I'd been chained to as a kid—the back-wrenching pull cord had been ergonomically relocated up on the handle, for one thing, thus eliminating the humiliating posture one used to assume before the instrument—kow-towing like an extra in *The King and I*—and with it the back-wrenching result of sadistic ergonomics. The mower's choke had also moved up the handle and had the sophisticated look of the starter button on a Bentley—the mower overall looked like it had designs on LeMans or Monte Carlo, especially compared to the rusted-out, greasy Briggs and Stratton of my youth, a battered tug so caked with the diced and juiced grasses that its undercarriage looked, when you tipped it up, like the mossy carapace of an alligator snapping turtle. But this slick new mower had that same smell, that intoxicating mix of chlorophyll and gasoline with overtones of burnt motor oil. As with Proust's Madeleine, the scent immediately and viscerally brought me back to childhood in the suburbs, when the growl of two-stroke motors was the carillon of a Saturday morning.

The first thing I did was scalp my lawn. The mower was set too low for the irregularities of my untended sod and the blades dug in, leaving an ugly spot of exposed earth and ravaged roots. I remembered this from my landscaping days. The mower deck is a planar surface which tolerates only level conditions—and, like Procrustes of old, it is willing to enforce its dicta. The world must adapt to the tool when the tool is this powerful—modern landscaping has to take into account the dimensions and proclivities of mowers. Part of the problem is a reduced feedback between tool and hand. It is said that a large percentage of roofing nails now fail to connect with the actual roof trestles, because the nail gun roofers use does not allow the nailer to feel the difference between a solidly clinched nail and one that points into empty space. The result is that roofs are much easier for tornadoes to pry off than they used to be. I felt the same disconnect as I wrestled this behemoth of a mower across my little lawn: it was like riding a bronco through a boudoir, trying to keep the roaring blades from destroying the hosta beds and gouging the fence posts. Every time I tried to slow down, the wheels began to churn a strip into the grass—finally I disengaged the drive and pushed the heavy, reluctant machine with my own muscles.

The mower did its job: it cut the grass evenly and swiftly. I was left with a respectable looking lawn, even and trim. But I felt as though I had done something slightly immoral. Something against my principles.

We use the gas mower for the same reason we drive our 6,000-pound Cadillac Escalades five blocks to the grocery store instead of walking or riding a bike, for the same reason gas leaf blowers have replaced the simple rake. Drunk with the energy of ancient sunlight, who needs elegant or subtle solutions? Brutality suffices, especially when we convince ourselves we are "saving time." The modern lawn mower is an example of the deformative effects of excess power: in its effects, in its operations, it is a crude machine, adapted to the whims of the lazy or distracted homeowner, not the specifications of the job. It is so vastly overpowered for what it has to do, it is like using a sledge to drive a nail. And such excess of power leads to ugliness. It can be said that necessity is the mother of beauty: the pressure of necessity makes the deer's haunch beautiful and the wolf's eyes intelligent. The factory chicken who cannot stand under the weight of her own breasts, or the milk cow overbred to the point of becoming a grotesque cartoon, are the works of a people more interested in efficiency than happiness, more obsessed with immediate profit than the fitness of means to ends. And we bear the weight of this ill judgment in our collective swollen waistlines, our inurement to ugliness, our distracted ethical sense. Oil—which is unearned energy of such density that it effectively gives each American the equivalent of ninety slaves—makes us as obese, distracted and corrupt as pashas of yore. I didn't—don't—want to be part of that.

Nick says, at the end of *The Great Gatsby,* "Gatsby's house was still empty when I left—the grass on his lawn had grown as long as mine." After Gatsby's death, the wilding of his lawn reflects the end of his dream, which Nick says was already behind him anyway. *The Great Gatsby* is a great book because it captures the intensity of our desires and the shallowness of our goals. Americans so often spend enormous amounts of energy to *look* successful, to be accepted, but we have so little capacity for defining what success or belonging might really mean. Our lawns are symptoms of this. We expend 600 million gallons of gas on our lawns each year. A four-horsepower lawnmower creates as much pollution in an hour as a car does driving 200 miles. To maintain our lawns we use thirty percent of the nation's water. All for a species of vegetable social credit, for the assurance we will look as though we have finally made it to the American dream. Perhaps we should step back and ask ourselves when enough is enough.

There are plenty of alternatives—in Germany, it is common to grow fruit trees instead of turf. Italians grow tomatoes and eggplants. Certainly we could begin to see our lawns as sources of food again—as gardens, rather than carpets. Los Angeles architect Fritz Haeg's "Edible Estates" project, launched in 2005, has transformed lawns across the country into organic gardens that feed their owners and confront the neighbors with alternatives to grass. His project is the tip of the hoe for a lawn reform movement that continues to gain momentum. In my neighborhood, this would be a return to our original ethos—in the nineteenth century everyone had a backyard garden.

But we are unlikely to rid ourselves of lawns completely: they have deep roots in our culture. At the very least we could learn to tolerate the yards our great-grandparents had, and mow them with the same technology. Perhaps one day I will wake to hear and see my neighbor's grass leaping in a "fount from the chattering mower." Then I'll be able to say, "God bless the lawn mower."

ONE HUNDRED FORTY YEARS OF PLANNING OPEN SPACE AND WHY IS IT NOT QUITE RIGHT?

KIM

In 2003-2004 I was working on comprehensive plans in the Twin Cities and was struck by the challenge of directing planning to promote good land use in an ecological sense.

O ne of the first planned open spaces was created for the burgeoning Island of Manhattan—Central Park, whose inventor, Frederick Law Olmstead, is the patron saint of landscape architects and planners. That was one hundred forty years ago. Since then the Supreme Court has established the legitimacy of land use planning as a tool to promote the common good. When it comes to land, the common good is decided by people who live in a township, borough, county, village, or city, as befits participatory democracy. The specifics of that common good, though, are debated. In 1970 the common good did not particularly include wetlands, though it did include the proper placement of billboards on highways and the hygienic siting of septic tanks. Decades later the common good encompasses a welter of environmental goods, including but not limited to replenishing groundwater, preserving the natural fluctuation in the levels of lakes and streams, preventing water pollution, protecting wetlands and trees, not to mention endangered species.

Underlying these common goods is the sincerely felt belief that, while we must provide living space for people, we also must protect and improve the environment. The entire movement toward sustainability has this as its most basic assumption. The U.N. Population Office projects that, by 2100, the world's population will have increased by fifty percent and, if all goes well, growth will slow down. Ecologists calculate that right now the world's population and consumption levels of its people require 2.5 Earths to satisfy us all.[1] By 2100, presumably, we will have figured out how to live sustainably and, despite the

The Jeffersonian survey grid laid down on a landscape of glacial ponds, potholes, and a river valley.

larger population and greater affluence, we will not require five Earths to satisfy us. When, however, more than a single Earth is needed to keep people alive and happy, the Earth has to give something up—environmental quality is what is sacrificed when too much is taken to satisfy people's needs.

With this as an assumed future, it is worth taking a moment to consider planning for open space in a crowded world. Open space in and around an urban or suburban setting benefits people tremendously, even though much of that goes unnoticed. These benefits include the psychological calming that vegetation has on the human psyche. Fish and fowl and beautiful settings where people camp, boat, canoe, fish, hunt, bike, ski, and otherwise take their innocent pleasures come without charge from natural lands and waters. Open spaces purify and replenish ground and surface waters that people depend on for drinking, industry, and many of life's necessities. There are many other benefits, greater and lesser, which have always been there, a by-product of the existence and natural functioning of biological communities comprising open space. These benefits are called ecosystem services, they are free, and they have been enumerated by several researchers over the years.[2]

It is this part of open space—generally defined as all the lands left over when the rest of the land surface has been claimed for direct human use—that is most in need of protection as a public good. In fact, because of the ecosystem services provided by intact wetlands (water regulation and purification, groundwater recharge, fish and wildlife population stability, among other things) legislation was passed at the federal and state level, beginning with the 1972 Clean Water Act, which emphatically stated wetlands were a public good deserving of perpetual protection. The details of what a wetland is are still being debated, but no-one now believes that wetlands are worthless because they cannot be farmed, built on, or otherwise directly used by people. The indirect benefit that people derive from wetlands, the free ecosystem services we enjoy, are enough to make us value them, but it took legislation to codify what had been increasingly understood by some and increasingly opposed by others who had a strong interest in believing wetlands had little, if any, common good.

If designing for good land planning—the architectural equivalent of designing for good energy and water efficiency—were commonly practiced, then ecosystem services and the common good they represent would be safeguarded for us and future generations. But in fact ecosystem services continue to erode and, worse, fail to be improved even when there is an opportunity to do so. The statistics on this are commonplace.[3] We know them well and want to look forward to solutions, not backwards to reasons for protest.

Land use planning is an institutionalized form of landscape design implemented by elected civic governments and their staff. As an institution, it creates solutions that, over time, tend to solidify and become institutions themselves. At its most basic, the type of design solution to settle people on the landscape tends to takes two general forms: dense and dispersed. In dense design, a variety of uses occupy as much of the surface of a municipality as possible, including large retail stores, office buildings, restaurants and consumer destinations, apartment buildings, multi-family dwellings, and neighborhoods of single family homes. When the development is finished, remaining open space consists of wetlands bordered by a narrow buffer, city parks, and boulevards or trail systems. Everything is otherwise used. In dispersed design the idea is that, by placing a single family home on a one-, two-and-one-half- or ten-acre piece of ground, the rural character of an area will be preserved and environmental damages minimized. The lower threshold of dispersed development is somewhere around one acre per residence, which is commonly believed to be smallest lot possible for the soil to successfully purify septic tank drainage before it leaves the lot and becomes someone else's drinking water.[4]

It may be that people born and raised in cities see nothing wrong with dense design, and rural people see nothing wrong with dispersed design, but the fact is that both have their benefits and shortcomings. The gap between the desired and actual effect of either perspective is what ecologists take issue with. Neither perspective takes into account the ways that landscapes and watersheds actually function, and hence continuously miss the mark in providing for the common good—assuming, of course, that people care about the common good delivered by open space in support of healthy ecosystems and watersheds.

Given the goals of providing for people's living needs and protecting and improving open space, dense design has several good qualities. First, it limits the development footprint in a region by concentrating the built environment in certain areas and leaving a greater portion of the land alone.

Secondly, dense design reduces the cost of building roads, utilities, and other public infrastructure, meaning less tax revenue is needed to support a larger number of people. The efficiencies of dense design are well known and studies have documented them.[5]

Thirdly, there is a social benefit to children and adults living near each other and to their schools, churches, shops, and other places they need to get to. Though much overused, the term "community" suggests what becomes of a group of people when they associate on a frequent basis. All these things in and of themselves represent additional common goods, which can be added to the common good of protecting the ecosystem services found in the large open spaces that remain. So dense design supports much in the way of common good and is something to promote.

On the other hand, dense design is an ecological and aesthetic disaster for the locations where it lands. The intersections of four-lane highways (with a fifth left turn lane and right-turn bump-out) are ecological deserts and net exporters of ecological problems. In the first place, the amount of impervious surface—a degrading force to wetlands, lakes, and streams—overwhelms the local environment's capacity to compensate. As a result, urban and suburban water bodies and wetlands tend to be polluted, or have no shoreline vegetation where important biological processes take place, or are simply unsightly due to large amounts of trash, bare soil and erosion. The widely employed stormwater pond bears little resemblance in looks or function to the natural swales and wetlands through which run-off passes in an unaltered landscape, and does not capture the fine sediments and dissolved phosphorus that eutrophy downstream waters.

Almost as profound a change takes place in the densely designed uplands. A total shift in wildlife, in populations of birds and small mammals, butterflies and dragonflies, in wild plants, and a host of other creatures follows the change from rural lands to densely developed settings. Some argue that this is natural, that these other species must make way for people. I would argue that if we cannot find a way to preserve the variety of species that are natural to a region, we will also fail to provide for other important ecological processes and lose ecosystem services along the way. These species are indicators of the extreme changes that are wrought on a piece of ground. They indicate that the balance has tipped too far in one direction, and entire assemblages of creatures and their habitats were wiped out over large expanses. No wise stewardship is taking place when this happens; it is a mistake, one that people should not continue to make given our current understanding of environmental issues.

Finally, dense design slivers and isolates open space. In these settings, the balm that nature confers on busy people's minds is taken away, replaced by the jarring juxtaposition of constructed objects. The subtle forms, shades, colors, and continuities found in nature are simply not available any more, unless one gets in one's car and drives to a more natural place. In fact, in dense design, the best open space goes to those most able to afford it. It has been well documented that buyers pay a premium for lots next to open space. It is a distinctly undemocratic way to design for the human community, and establishes a subtle form of aristocracy in the land of the free.

Dispersed design is the darling of 1970s environmentalists. The idea of each of us living on his or her own two-acre or ten-acre lot, growing vegetables, free from society's expectations and constraints, appeals to freedom-seeking individuals. Its greatest common good, the argument goes, is that it preserves an impression of open vistas and the agrarian past. This is a calmer, less expensive way of life. People's property taxes are much lower in places where public services are few, administrative overhead is minimal, and the need for services greatly reduced because of a smaller, more self-reliant population. All of these are superior alternatives to the dense design model as a way to create an affordable and sustainable living space. Dispersed design has a reputable advocate in Thomas Jefferson: an ideal democracy in which every man's character was established by ownership of land that he worked himself.

On the other hand, there are subtle ecological downsides to dispersed development. For one, everyone must drive a long distance to get to any place where people or events or objects of desire are to be found. In the horse-and-buggy era, this didn't matter except in the expense of time, but today the implications for global climate change are profound.[6] Moreover, many of those living in dispersed design settings are just as harried and busy as the rest of us living in cities. This is a cultural phenomenon that has more to do with the evolution of our society, economy, and technology, and less to do with the density of homes in the landscape. The preservation of a rural feeling doesn't pan out either. Homes on one or two acres, or even five acres, stand out and appear like so many Easter Island heads set in former cornfields or tucked back against a woods. Driving by, yes, it is not a wall of houses, but one sees very visible houses just the same. With the sizes of homes now at three stories or 3,500 square feet, with a basement walkout, the effect is jarring. The actual rural landscape of four farmhouses per square mile is destroyed when up to 320 homes might go in on every square mile.

Then there are the larger ecological consequences that play out at regional scales. Because dispersed design spreads the same number of homes that could be accommodated by dense design across fourteen times the area (one per two acres instead of five or six per acre), the influence of people on nature will be that much greater. Two things happen then. The landscape is broken into many small management parcels which contain buildings, lawns, driveways, and the other accoutrements of settlement. Ecologists call this "habitat fragmentation" and it is a driving force behind species extinctions worldwide. Here in America, habitat destruction and fragmentation are responsible for the decades-long downward slide of many songbirds, including certain warblers, various grassland sparrows, bobolinks, red-headed woodpeckers, and others.[7] (In rural areas, habitat change due to changing farming practices is another factor.) Each home built in a woods, or in a grassland, or at the edge of a wetland, spins out its own web of influence. Housecats and dogs make forays into the surrounding landscape, killing voles, mice, songbirds, and other species that make up the bottom of the food chain for hawks, owls, and larger animals. Plantings of nursery-purchased stock introduce new types of plants to the neighborhood. Some of these plants are capable of spreading into nearby wildlife habitat and making it less suitable.[8] Each small parcel-holder manages the land according to his or her individual vision of sustainability, if indeed they have one. This may represent great freedom for the individual, but it also represents a tyranny of small decisions for all of us because standards of ecological health are not applied evenly across ownership parcels. The resulting patchwork of habitats may or may not support a region's wildlife. There is also the loss of productive land that could be used to grow food, raise livestock, or supply timber. It appears at the moment that we have enough to eat, but in 2100 will that be the case? Or will the price of land be so high that only the wealthiest corporations can afford to own and farm it? That future is already being glimpsed, and is it one we want to cement in place by the decisions we make today?

Both dense and dispersed design help and hinder our efforts to create human living spaces and protect and enhance the environment. Your choice of which path to follow may depend on nothing more than what you are used to. In some ways, that choice represents a spiritual divide, difficult to bridge because of what is perceived to be at stake. Growth itself is part of the problem—a doubling or tripling of an area's population in a couple of decades is wrenching to local customs and institutions. Yet the growth will not abate—nor will the need to build houses disappear—for a hundred years. It is fruitless to argue against growth at this point in our cultural development. Far more useful is to debate the details of how the growth will be handled.

It is generally understood that greater density helps preserve open space. In actual developments designed for minimal environmental impact—termed low-impact or conservation developments—as much as ninety percent of the land surface has been protected as open space. More typically, twenty-five to seventy-five percent of the land surface has been protected, the actual amount depending on the location of the property, the profit margin required by investors, and the size of the property. Small geographically desirable (and expensive) parcels in the hands of people who wish to maximize return on investment will struggle to achieve twenty-five percent open space. Below twenty-five percent open space one begins to approach a conventional development in the amount of open space remaining. There are biological reasons why twenty-five to seventy-five percent open space is a target for conservation developments. It seems to represent a threshold at which ecological processes rapidly shift in their function and form, with significant losses in ecosystem services as a result.[9]

To reach the twenty-five to seventy-five percent open space threshold, the design of developments must be compact. Multi-family buildings, underground and multi-tiered parking structures, and multi-storied commercial and consumer product buildings all must become tools in the design toolbox. Homes must have smaller ground floor footprints on smaller lots. That is how one gains the flexibility to balance land costs and open space. At this point, the advocates of dispersed design cringe—what is being created is nothing more than the standard urban or suburban space with its social issues and expensive overhead. They are correct—

why replace one set of problems associated with dispersed design with a different set coming with dense design? An ecologist on the whole would prefer dense design because it minimizes the extent of the human footprint across a region. But where the foot steps, the impact is enormous. That is the central problem with dense design. The solution, then, is to make dense design more environmentally benign. That has been done, and can be done, by first viewing the challenge from two perspectives, regional and local, and then designing with principles appropriate to each scale that minimize the unintended environmental consequences of dense design.

A regional ecological perspective takes into account how much wildlife habitat there is for different groups of animals (forest-dwellers, grassland-dwellers, wetland-dwellers), how big the individual patches of habitat are, whether they are connected to or at least near to each other, the major barriers to animal and plant movement that exist or might be built, the total amount of impervious and less-pervious (e.g., mowed turf grass, cropland) surface, and the degree to which streams, lakes, wetlands, and other aquatic habitats are cushioned against adjacent land uses by permanent vegetation.

A local perspective pays attention to:

- the management of stormwater leaving impervious and less-pervious surfaces
- the amount of open space next to each home
- the creation of natural conveyance channels and storage structures for managing stormwater run-off
- the quality of that open space and the provision of long term management of the open space
- the creation of small wildlife refuges inside and around the developed space
- the visual impact of the development on travelers and neighbors viewing the property

Paying attention to these things at regional and local levels is no small task. Each municipality's and landowner's view of the world stops at the boundary of their domain. No-one really has an ecological big picture in mind when a piece of property is zoned rural low-density residential or commercial, neither the city planner nor the private developer. It is enough to try to make sense of one's own transportation, housing, business, and emergency services needs without worrying about how that intersects with the neighbor's. Worrying about regional networks of open space and the flow of water across tens of miles is not even considered.

In my experience, the two levels can be, and must in fact be, integrated in order to accommodate population growth for the next hundred years without eroding the current free benefits we enjoy from functioning ecosystems. In essence, dispersed and dense development must be implemented in the same place, where the best of each approach is used. Simply put, a municipality's comprehensive plan can steer new development toward a form that supports ecosystem services. I've seen it done, so I know it can be done. Politics, though, weigh heavily in the equation. The city's lawyer tells the council members, "You will be sued if you try to support the public good in this way," and more often than not, the council members vote against such a plan. A prominent citizen says, "I was counting on a road intersection right there so I can maximize the value of my land when I develop it—you are taking my property on which I've paid taxes for twenty years." Or a council member simply doesn't believe in the expression of public good represented by stable streams, clear water, and continuous green belts. He believes the community's character is defined by one-acre lots—nothing else. All of these objections, and more, confront the city planner and council that attempts to extend the public good to a healthy environment. They hear from constituents, "Forget the National Environmental Policy Act—this is about land use decisions at the scale of an individual vote—do what benefits me the most, or I'll vote you out."

But the tide is turning in this regard. There are communities across the nation which know that investment in open space returns more on that investment than investing solely in new roads and sewers.[10] In fact, open space and a less expansive infrastructure, in the long run, save communities money and elevate the mood of citizens. Who doesn't love biking through nature, seeing it out their back door, walking to a park where children splash in a brook or pond? What individual isn't calmed by a backdrop of plants and the song of birds? Well . . . there are some, certainly. But by and large the behavioral psychologists say that nature is good for us. E.O. Wilson, scientist and legendary conservationist, wrote a book on the subject—*Biophilia*—which argues that people require contact with the natural world in order to be fully human.

The other piece of the puzzle is site design. Where do the roads go, where should buildings be, by which path will rooftop runoff flow to the nearest stream? These important decisions at a specific locale ripple outward from the pebble thrown in the pond—the pebble being, naturally, a sheet of pavement and turf, studded with buildings. The landscape around every development absorbs the effect of that development, whether or nor it is noticed by council members, developers, or the public. Ecologists will tell you it has an effect, and ecologists will further quantify that effect for you.[11] The overall evidence is that development, done badly, does badly by the environment. There's no way around it. Given that, and knowing that people have mostly figured out how to avoid many of the harms caused by development, why does development not pattern itself to preserve, even restore the natural world? Well, sometimes it does.

Conservation design and low impact design are two modes of development that pay attention to the details of how to live more lightly on the land. Where a municipal comprehensive plan identifies a regional stormwater treatment train, development in this vein seeks to enshrine that regional flow path by adjusting the location of roads and buildings. Where wildlife habitat is identified, and is continuous with or near wildlife habitat on adjacent properties, a sensitive development plan secures and buffers that important refuge with similar vegetation—even creates connections to bind two habitats currently separated by cornfields. Of course, the price of land—climbing as it always does—pushes back mightily on these types of developments—wouldn't a nice wooded neighborhood be just the thing to cap off this development, and bring in a tidy sum? That impulse is driven to the fore by the cost of land, but it could be dealt with by the types of housing offered. The developer objects: "I can't sell that type of housing. Nobody will buy it." That is a good argument, one that in the end decides whether a project lives or dies, but why does it always have the last word? Surely there is a way to balance the price of land, the need to get so many houses out of it, and the price offered for the type of housing—surely these can be balanced against the public good that sensibly asks, for our own and future generations, that streams not be degraded, wildlife not be extirpated from a region, lakes and ponds not be polluted, and everybody have ready access to nature. That is the challenge, but also the payoff in thinking of the public good in larger terms, and codifying that in municipal zoning and ordinances.

So far this has been mostly about the nuts and bolts of ecosystem degradation caused by development, and what can be done about it. At the start of this I presented the idea that, we've been doing land-use planning for at least one hundred forty years, yet it is still not right. Why? What are we missing that ecologists, in their studies and publications, point out to society at large—that our development patterns are not sustaining the public good as far as the very big issues of ecosystem health and services go?

I attribute it to these things:

- Little appreciation of nature's support of our existence
- Lack of ecological intelligence about our region
- Timidity in standing up for the public good

Planning as practiced by the vast majority of planners going back over a century is largely devoid of ecological thought. I can't blame them—ecology wasn't even a cohesive science until around 1900. By comparison, mathematics goes back several hundred years. Let's not forget the Egyptian engineers who build the pyramids. All this is to say, perhaps in the next twenty years an ecological perspective will creep into planning. It already is doing so in landscape architecture—the discipline of drawing from multiple disciplines and expressing it in forms we build on the landscape. Landscape architecture is a lot like ecology in that way—multi-disciplinary, integrative, holistic—but an ecologist would emphasize the underlying science more. I suppose geologists and pedologists view an ecologist's use of their data with a scant eye—what does this biologist know about the workings of solid ground?

That said, planning fails to protect the public good because it is ignorant at this time of the public good related to the life support systems of the planet. But even if planners had been educated as landscape ecologists and aquatic biologists, would they be able to shift a municipality's attention from the price of land, kinds of housing stock, buyer's preference, and local politics sufficiently to make it stick? Could they lead a community to the understanding that its character, well-being, even its economic health is tied to the public good represented by ecosystem health and services? Good question. Time will tell whether planning graduates to the next level, or whether another hundred forty years will pass doing business as usual.

Bleak House

Jim

The grass is steel wool under the swing set
and the walnut sheds leaves of anachronistic yellow;
the hosta are burnt as though with a welder's torch.
The canoe lies hull up against the rusty fence,
a green tapered shape, inverted and idle.

I think of blue Superior,
noisy with all that water
and cold as a snowcone.
I think of the reams of data
in some NOAA conference room:
the average daily temperature,
the means and extremes.
I think of a parking lot
in Christmas, Michigan,
the trailers, with their powerboats and jet skis,
yoked to their Yukons and Navigators
and Cherokees, shimmering in the heat: inside,
their owners, rampant for risk and
dissolution.

What I have done this summer?
Why have I shown my children
the secret cove, its glassy minuet?
The stage laugh of the loon?
The sough of wind in the pine crown?
Like Jarndyce in Dickens,
they will be hopeful while others
gamble away their inheritance,

throwing down what they cannot
afford to lose.

THE BOILER

JIM

On Muskrat Point, a riveted drum
wets its ankles in the calm
like a fat lady bathing.
Hard to picture it as the original lung
of a donkey-engine,
a purse of furious vapor
cranking a winch on a salvage boom—
wresting some sodden timber off the
dark lake bottom.
Now it's a curiosity,
forensic and rusty,
on which the gulls
sit and preen.

This is the same sand spit
where an Ojibwa war party
drank itself mad with trader's whiskey:
three days of slurred singing,
firing muskets into the air.
Then silence.
The trader saw them through his spyglass,
lying on the wide beach
as though dead.

Every spree runs aground eventually;
there are not enough spirits to float us
into paradise.
The sandbar itself is a
child of inebriation,
cast up by a drunken lake
which the east wind
lashed to idiot foam.

But what if a spree
defines a civilization?

It was a roaring night
that dragged this barrel of iron
out of the lake depths—
forged in some ironworks downstate
and cribbed in white oak,
then burst by the wave-paw
and rolled like a plaything.
Now the minnows flicker like confetti
in the sun-dappled shallows.
The boiler grows warm and empty
and red with rust.

Somone places a rock on its dented lid
like an afterthought.

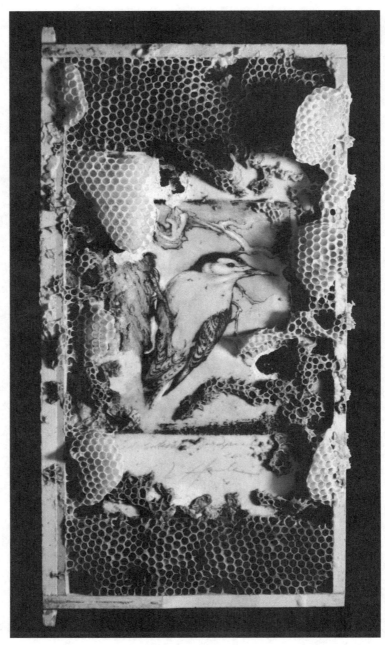

In the Red-Bellied Woodpecker,
the handiwork of bees and Ladislav Hanka merge.

STILL TALKING
AFTER ALL THESE YEARS

JIM AND KIM

A quarter-century of conversations between us makes us wonder what to make of it all. What did all that talking mean? Here we conversed yet again, via email, as a bookend to that first email conversation we had so many years ago.

Jim

I'll open with some questions: now that the shape of the millennium is appearing, like a picture under the darkroom light, one question would be: did we waste our time? We could see what was happening and what needed to be done, but was there something we couldn't see—that shape of the human tragedy about which our religious elders were well-informed? So many conversations during which you and I solved the problems of the world, and the problems of the world kept getting worse nonetheless. I suppose I meant more than I knew when I used to tell you that human beings were vermin— remember that? Driving in the rain, I think coming back from Drummond Island, looking for ducks?

Is the problem that we were ahead of the curve, like all those guys who invented cars before Ford and watched him steal the world once he figured out how to scale things up? Will the generation after us be clever enough to begin to pull up on the stick, or will we just auger in and leave our bones for the next species to ponder? Right now I don't have much hope. But is that because I am not in the fight, really? Maybe you are optimistic because you are in the trenches fighting, and that always helps with anxiety: the illusion of control.

I have had my heart broken I guess. In the '80s I discovered the natural world. I fell in love with Michigan, with the swell and fall of the old seabed, the dark-columned forest coming back from a century of depredation, the spring woods full of trillium and Dutchman's breeches and the sound of spring peepers.

The chortle of water in a spring-fed creek. The overgrown fields smelling of knotweed and wild carrot and crackling with grasshoppers. The snow—the snow that came and stayed and gave me afternoons of skiing. Winter sunsets through the bare branches, the happy call of the chickadee. And all that beautiful consortium now to be scattered like a Lego tower meeting a baseball bat. The heat, the storms, the invading pests, the ugliness of algal blooms and diseased forests; the fires and floods.

Yet this is nature too. Nature as Shiva, not as Aphrodite or Diana: not the pleasant postglacial maiden/mother of the tigerless north, where the lakes were devoid of alligators and were clear enough to make you think that nature was synonymous with purity and benignity. We are about to meet the Mother of Catastrophe—the Empress of Extinctions. As in a Greek tragedy, we are about to get existentially schooled. So what have we learned that will take us over the falls? What's at the bottom? Will we survive in some sort of technological barrel?

Well, that is negative. But it is a fair question to ask of ourselves.

Kim

I read your email just before heading outdoors to weed the raspberry patch. I wanted to ponder what you said, and especially think about your doleful tone, dire vision, and sad-sack demeanor. As my son William used to say, "Snap it out!" ("Snap out of it," he meant.) I pondered your perspective and, in response, decided to talk about my raspberry patch.

It's a tiny patch—twenty-four inches by twenty-four feet. I think you know it because we've sent the children back there to pick berries. (Cruel of us, since we both know that raspberry patches are a mosquito's best friend.) Since it's between the garage and our neighbor's cement basketball court, the patch gets sun in the afternoon and, on a typically hot summer's day, is several degrees hotter than the ordinary open air, thanks to the urban heat island effect of shingle rooftops, hot concrete, and black alley asphalt. The soil bakes to a hard rind that you have to peel back now and again—with a rake or hoe—just to get rainwater to soak in. There's no overland flow from the land next door, no extra allotment of moisture. And the garage roof and gutter overhead divert what rain might fall and send it pell-mell down the depressed alley centerline to the storm drain at the bottom of the hill, where it's whisked away to the Mississippi River. A desert in a hot place, and deserted—that's my raspberry patch. You could say, what doesn't kill it, makes it stronger, except that last year, with the summer 2012 to winter 2013 drought, it was pretty much toast . . . or toasted.

What is trying to kill it? Let's start with my favorite non-native weed to hate, creeping bellflower (*Campanula aparinoides*). You know it. Purple, five-petaled, tubular flowers growing at the end of a leafy stem. The toothy leaves alternate up the stem. The wand of flowers begins blooming at the base around now, early July, and continues up the stem to include the little green buds unfurling even now. Each seed pod holds the tiny seeds, like mustard grains, only black—there are thousands in each pod, and there are dozens of pods on a single plant, and a single white rootstock—like a white beetle larva—sends up half a dozen or so stems. Like the proverbial mustard seed, these seeds blow on the wind far and wide. Needless to say, you've got a formidable competitor in this pretty little plant. Did I mention that the rootstocks are about six to twelve inches below ground, and connected to the leaves and flowering stems with a threadlike rhizome? Well. . . this clever evolutionary gizmo makes it certain that, a) if you pull the stem or basal leaves (which I'll get to in a minute), the plant will resprout, and b) if you cultivate the ground to kill the plant, you'll miss the rhizome. Brilliant! In other words, to eradicate the plant you have to a) dig deep to get the rhizomes, b) cultivate often every year for five to seven to expose the tens of thousands of seeds waiting in the soil for a little extra light to signal the all-clear, and c) pull, pull, pull the basal rosettes until you've exhausted the seed bank.

Yikes! All this is just more evidence of a super-competitor. But wait—there's more! Basal leaves. Do you want to hear about basal leaves? Creeping bellflower got its name because it creeps. It creeps all over the place. It creeps along just beneath the soil for a distance sufficiently far from the mother plant, then sends up a basal leaf or two. The basal leaf expands in size to catch as much light as possible, and sends the luscious glucose generated by photo-synthesis into roots that it is growing, and also into. . . you guessed it, a new rootstock. Several inches, down, don't forget. Now this wouldn't be so perni-cious (okay, a value judgment on my part), but for its predisposition to send its rhizomes beneath pavement, into the cracks of stone walls, into the heart of rose bushes (a commensal-like relationship with a thorny protector), and, oh, woe, into the growing centers of wildflowers and ornamentals we are trying to cultivate for their diversity, beauty, and helpfulness as food for butterflies, bees, birds, and other life forms. The basal leaves are prolific, and if not weeded, produce a bountiful crop of stems, which generate thousands of seeds, which close the circle of creeping bellflower life by generating thousands of new seedlings. There must be a weakness in this plant's prodigious will to live, but I haven't found it.

There's a theory now that the tens of thousands of invasive plants and animals should be judged by a new standard. Creeping bellflower and the many you know—leafy spurge, garlic mustard, European and glossy buckthorn, Tartarian honeysuckle, reed canary-grass, giant reed (the pan-oceanic hybrid), not to mention the many animals like the common earthworm (*Lumbricus terrestris*) and red worm, brown tree snake (scourge of oceanic islands) . . . what's the point in listing them . . . they are here by the thousands and here to stay. Though in evolutionary time, and with help from our own biocontrol ingenuity, they may acquire the pests and diseases left behind in old Europe or Asia, and, tamed by weakness, join the majority of species that manage to fit in without disrupting the lives of the species around them. (Although, to be fair, given the right management regime, even sugar maple from which the Iroquois for thousands of years drew a delightful, delicate syrup, even big and little bluestem and side-oats grama grass, the foundations of the sixty-million-acre mid-continental prairie ecosystem—even these can dominate the landscape. And even *Cladophora orbiculata*, a usually benign green alga that, in recent years, coats our beloved Great Lakes beaches with a green scum that turns to gray, webby masses on plants and cobbles in mid-summer, is one of these, though, I must emphasize, only under the unique management conditions set in motion by people, including the release of zebra mussel. This plant and hundreds of other native building blocks of North American ecosystems can be aggressive against their neighbors.)

The theory I mentioned of neutral invasives is this: there's been no documented species of plant driven to extinction by an invasive plant or animal. Therefore, there is no ecological or scientific reason to be angry at the invaders. Rather, to be angry is to place a human value atop a nature that neither cares about nor favors one species over another, but simply "is." (The brown tree snake, pigs, rats, cats, goats, and other invaders of oceanic islands, of course, have driven species to extinction—and the theorists allow that, in this narrow case, invasives are perhaps ecologically bad.) In other words, nature abides. The earth abides. We can't drive the earth to extinction, despite everything we do. Asteroids were able to extinguish, what, from ten to ninety percent of the earth's living creatures in any one spasmodic, catastrophic episode? Yet each time, out of the burnt, depopulated earth sprang even more species than existed prior to the extinction event. The latest predictions resulting from the current anthropocenic extinction spasm which I've seen are, one-quarter to one-third of the earth's species going extinct by 2100 or 2150. Out of ten million, I believe is the latest best guess of the total number. We'll go from 10,000,000 to a range of 6,600,000 to 7,500,000 species. Naturally, a lot of those to go are the ones we know and love best:

- anything that can be eaten or harvested for medicine, magic or prestige (think rhino, elephant, shark, turtle, tuna, even some tropical trees);
- animals like big cats, canines, bears, and large primates—all of which need big spaces;
- anything that depends on unique habitats and specialized climatic conditions (alpine species for example, and even those mid-continental grassland plants we studied on Drummond Island); and
- the fifteen to fifty percent of just plain uncommon wildflowers, birds, butterflies, frogs and toads, dragonflies, freshwater mussels, and the like that are not rare enough to be endangered, but not common enough to be ensured a future unless land use and management practices across millions of acres of settled landscape are fundamentally altered.

Unfortunately, species that will remain include many crowding out other species and reducing the natural variety of the earth's species—shrinking their abundance and range—the introduced pasture grasses and soil-holding plants like cheat grass and crown vetch are good examples. Or they are making once-benign ecosystems hazardous. I've been watching the spread of wild parsnip (*Pastinaca sativa*) along the mid-continent's roadways. You know all about this—this yellow-flowered relative of parsley and celery forms a yellow cloud along the roadways in July, is dispersed by the mowing equipment, and was brought to America for the best of all reasons, to eat. In a strange twist, as it spreads along the highways, and from there into every adjacent pasture and field, it now makes people ill. The plant tissues contain a substance (with the elegant name of furocoumarin), which is absorbed by skin. The sun's rays then transform the chemical into a material that raises blisters and permanently darkens the skin. So now, as with so many other introduced plants and animals, our natural ecosystems are just a little less pleasant, just a little more hazardous. I'm not saying it was an Eden here before the rash of introductions, but I do know that the Last Child Left in the Woods (to use the title of a recent popular book) now has to be a little more careful about going into a field. We've added "natural hazard" to the cultural and economic reasons Richard Louv gave for why people don't head first for nature before turning to a glowing screen.

The theorists say, in their dispassionate way, the only reason to care about invasives is if they threaten people or we hate them for what they do and who they are. There's no other reason to worry. If they don't threaten us or our psyche, don't worry about them. Even if they threaten the inner workings of ecological systems, don't pay no mind, and if you do, acknowledge you are doing it because you care, not because nature needs you to intervene. And if we want to eradicate them because we don't like them, then don't clothe your purpose in phony science and ecological pure-speak . . . Botkin's *Discordant Harmonies* married to a new wildland aesthetic that accepts invasives as part of the new ecology. You know, no doubt, about "Urban Ecology"—new branch of ecology—but have you heard about the science of novel ecosystems? It is now worthy of study and papers are being published. In some ways, that's a good thing. The corn-soybean agroecosystem is now worthy of scientific study. People will now start looking at how fast nitrogen moves through the organics-depleted root-soil system, for example. They will now investigate the speed at which water moves through a tiled and ditched landscape and what that does to the amount of water a stream system can handle before its bed and banks begin unraveling—sending a muddy slurry downstream with every half-inch rainfall (which ain't much).

I used to joke about a novel ecosystem that the USFWS office was tending next to its Minnesota River Valley Refuge. High above was a canopy of black locust (*Robinia pseudoacacia*) imported from the South because it bears a fragrant white blossom mid-summer and grows like a weed. Beneath this was a subcanopy of European buckthorn (*Rhamnus cathartica*), first planted as a hedge and now escaped to every woodlot within spitting distance of one of those hedges. And covering the soil was smooth brome (*Bromus inermis*), assiduously distributed, Johnny-Appleseed-like, by federal and state governments through soil-protecting and road-building agencies, as a soil-stabilizing grass. All good intentions, all gone so wrong as far as unintended consequences. The Soil Conservation Service guys of the early to mid-twentieth century only wanted what was best for America—stable soils, healthy crops, prosperous farmers. They didn't want to unleash ecological super-competitors against which tens of millions of dollars and tens of thousands of hours are expended each year holding them at bay, keeping them out of museum-scale benchmark stands of native ecosystems (which we use to understand the workings of the natural systems being displaced by novel ecosystems), and controlling them in the larger productive forestry and grazing systems of the continent. It always strikes me as funny—if you go searching the globe for super-competitors to hold the soil (think kudzu, my friend), why are you surprised when they behave as super-competitors when released in a new land, *sans* diseases, *sans* pests, *sans* serious competitors?

Back to novel ecosystems and, to tie up some loose ends, back to my raspberry patch. My raspberry patch is, as you've guessed, a novel ecosystem. I am growing our families' highly sought northwoods fruit, red raspberry (*Rubus strigosus*). I decided not to plant the blackberry (*Rubus allegheniensis*) because of its fearful thorns in aspect and effect. Give me the prickly *R. strigosus* any day. Plus I have always been partial to the tint and hint of red raspberry juice over all the other *Rubus* berries. So I have my patch. It's a nice patch, though because little tended, it's not a particularly productive patch. Oh, well. I head back there in mid- to late July, pluck my few berries and am content.

Once or maybe twice a year, I pull the weeds and clip the dead and three-year-old canes—to bring on new canes that will bear well in the second year. My edible, novel ecosystem. I like it (high desire). It's already there (capital investment several years ago). I like not having to put much effort into it (low maintenance). It is the fruit of my labor, in the exact sense. It is this attention to detail, an economy of labor, that produces the desired effect. There's a simple equation for this, me being a scientific reductionist and all:

Desire + Capital Investment + Maintenance = Food, Shelter, Clothing, Safety, Time, Beauty, Health, Sex, Better Sex (or the Income to buy all this)

It seems to me, in a simple-minded way, that people tend their garden, plant their corn, selective-cut their trees, build their grape trellises, invest in their boats and lobster traps, hunt their bush meat, construct their buildings and roads, run their cattle on public land (at below market prices, lest we forget), overfish the ocean's catch-of-the-day—and whatever else people do, like wrest oil and coal and natural gas and silver and nickel and you name it from public land (again, at below market prices—and then sell the unused land for condos!) . . . in order to win or earn what they want. (Now I've gotten negative, which one will do getting into the details . . . but I take heart from the fact progress has been made in all of the aforementioned ways of earning a living, plus others, and much is being done in a "greener" fashion.) I'm no different. I like the idea of a raspberry patch because it brings back my childhood and gives me something interesting to do. I like the idea of a catbird stealing a few berries (and stealing from the red-stemmed serviceberry nearby) because I like the mewling whine of catbird in the evening. I like the taste—that's a bonus.

I ask you, what's wrong with that? By extension, what's wrong with anybody doing anything they want to in order to gain what we seek to gain? How can we begrudge any person that right? Isn't the pursuit of happiness undefined in our Declaration of Independence? I think it's amazing that the right to private property was first installed there, and, in their wisdom (I like to think in Franklin's wisdom, because the southern slave-owners had an especially big bone to pick about property rights)—in the wisdom of some of those men, it was more important to leave it up to us to decide what happiness meant. For some, it was a two-thousand-acre plantation managed by human property, for others it was a homestead at the edge of civilization—think of our bee-keeping friend, Ben Boden, in his dotage on Prairie Ronde, enjoying visits by those wanting to hear of "the old days" on the frontier. Jim, my friend, we can't interfere, except when we have a good reason.

What's the reason, you might ask? That's the $10,000-dollar question, the 900-pound gorilla in the room, and whatever other suitable metaphor you might propose.

Jim

Doleful tone, dire vision, and sad-sack demeanor are what people have always said about environmentalists. Remember what Leopold said about becoming an ecologist: it opens you to a "world of wounds." I think it is important to honor the feelings rather than just brushing them aside—if it is okay to love a landscape, it is okay to mourn its passing; in fact that is psychologically necessary. If we are living in a time of massively accelerated change we can't let the inevitability of that change push us into repression or self-serving stoicism or indifference. To say, "Snap out of it," is useful if you mean: "Don't just stand there, do something!" But that implies there is something to do. I mourn the climate of my youth, which won't come again. I know that climate was full of problems, had been rather horribly despoiled by mankind, and was a brief (from a glacier's point of view) interval of pleasantness between much harsher times, as the world oscillates between glacial hell and interglacial steam bath—but that is like saying, why feel sorry if your wife dies? All humans are mortal. And what does it mean if you actually, through negligence, hastened her death?

Your meditation on your raspberry patch is very apt: a deep understanding of nature is a good cure for pastoralism, the view of nature as some kind of "paradise," free of strife or tragedy. That is a tendency we humans have, as we look out from our cities, whose feral reality we understand pretty well when we read the papers, and sigh for the simple peace of the green fields. Scientists such as you know that is a problem of scale and distance: up close you can see the ferocious warfare going on at all times, the ebb and flow of species tightly interlocked in their struggle for existence. The reason Victorians were so shocked by Darwin was that this teeming violence denied them their pious meditation on God's goodness, back when Natural Theology was a storehouse of sermon ideas. And, yes, we humans always insert ourselves in an already-in-progress complexity; to live we must disturb the universe. You plant raspberries. I plant tomatoes and beans. You fight creeping bellflowers, I pull snakeroot— a native, with more right to be here than me, but an annoying invasive in my little yard. We are part of the world and not apart from it, gazing through our lorgnettes and sighing at nature's beauty.

But you are evading the elephant in the essay, my friend. Our problem is not invasives. Our problem is our own waste: we are pumping carbon into the atmosphere at rates that will most probably destroy our civilization. You say latest estimates are that we'll only lose "one quarter to one third" of the world's species—as if that were an acceptable loss. What you don't say is that we are on track for a three- to seven-foot sea rise in just a century, a growing desertification of large portions of the American interior, the acidification of the world's oceans (and resulting food web collapse), a lowering yield for much of conventional agriculture, a rising heat-death toll in the broiling cities of the world, and the destruction of infrastructure due to catastrophic weather. Look at the floods in Europe, look at the evacuation of Calgary, look at the wildfires out west, look at the dire planting season here in Minnesota (not just the slow corn growth, but ask any of our vegetable farmers down here how they feel about the unseasonable rain and cold, finishing up in drought—they have *never* seen a season like this one, in their lifetimes—think how vulnerable our food is to atmospheric variation).

So I have a right to be a bit mopey. It will be a head-on, full-tilt struggle to survive on this planet from now on: the heat we are experiencing is—because of the way the oceans have been keeping us cool until now—the result of the carbon of the 1970s, when you and I were coming into our own. What is to come is only stoppable if we actually begin drawing carbon down—otherwise the catastrophe is a cake already baked—the only question is *how bad* will it be? Remember, every single prediction made by the IPCC is coming true much faster and much more seriously than predicted—or, is coming in at the extremes of prediction rather than the mean. So when you say everyone has a right to his own pursuit of happiness, you lose me. The essence of a system of law is that everyone has the right to his pursuit if it does no harm. Clearly every pound of carbon now rising into the heavens is doing me and all other human beings incalculable harm. My question is really: does this mean that we, as a species, are not any more intelligent than pond scum? Never mind creeping bellflower: we are rapidly filling our environment with our own wastes and may soon choke ourselves into a mass die-off. You might still plant raspberries in the Arkansas heat that is the future for your St. Paul backyard—I say might because they grow in zone seven, not in zone eight, and Arkansas straddles the line—but will you enjoy them as you watch the peoples of the world drown and starve on television? Less laissez-faire, more sympathy, my friend! The earth will endure, but saving the earth was never our mission. Trying to preserve our way of life, our little mild interglacial epoch and its associated species—if that is what we intended, have we succeeded in any way? Has the target shifted now, so we realize we were unconsciously preparing for, not the prolongation of what we thought was paradise, but the putting into place of certain technologies of survival? Is that our consolation? From saving the "wilderness" (our youthful passion) to keeping stormwater from washing us all away? From preserving the prairie to understanding how the prairie survives in a highly stochastic environment—which is our future everywhere?

Kim

I know the quote well: "One of the penalties of an ecological education is that one lives alone in a world of wounds." Jim, I've lived in that world for thirty some years. You and I already knew in the 1970s just how tragically destructive of nature people are. But here's the thing . . . we've always been tragically destructive of nature, throughout our existence, beginning some 200,000 years ago when those first people like us emerged in east Africa. Everywhere we went, we destroyed something . . . soil in Mesopotamia, soil in Meso-America and the American Southwest, grassland in the Sahel, dozens of large mammals in North America, dodos and the great auk at the hands of hungry ship crews . . . and that's just a taste of the bygone destruction. We ramped up the scale after the Industrial Revolution . . . on a brief tour let's start with beavers for hats, go on to buffalo for their tongues and robes, and end with the passenger pigeon—gobbled down, chicks and all, in fine restaurants from New York to Chicago. The passenger pigeon was actually doing okay despite being brought down with birdshot in the hundreds of thousands, until the railroad and telegraph penetrated their breeding grounds. At that point, it was game over because the "hunters," or whatever you want to call them, could discover within a day of a flock's alighting in a forest just where they were, jump a fast train to the nesting ground, smoke out the squabs (the chicks), pack them in barrels, and ship them to market. Need I go on to whales (many verged on extinction before the hunting ban), orange roughy, Atlantic cod, and a host of other table fish, shark, elephant, tiger, rhino, bear . . . ? They all are being eaten up or poached to cure dyspepsia, ensure pregnancy, or make a guy's erection last longer. We are happy destroyers of nature, wittingly or unwittingly.

So what's the big deal? Why does all of this not-so-new news about people's inherently destruction effect get you madder now than before? We used to rail against the timber giants who clear-cut North America, let the cutover landscape burn up, then went tax-forfeit on their land to avoid property taxes—having sucked as much out of the land as they could. Talk about a vast transformation of millions of acres! We still see the effects today in the stumpfields—think Kingston Plains—in the depauperate organic layer of the soil, in the lack of conifers over much of the northern forest, and the lowered productivity of the landscape compared to the Menominee tribe's forest, which is still producing like gangbusters despite three complete selective harvests since the Civil War. We also were irritated by the crafty foresight of those timber giants who knew what they were doing to the land . . . why else did they set aside their exclusive tracts of old-growth wilderness in the northwoods?

You might call this venal, or you might call it human nature, which is actually wild nature—it's nature in action, nature as nature meant us to behave. We are no different than the paper wasp trying to nest in my eaves and raise there a half dozen or so youngsters . . . she may damage my eaves, without regard for my feelings or wallet, if that's what it takes for her clan to survive. We are not different than the elephant family raiding a farmer's field in Tanzania to get that extra bit of protein that might make a difference between starvation of a youngster or ensuring there's a next generation. We differ not in intent or, at some level, even effect (think plankton in the ocean and plants on land that fundamentally alter the atmosphere), from every other species on the planet.

Maybe it's because this time, it's not nature destroying Herculaneum by volcanic ash, or washing away Aceh in a tsunami (170,000 in that one!), or wiping out San Francisco, it's just us. It's we the people, acting as we instinctively must act, as nature has instructed us to act from the moment we first spoke a human word and could organize ourselves to kill prey, construct a communal hut, eventually a pyramid or Burj Khalifa, or sail around the world to kill a sperm whale . . . and let's not forget landing a man on the moon. We are giants now, is perhaps the problem—7.1 billion giants, striding the globe, leaving a big footprint.

It's also personal with you, I know. Your essay on the pines suddenly comes back to me. It was that particular stand of oaks and maples, the individual trees perhaps, the rustling in the branches you only hear in oak stands in fall . . . that was taken from you, from your backyard, from the place you called home. The poet John Clare's insanity, it's said, was partly brought on by the enclosure of common land in England—dissolution of communal rights to pasture, replaced by industrial scale agriculture for commodity production—and with it, tearing up thousands of miles of hedgerows and forest patches that not only provided the people with fuel and building material, but enlivened their days with birdsong, flowers, and animal life. (Of course, there was the general dispossession of farmers from the land. . . but that's another story.)

Believe me, Jim, I still live in a world of wounds. What did I study for my master's degree? Michigan's prairies and savannas, as much an ecological basket case as anything you can imagine. For my doctorate, more of the same—figure out which species of birds disappear from the landscape when you add agriculture, and then when you lay down on that pastoral landscape a blanket of houses, gas stations, and shopping malls. Sigh. On a positive note, I found that, if you add just a touch of agriculture and settlements to wilderness, it actually increases the variety of birds at a regional scale.

All that climate change represents is a ramping up of the scale of destruction. I find it ironic. It took possibly this most destructive effect of people going about their business—having kids, making money, doing fun things in cars—to finally get enough people's attention at high-enough levels about lifestyle effects on the environment—when for centuries people's lifestyles were not considered the problem. Even water pollution, which people care most deeply about among all possible environmental ills, didn't take front and center in policy circles despite decades of evidence that it should have. It took the Cuyahoga River catching fire to ignite enough passion in Washington, D.C., for politicians to pass the Clean Water Act. Before then, not so much passion. Even here, though, they first went after the industrial polluters, not lifestyles. That law was passed in 1972. Forty years later we're still trying to control the polluted urban runoff that washes directly into our nation's waters. We haven't even touched agriculture, largely exempted from the Clean Water Act despite its profound effect on mid-continent streams and lakes—and the Gulf of Mexico. These things touch directly on lifestyle and cost of living. To whit— it takes a long time to change the way people live.

There's a simple reason for this. People don't want their lives disrupted, they want a good life, and they want a good life for their children. They don't want to see the price of corn, and hence meat, double, because farmers are made to stop destroying our nation's waters. It's easy to image why people don't want to pay a tax on stormwater running into a street sewer—it's just rain. It's not surprising to me that a carbon tax has so many people freaked out—are you kidding? We are carbon-based lifeforms.

If we fixed all these problems, it would narrow our lifestyle options—we'd have to eat less meat, have less to spend because Winona is taxing the amount of rooftop you have that sheds stormwater, we'd have to drive less, or get a job we can walk to, or spend our money on gas rather than a trip to Cancun. What about the Chinese, Vietnamese, Indians, Africans, and everyone else who is striving with all their might to enter the middle class? Impose on them all the strictures of a western regulatory framework to protect the environment? We can barely do that to ourselves, a highly evolved economy and lifestyle. Do you think Robert Mugabe is going to let that happen in Zimbabwe, or the Politburo in China, or the capitalistic, democracy-inhabiting peasants of India?

Where does that leave us? Maybe with this question—how does conservation happen? How do people live lightly on the earth? (Not how *can* people live lightly, but how *do* people live lightly. We already know how we could if we wanted to.)

You frame this differently, I think. You cite the statistics, emphasize the worst possible outcome, and say that nature will instruct us in the end. Maybe, maybe not. The world is a crazy, complicated place where anything can happen. Perhaps Aldo's land ethic will take hold—it seems to have done so among the pre-contact American Indians, who were perhaps "existentially schooled" when they helped drive the giant mammals of the Pleistocene to extinction and lived in poverty until they figured out another way to live. On second thought, even the Plains Indians were happy to wipe out one of the last bison herds (which they did near Yellowstone) or, in happier, more abundant times, drive hundreds over cliffs at one go. Perhaps the "techno-fix," as you imagine it, will save us—carbon dioxide scrubbers on every smokestack and tailpipe. I reject the idea of millions drowning and starving. We have ample evidence that people are more resilient than that, more creative and able to adapt—and one thing is certain, we will not go extinct... too many of us. We could lose half the human race, and still have plenty left over to reproduce our way back to eleven billion (which is the latest prediction, to be reached by 2100). We know that we can grow enough food to feed the entire state of Iowa on just a couple square miles ... it all depends on how it's done. And people will migrate away from the coasts, as the Doggerlandians did when they abandoned the North Sea, Baltic Sea and English Channel 8,500 years ago. They are now living in London, Hamburg, and Copenhagen.

So, what's the future going to be, and how to get there? That's my question, which inclines me to act, not cry in the wilderness like Jeremiah at the gates of Jerusalem.

Jim

I still get the strong impression you are rationalizing to keep yourself from feeling the full extent of the emergency. Paper wasps build their nests without a thought to your eaves, yes: but paper wasps don't bring down whole ecosystems and change the composition of the atmosphere. It is possible to believe that humans are nature *and* to feel outrage at their venality and blindness. I said from the outset that nature loves destruction—if you look at the history of the earth you can see that every few dozen million years she likes to shake the snow globe. That this is the sixth great extinction event is not a surprise, from that perspective. But this time it is caused by sentient beings who make conscious choices. It is the paradox of being human that on one hand we are nature, we are animals participating blindly in an intricate but goal-free system of interlocking activity called an ecosystem, and on the other hand we are capable of understanding and influencing that system, making choices which lead to different outcomes. The essence of your career, over these many years, is that humans can understand and to some extent manage their life on this planet. You have spent your life outracing the forces of entropy. It is disingenuous to claim we are no different from the paper wasp: you switch to a perspective too broad to acknowledge distinctions in order to seem objective, but if you really believed there was no difference you wouldn't do the work you do. And I would give up writing and thinking and teaching. We would both just start chewing wood into pulp and putting another layer on the colony's nest. The fact is, you want to act and you do: indicating there is a point to action. And if there is a point to action there are good and bad ways to act, and if that is so there is accountability for bad action, which implies morality. Just because humans often fuck up doesn't mean they always do: what makes humans so agonizingly tragic is they sometimes know the right thing and do the right thing. It's like intermittent reinforcement. We keep going because there is always the chance something good will happen, even if the chance is small.

So why am I madder than before? Because we once had a coalition across political boundaries that actually got things done—corrupt and weak as solutions often were, they were solutions. What made the difference was the left and the right agreed that science could be trusted. The creation of the EPA and the passage of the Clean Air and Clean Water acts were examples of politicians conceding to reality. We led the world in this, actually. When you and I first began talking about these issues in the '80s we never could have imagined the rise of a political class that would actively seek to discredit scientific data, especially data making extremely dire predictions about the future. A political class so completely blinkered by its ideology that it would shut down research and seek to gag researchers. A political class that would not only not act prudently, but would do just the opposite—double down on the destruction. I don't mind hapless destruction nearly so much as willful self-destruction. No paper wasp ever worked for the ruin of its own colony because of the seductions of faulty syllogisms or the lure of short-term profit. Again, you give yourself false comfort by blurring the distinction between human and animal: there is a reason human beings are the only species with lawyers. We are the only species that can be found guilty.

Your mention of Botkin's *Discordant Harmonies* made me go back and pull out my copy. That book very eloquently summarized a change in our understanding of nature. Botkin pointed out our tendency to view nature as either machine, or as divine and changeless order, has obscured the truth about nature, that it is an organic, stochastic system, constantly changing. Nature can and does constantly shift from one equilibrium to another. Scientists have been able to negate the ideological, theological uses of nature and have constructed a truer narrative . . . but this has not penetrated the political life of the nation. The far right still assumes that nature is either a divine order God is in charge of (hence Rush Limbaugh actually claiming God would not allow global warming) or a machine that churns out the best of all possible outcomes (this is the sunny teleology behind libertarianism and neoclassical economics—both of which ignore history and biology). Libertarians sound close to your own pronouncements when they say: just follow your cravings and everything will work out fine. No need to sweat the management of the world, because it will naturally seek equilibrium. You are too smart for that, because you know there is no equilibrium point, no final state of perfection—but your wish to excuse mankind as if all its actions were instinctive and could not be interfered with comes dangerously close to the libertarian denial of evil (let the market decide!).

The main reason we are in trouble right now is that humans discovered an energy source so incredibly rich it has allowed them to throw off the restraints of necessity and develop a hugely wasteful infrastructure that is poisoning the air and degrading the environment at rates that could not have been imagined previously. And this same energy source has enabled the growth of a population far beyond what can be sensibly maintained on a finite planet, if by sensibly we mean without cannibalizing most other species and their habitats for our own maintenance. This development need not have proceeded in exactly this way. One can imagine a variety of scenarios, some worse (nuclear winter) some much, much better. Given that choice matters, one can meditate on the moral status of mankind, its psychological fitness for its godlike abilities, and its likely end state. I am immensely more pessimistic than I was when I was young, not because the risk of annihilation is greater (after all, for much of my youth we practiced crouching under desks to hide from nuclear blasts) but because the method of annihilation is so shamefully stupid. To drown in your own waste, and to do so knowingly, is worse than to die in destructive combat.

You claim that we can lose half our population and still keep going, and I believe you: I don't think we'll go extinct soon. But I do think the everlasting shame we bring down upon ourselves will have consequences for the survivors. And I do think we owe it to the mostly poor and wretched of the earth who will do most of the dying not to ignore the injustice of the outcome. You are already seeing people starve and drown on television as a result of the American way of life—pumping the air full of carbon to subsidize shopping malls. They are drowning in the Brahmaputra and the Danube and the Root River here in my backyard (which wiped out most of a town recently). They are starving in Africa and South America and the Middle East (climate change is behind conflict in Darfur, Somalia, and Syria because as the world warms the deserts expand and formerly self-sufficient villages move to the cities to survive). People can't just move somewhere else when the rains cease or the seas rise because we don't live in an empty world any more: other people are already on the land farther inland. There will be war. The Pentagon has been saying this for a decade, that climate change will destabilize the world even further and presents the greatest risk to national security.

You claim we can't change because that would limit our lifestyle. But we must change. We will change. The only question is how wrenching will the change be? How much blood will it take? I don't believe that the choice is between self-destructive wealth and stultifying poverty. If the U.S. could become as energy efficient as Europe, for example, it would be a huge step forward, and yet the European lifestyle is arguable superior to our own. We are so far out of whack that we could stand to cut our energy usage by eighty percent and still live full and exciting lives. If we stopped eating such vast quantities of meat we would not suffer: we'd be healthier. If we ended the subsidies to corn, farmers would figure out how to grow food that didn't kill us, and we'd have healthier water and healthier bodies. Yes, the price of food would rise, but we already pay less for food than our parents or their parents—we have unrealistic expectations for what food should cost (that is all the result of Earl Butz's "reform" of crop subsidies in the Nixon era—we started "modernizing" agriculture so as to focus on the cost of food rather than its healthiness, and the result was the "diabesity" epidemic). Americans would be a lot happier without the diet you say they won't give up. And we'd have to have a lot more farms, which would mean a lot more farmers, which would be jobs for people and economies for communities currently devastated by industrial agriculture (big corn takes so few workers the entire Midwest economy has been restructured, depopulating and impoverishing the countryside).

The problem is not how to save the world. The problem is facing the data squarely and deciding it needs saving. People in America are being encouraged to live in denial by a political class that sees only its own enrichment. That won't change if people don't get both scared and angry enough to demand change. Jeremiah wasn't whining in the wilderness: he was calling for action.

Kim

How to react? That is what you're needling me about, isn't it? You are right, Jim, this time it's different because the scale is vast, almost incomprehensible, and those profound changes have been unleashed because of the choices we've made—or decided not to make. But even here, Jim, even here, I put it in perspective. This won't be the first time civilizations have been dismantled or disrupted by climate change. The Anasazi, or Old Ones of the desert Southwest, unraveled when the rains stopped supporting their irrigation agriculture (though other factors contributed). The Mesopotamians of the world's first grain belt impregnated their soil with salt thanks to their irrigation scheme, perhaps accelerated by weather changes—and Babylon ceased to be the center of the world. Drought especially is a driver of social change—the Okies and their trek to California come to mind. Those were local perils, I know, but we are not the first to transform vast swathes of the Earth's surface, either. Fire. People wielded it like a planetary sword and transformed continents, perhaps helping to drive mini-spasms of numerous species extinctions. It wasn't just the Clovis point, that technological breakthrough for big game hunters, that helped exterminate the mastodon, mammoth, cats, sloths, ungulates, and other big mammals of the Americas, it was habitat change, wrought by fire, abetted by climate change. Similar events played out in Australia when the Aborigines landed their little boats there 40,000 years ago. As for global effects—just look at plant life that transformed our atmosphere from a CO_2 dominated one, to one with plenty of O_2. Let's also not forget that Florida was mostly underwater 15,000 years ago, after the Indians arrived from Asia to begin their transformation of the continent.

The point of all this is, profound changes to the planet have always occurred, caused by climate and not caused by climate, many within written history. Now that people are fully in charge and driving a profound change, by changing climate, what should be our reaction?

I worry for my children's future, as you do for yours. I feel great sorrow for the species that are inevitably going to be lost—though many are being lost anyway not due to climate change, but because the whirlwind from our immense and growing population is sweeping them away. I am upset that so many human lives will be disrupted, maybe ruined. I am not, certain, however, that in this instance I should feel moral outrage at the behavior of the human race.

People are frail and flawed creatures, without doubt. But venal? I am not convinced. We have models of how to behave, both in persons and in admonitions. Aldo Leopold and his land ethic—let's take that for starters. Do unto the land as you would have your neighbor do unto his, and love the land and its creatures as yourself. Beautiful, though unrealized words. (Yet he, too, took out the trash generated by his five children, wife and self, drove a car an hour or so north of Madison to his shack, belching not only CO_2, but lead in the process, and ate meat—that he sometimes caught himself. Not very virtuous, as defined by some.) Kant's moral imperative: act as if your action were to be a rule for the human race. Jesus' two greatest commandments— love your God, and love your neighbor as yourself. Since humans first started spouting aphorisms and writing them down, we have heard these wise words and seen the acts of these exemplary people, and to greater or lesser extent have tried to embody their wisdom and live by their example. How is that venal? We are flawed and frail creatures . . . just like every other species on the planet. Some individuals rise to the great challenge of their time, some resist, and some just go with the flow. Out of that dynamic, the species advances, one small step at a time, one individual at a time.

Ultimately, who are we to judge? You and I have spent a lifetime judging the human race. Maybe it's time to join it. You and I, for all our recycling, composting, vegetable-growing, bicycle-riding, reel-mowering, and the myriad other ways we try to reduce our footprint—you and I are embedded in an economic-technological system that has been created over the last hundred, hundred fifty years and has philosophical precedents going back a thousand years. As a result, you take one plane ride, Jim, and you undo all your good works. In one flight from Minneapolis to Detroit, you emit as much CO_2 as two Bangladeshis do in a year. That is the burden—and privilege—of living in our society.

My point about changing our lifestyle was not to excuse it, nor to resist changing it, and certainly not to accept that it must remain as it is—it was merely to point out that we are captives of an economic and technological universe that forces on us high CO_2 emissions and all the other negative environmental consequences of modern living, such as generating 4.5 pounds of trash per person per day, to cite one example. Then there's wastewater and its downstream effect on aquatic life. Then there's agriculture and the effect on the Gulf of Mexico and the hundreds of other dead zones around the world. I could go on. Bottom line: those are all the externalizable costs of living in a society of our economic type and technological prowess. The environment has for centuries simply been expected to absorb it all—assimilative capacity, it's called. You have to undo one hundred fifty years and more of ideas, inventions, and infrastructure, capitalization and banking schemes, production and delivery systems, and all the rest to undo what we have wrought. To use an old cliché, how do you turn an ocean liner—one degree at a time.

Which takes me to the topic of "hope." Knowing that the future will be better. Can you imagine raising your children in the belief that the world will end, that their lives will slowly become more miserable because of decisions made years before and irrevocably by our actions? Of course not—why pile doom upon doom in their small world, when their job is to grow up to be strong, moral creatures, forces for good in the world? A dire world outlook drags you down, keeps you from being an effective actor in the world. The media dish up plenty to fear without parents adding to it. Despite seeing all around me "a world of wounds," I did my best to not infect my children with my own despair and rage. If they asked about an environmental issue, I didn't sugar-coat it, but I didn't close the door on hope that people were working on the problem, or if it was intractable, that eventually we would fix it. I had to do that for my own peace of mind. Luckily for me, children are resilient and optimistic anyway, so my lapses into negativity weren't scarring. I have to say, though, that teaching environmental studies at Macalester opened my eyes to the harm that could be done to young, impressionable minds by the constant drum-beat of ecological crisis. Most of the students were pretty downbeat about prospects for environmental improvements in their lifetime. They were resigned to the idea that things were only getting worse. But because they were young, happy to be alive and keenly interested in each other and the world, they were buffered against the wearing effect of their intellectual construct about the environmental future. I never did reconcile what it all meant, except that they were probably conflicted about it all. I remember from time to time delivering a couple mantras as a way to impart a "long view" about environmental history in human history—first, that population growth would stop in the next hundred years, and, second, that environmental conditions improve when people put their mind to it. I liked to quote Donella Meadows, an ecologist and superb writer who was lead author of the first *Limits to Growth* study in the 1970s. She said, in response to reporters asking whether we can fix the environmental problems of the age in time to prevent utter devastation: "We have just enough time."

Years ago, judged by the acceleration of human advancement from hunter gatherers to the present, I estimated that global society would become fully an ecologically minded society by the year 2125—ecological thought penetrating everything we do, just as the concepts of mass production and electronic media penetrate all we now do. (I put a little chart about that in a book of my poetry and you, sharp editor that you are, struck it.)

I still think that's the time it's going to take, another hundred years—meaning we have a lot of damage to do, a lot of problems to fix, between now and then. You and I will be long gone, and so will our children. Our grandchildren will be old men and women. Yes, in our lifetime we can rage against the machine, but the machine is us. We are only at the beginning of that change, which started in the late 1800s with those early ecologists like Cowles studying sand dune succession on Lake Michigan—integrating all physical and biological elements operating there to develop a concept of how the world works, and what it means for people. Eventually, every political leader in the world will carry just such a concept in his or her mind when they make decisions to benefit their society—and that concept will unify their action and the effect on their society with the interactions of the physical and biological world. The good news about climate change is that it may spur us to action faster than if there were no climate change. Climate change is shaping up to be the great environmental unifier, the one problem that permeates much of everyday life—food production, infrastructure integrity, human health. Strangely, it may save the environment from "death by a thousand cuts"—which is what Aldo Leopold witnessed in the early 1900s, Rachel Carson in the mid-1900s, and you and I in the late 1900s.

Still, there are those pesky Chinese and Indians to worry about—why does this third of humanity want a middle class lifestyle anyway? Africa is next,

Jim. As soon as the Africans fix their president-for-life, tribal winner-take-all governing problem, they will surge. Add another billion middle class people with middle class consumption habits.

Along the way they will create, just as the United States created, a military-industrial complex, which will morph into a government-corporation complex. (Did you know that Dwight Eisenhower actually wanted to warn us, in his farewell address, of the "military-industrial-academic" complex? He was talked out of it by a P.R. guy.) How to overcome that? Then, just as with every animal species, there are the cheaters and greedy ones—those who take without fair compensation, and those who take much more than they should. That problem has been with us for 200,000 years, so I don't think we'll be solving it any time soon. At best, we pass laws to subvert their aims. As long as we have a government-corporation complex, though, our shift to ecological thinking will be slow, if not stymied entirely.

I guess I'm at a point in this conversation where I wonder at whom your rage is directed. You and me for doing our fair share of polluting? Others for not being ecologists or climate scientists—or for not listening to those experts (among the thousands of "special interest" experts clamoring for attention)? Politicians for their timidity and big corporations for their opposition to change? Democrats for being as silent as Republicans on the issue—note, Jim, that the first president in our history to mention climate change in a significant speech was Obama, and that only in his second term. The science of ecology was eighty years old before a president, George H.W. Bush, said he was an environmentalist. Before him, no president was. Change comes slow at the top, my friend. We little people see the light and the path forward, but our voices filter upward through dozens of layers of obfuscation and distortion, reaching the ears of the powerful as brief whispers that could be mistaken for only the wind. Yet I don't believe the rosy poll numbers giving climate change the majority of American minds. I have said it dozens of times before, and repeat it once again: environmentalism in America is a mile wide and an inch deep. Just one little thing, and it evaporates. Gas prices. Recession. Debt. Children. 9/11. You name it, Jim. It's number twenty-one on a list of twenty major concerns. Now, if by environment you mean the health and well-being of one's children, well, that's a different story. In America, the environment is important to the extent that its tragedies personally hurt you.

What I find most positive are the millions of small experiments going on. There's a newsletter I get from an organization called PERC—Property and Environment Research Center. It was started by an ideologue for property rights who ignores the idea of public good (and misunderstands ecological science), but the newsletter itself is full of interesting experiments in marrying free market ideas with environmental protection and restoration. That's just the tip of the iceberg.

Look to those types of ideas as the future. Your own experiment at Winona State is a great example—build a curriculum around the Mississippi River. There's a world of issues there—food production, invasive species, people's mental health and physical pleasure-taking, transportation and energy use (the barges and trains, Jim), Mark Twain, the whole ecology thing. Professor by professor, student by student, administrator by administrator, the issues of the day are surfaced, fleshed out, debated, and taught. In the end, a generation of young people participating in that program will have developed a holistic, ecologically grounded concept of that river, its watershed, and the relation of both to upstream and downstream places, people, and things—such as the tendrils of causality spreading from the Gulf of Mexico dead zone. Imagine shrimpers and farmers being unified in the minds of a Winona State student. That's something new on the earth.

Do something. I think that's the only solution, Jim. We just have to do something to show the way. The politicians will catch up eventually, and corporations will follow. We do something ourselves to transform the economic-technological system, or we look for where something meaningful is being done, and copy it. It's really that simple.

When I read your last response, I worried you were going to call me a libertarian outright. You would have been technically wrong if you had—they have no concept of the public good, but I'm a sucker for that idea. I used to be pretty pissed off at capitalism as an economic system, but after years of working in non-profit, government, and private sectors, I've changed my perspective. Capitalism is a natural outgrowth of the human spirit, able to accomplish great things by reducing cost, but it's terrible at producing a good society. It should not be revered as an icon of our civilization, nor held up as a standard against which all good is measured. Yet it has its uses. Working for years in the heart of the non-profit, conservation-advocacy world, I often wondered how we could effect change in the private sector because, I'd noticed, the private sector so often is the driving force beyond social change and advancement—or social stultification and regression. The private sector is simply huge and has an immense global effect. Certainly, the Panama Canal and other great public works projects would never have been built by private enterprise alone. The slaves would not have been freed but for a presidential decree. Yet fifty-five percent of spending in the world is private sector spending. That is huge force for change. We used to pride ourselves at The Nature Conservancy in setting aside ten thousand acres here, even a hundred thousand acres there . . . but that and everything else anybody did to set land aside—"protect" it from human rapacity and depredation—amounted to less than ten percent of the continent's total land surface. And that effort took a hundred years and billions of dollars. What about the rest of the planet?

As tough as it is to swallow, the medicine is not just government policy and regulation, it is not public sector spending, it is not blog postings on the damage caused by climate change—it is the private sector becoming aware and educated about climate change and its effects, and then acting in its own self interest. Whether morality needs to be attached to that or not, I can't say. Leopold articulated his land ethic seventy years ago. Are we any closer to seeing it embedded in the fabric of society than in his day? I think not. Hell, it took 350 years for Jesus' philosophy to become the law of the land, and that was a much more powerful message than the land ethic, prefiguring as it did the Declaration of Independence and other great documents of human emancipation.

Jim

Well, that was an eloquent response. All the more so because you can back it up with so many years of real service to the environment. I am aware that you have had more positive effect on the world in one land deal than I have in twenty years of opining. Not that I'm not doing my part, but it does mean something that you have a boots-on-the-ground perspective. You are right, that we are all enmeshed in the system—that's what makes it so hard to change. During the Civil War the North could march into battle knowing it had no part in the slavery system—it is easy to crusade against someone else's livelihood. What if both sides had held slaves, though? What if it wasn't the small northern farmer, resentful of the economic advantage free labor gave the southern plantation farmer, but one plantation owner versus another? Would we have been able to stop slavery? We all have the equivalent of ninety slaves now—that's roughly how much fossil fuel energy each person in America commands. How can we give that up? Like southerner slaveowners, we tend to say our lifestyle is not negotiable (as the Republicans say now about attempts to legislate better gas mileage or more efficient light bulbs). I do understand when you question the moral critique: how realistic is it that we will curb our privileges and freedoms until we are all confronted so clearly with the consequences that we can no longer deny them? And yet I don't want to let go of the fact that there are moral choices here: we aren't guilty until we know, but once we know . . .

Yet I am guilty of many knowing excesses. If I lived alone, I would be much more frugal, but I have a family and children who need to be transported places. I managed to live with only one car for most of my married life but recently I relented (having inherited an old car from my mother). Now I am in the same trap as everyone: I used to bike to local stores, but it is so easy just to jump in the car and go. So the solution to climate change will not be a mass conversion to frugality. It is in the nature of any species to maximize its power, relative to the environment. The problem is our power is borrowed, and by the time the environment pushes back it will be *such* a push we may not take it well. Our systems are powerful, but very brittle—our supply lines are vulnerable, our infrastructure decaying and hugely inefficient. We have been living in what Andrew Zolli calls a "vacation from history," because our insanely rich energy source has insulated us from necessity ("us" meaning the West). We have come to think ourselves invincible. Our energy-wealth has made it seem like high-risk choices and behaviors have no consequences. And that is what you mean when you say that capitalism must come to terms with its limits for things to change: the business model is predicated on free energy and minimal pushback from the environment. That is what makes the ethos of "endless expansion" tenable—both the inputs and the outputs of the system are somewhat mystically considered to be "external." As you say, this is a big mistake: it is against the laws of physics, and nobody can violate those for long. You have great faith that things will change, because they must change, and I agree. The question is, how bad will things get before we reach that point, and how far can we recover? Will we be able to regain enough organizational power as a species that we can continue the work of civilization, or will we collapse to a much simpler, more stable social level—post-apocalyptic hunters and gatherers, like we were ten thousand years ago, scrounging at the edges of the glaciers?

Zolli's book *Resilience: Why Things Bounce Back* was good reading while I was thinking about our conversation. His thesis is that we are natural, and as such, for us to be successful we must do what all natural systems—whether individual species or entire biospheres—do to endure: we must learn to maintain our core purpose and integrity in the face of dramatically changed circumstances. That is the story of life: constant adaptation to disruptions and catastrophes. To know that is perhaps to step aside from moral outrage and become at once more spiritual and more practical. Life is resilient—that is the spiritual affirmation—and we can learn from its resilience and echo life's successful strategies (that's the practical part). We need to view our current status as perilously "robust yet fragile"—Zolli points out that globalization has allowed us to "optimize a single variable—for example, resource extraction or consumption—and temporarily delay or hide the environmental feedbacks associated with it" because those feedbacks occur far away (the sick skies over China's cities, the poisoned rivers, are invisible to the Walmart shopper who revels in the personal expansion he or she gains from, say, iPhones or wheelbarrows or stone-washed jeans). Zolli adds that globalization achieves its successes by binding together "systems with radically different time signatures—financial transactions that happen in milliseconds, social norms that evolve over years, and ecological processes that normally take millennia." These interactions magnify the disruptions in ways too complex for anyone to follow—and the result is a crisis so vast and intricate that it defies the imagination. So maybe I can't simply blame the venality of humans for this: the distorted feedback, the distances involved, make it hard for a person not attuned to the possibility of catastrophe to sense the warning signs. Even I go out on a beautiful August morning in Minnesota and think, "well, maybe nothing bad will happen." I can't see the wildfires, the bark beetles, the melting glaciers, and methane-bubbling permafrost.

But the only way out is through, and interestingly Zolli identifies as one of the hallmarks of resilience "cognitive diversity"—that is, there need to be people inside an organization that provide alternatives to consensus thinking. They provide an antidote to groupthink, which brings companies and governments to disaster because it prevents them from adapting. That is us, Kim: we are little antibodies in the system, constantly trying to get others to frame issues differently, to pay attention to worrisome data, to look at alternative strategies. We may not be able to claim we've solved the crisis, but we are doing what we are supposed to do.

I just came back from the North Shore of Lake Superior: a landscape I consider holy ground. For many years now I have been almost afraid to go up there, knowing all that I know about the coming environmental disruptions. I have been reluctant to get hurt, like a lover afraid to visit his beloved in the hospital, wanting to remember her as she was. I was especially horrified by last year's Mother's Day storm, which filled the Duluth end of the lake with sediment and turned the formerly crystalline waters to root-beer. I felt such a sense of violation—the hand of man turning everything to shit.

Yet this time we camped at Tettegouche, above the stone beach, and the water was northerly enough to still be clear (though warmer than in my youth). And as I looked around me I saw the beat-up, dying birch forest clinging to the gray basalt, and I thought: "If I had seen the pristine shore of 200 years ago, before it was summarily logged and developed, I would think this was an ugly violation, an impoverished scrap. Yet I am utterly enthralled by this landscape. I am spiritually empowered by it. I wrote a whole book of poetry about it. It isn't pristine, it isn't a thing to be kept: it is a world in motion. There is no stillness in it at all: no stopped state one could point to as an ideal. A wavering field of energy and not a tableaux." I felt I was seeing a pattern, not a thing—a living field of nodes, niches, pulsations, interlocking feedback loops, and all these patterns existed in tension with conditions that always change. This doesn't excuse the heedlessness of humans, but it does help see where we stand: in a river, not in a museum. The human mistake is to imagine the world as artifact. It is an emanation. So if we disturb the system we are pushing change, not ruining a painting.

The moment is all we have—and that moment for me, sitting atop a beach of rhyolite and basalt cobbles, lapped by a post-glacial sea, was a spark in the abyss: think of the vast stretches of time between the vesicled rocks, cast up from an ancient continental rift, and the delicate blue harebell nodding in the crevices, and the call of the gull, and the roar of the car on Highway 61. We are all, like that harebell, a brief fluorescence, and in that depth of time there are so many earths, vastly unlike the one we were born into. We must have the consolation of philosophy, which is the recognition that the world is bigger than we are, without losing our moral compass. We must balance the valueless processes of natural history and the ethical life of man. Free will and fate. I remember the advice of a wise man, a spiritual counselor for the Fransciscan Center in LaCrosse: I asked him how he kept his equanimity in the face of so much bad news. He said the key to an ethical life was "show up, speak your peace, and realize you are not in charge of the outcome."

That seems to be where we end up, we two antibodies, we two philosophers and poets. That will have to do.

Kim

Eloquent, maybe, but cribbed from a hasty outline. All logic, not much emotion. You, my friend, got to the crux of the matter, with a more powerful expression of its sheer essence. Simply put, knowing our human lives are not only embedded in an economic and technological system centuries in the making, and knowing that our lives, embedded in our self-created ecosystem, are still further enmeshed in a natural system that is constantly changing—knowing all that, what is the right frame of mind to meet disruption? You say, acknowledge disruption, be flexible in your response, and keep the antibodies circulating in the bloodstream. Yes.

What's most interesting to me, Jim, about this point of view is that it suggests the root solution to environmental degradation is all mental. It's about a shift in human consciousness to one—using Leopold's idea, since it's a good one—where people see themselves as part of a local and global natural system—not apart from it. The land ethic, is one phrase for it—but that implies live and let live. It's really beyond the land ethic, to a point where we understand that our future and the future of nature are entwined. Not that nature cares a whit—it will go on without people—but that our fate will be easier or harder depending on what we do to nature. I think you are saying that, too. Pay attention to the feedback loops and indicators in nature, respond to them as if they were signs of our own bodily health, and take action to stem or reverse what we know to harm nature. I use "harm" in full knowledge that, to nature, there is no harm, only change. A temporary loss of biodiversity (in geological time scales) is not harm, merely an opportunity for some other group of organisms to come to the fore. I think I really mean "harm" in terms of, changes to nature that will in the end hurt us.

There's an intellectual effort afoot to place a monetary value on the goods and services given to us by fully functional ecosystems—so as to point out how we're hurting our own pocketbooks when we degrade ecosystems. Ecosystem services, is the idea, which you know all about. I'm not convinced that, in the long run, it will help us much, merely because only economists care about the monetary value of wetland services and the air-cleansing properties of trees. The attitudinal change has to be as fundamental as the one wrought by Jesus when he pointed out, perhaps for the first time in human history, that God is love. With that one idea, in a few words, he set in motion the overthrow of millennia of despotism and institutional cruelty—the innate tendency of the power-hungry and greedy among us.

Such a shift in attitude is so far out, I can't imagine how it begins to take hold. I do know this—*Ars longa vita brevis*. The famous aphorism—art lasts, life is short. In our words, Jim, in part artistic and poetic, in part fact-laden and linear, we are trying to make art that will last beyond our allotted four score years and ten. In fifteen years I think we should do this again—have another little talk about where we've been, where we're going—not just you and me, of course, but our culture and our beloved natural world.

Speaking of words, you should have the last one. You told me of Lad's latest art pieces—sculpted and etched material that he places in bee hives for the bees to incorporate into their honey-making, or just to devour . . . which he then removes and works on again before showing them to us all. A metaphor for the way it should be—people and nature teaming up to move everything along without undue disruption. Change, yes, back-and-forth productive-destructiveness, but catastrophic change (short of hive collapse syndrome, that is)—no. Is that possible in real life? Is Lad merely exercising wishful thinking? Is he even conscious of the model he's creating? We'll have to hear back from him about it. In the meantime, my thinnest of scaffolds built here to support a description of his work is not strong enough to continue. If you would, Jim, get a photo of some of Lad's latest work and tell me what you see. Look at that work of our friend and tell me what it is saying to you—what it might say for all of us. Send that my way and I might find in it a message to tell somewhere down the road—a message in a bottle for whomever happens to pluck it from the ocean of time.

Jim

If you look at this piece by Lad, you see the interesting new direction that his work is taking. He is inserting his prints into wooden frames which he uses in his bee hives—Lad has become an avid beekeeper, with something like eleven hives (he has also gotten involved in breeding queens, helping to develop mite-resistant and winter-hardy strains of bees). He inserts the sections into his living hives and lets the bees go to work. The result is a fascinating collaboration—the bees of course begin to build comb on top of his work, laying their art over his; they also begin to chew the paper, incorporating it into their wax. Here we have, not just the artist at an aesthetic remove, reproducing the forms of the natural world, but, in a rebarbative movement, the bees appropriating and using the artistic product—even critiquing it, in their own way, by effacing parts of the image. The overall feeling is that the nature/culture divide is dissolving, and the bees are revealed to be artists, as the artist himself is a species of bee, a builder of structure. Both are rearranging the world to suit their purposes. Somehow this feels very much of our moment: we, who have wanted to live above the world, at a remove from the seething plenitude of nature, now find ourselves insuperably intertwined with its processes, caught in its web, and it has begun to erase our efforts even as we are at the apogee of our arrogance. Yet there is hope here: if we are a species of artful bee, a busy builder race, might we, here at the last possible moment, begin to accept our origin and our fate, and begin to work in concert with the source of our being? Let's hope so!

NOTES

From the Darkness, Light: What an Ecologist and Poet See in an Artist's Work

1. The Wise Use Movement faded by the mid-1990s, but its essence was institutionalized in conservative political movements of the 1990s and 2000s.

Working From Memory: Prairies, Savannas and Land Restoration

1. H.S. Taylor, 1855, Ladies Library Association quarter centennial celebration of the settlement of Kalamazoo, Michigan (Gazette Printers, Kalamazoo, MI).

2. R. Hoppin, 1893, Personal recollections of pioneer days (Unpublished paper read at the Annual Meeting of the Pioneer Society, Centerville, MI).

3. L.I Wilder, 1939, *By the Shores of Silver Lake* (Harper Collins, New York, NY).

The Landscape of Nostalgia: Michigan's "Oak Openings" in the Scientific and Literary Imagination

1. S.W. Durant, 1880, *History of Kalamazoo County, Michigan* (Everts & Abbot, Philadelphia).

2. L.L. Tucker, 1961 (1831), "The correspondence of John Fisher" (*Michigan Historical Magazine* 45:219-236).

3. C.F. Hoffman, 1925 (1835), "A winter in the west" (*Michigan History Magazine* 9:221-228, 413-437).

4. B. Hubbard, 1928 (1838), "Report of the state geologist" (Michigan State Geologist, Annual Reports 1-7, 1837-1844. G.N. Fuller (ed.), House Document No. 24, Lansing, MI).

5. Hoffman, 1925.

6. A.D.P. Van Buren, 1904 (1884), "Pioneer annals and early settlers of Calhoun County" (*Michigan Pioneer Historical Collections* 5:237-259).

7. Now known as "Prairie Ronde," it lends its name to a township. There is also a Cooper Township, which by one account is said to be named after Cooper himself (Durant, *History*, 101).

8. J.F., Cooper, 1968, *The Letters and Journals*, James Franklin Beard (ed.), Vol. V (The Belknap Press of Harvard University Press, Cambridge MA), 219-220.

9. After Oak Openings, Cooper published two more books: *The Sea Lions* (1849) and *The Ways of the Hours* (1851). Cooper died in 1851.

10. Cooper, *Letters*, 245.

11. J.F. Cooper, 1892, *The Collected Works, Vol. 8-1* (Collier and Son, New York, NY), 35.

12. D.A. Ringe, 1962, *James Fenimore Cooper* (Twayne Publishers, New York, NY), 122.

13. Cooper, *Collected Works*, 308.

14. Cooper, *Collected Works*, 11.

15. D. Peck, 1997, *A World by Itself: The Pastoral Moment in Cooper's Fiction* (Yale University Press, New Haven, CT), 54.

16. Peck, *World by Itself*, 189.

17. Peck, *World by Itself*, 49.

18. Cooper, *Collected Works*, 248.

19. Cooper, *Collected Works*, 6.

20. Cooper, *Collected Works*, 495.

21. Cooper, *Collected Works*, 504.

22. Cooper, *Collected Works*, 504.

23. J.T. Curtis, 1971, *The Vegetation of Wisconsin* (University of Wisconsin Press, Madison WI).

24. R.F. Noss, E.T. LaRoe and J.M. Scott, 1994, "Endangered ecosystems of the United States: a preliminary assessment of loss and degradation" (U.S. Fish and Wildlife Service, Washington, D.C.).

25. S. Packard, 1988, "Just a few oddball species: restoration and rediscovery of the tallgrass savanna" (*Restoration and Management Notes* 6:13-22).

26. R. Hoppin, 1893, Personal recollections of pioneer days (Unpublished paper read at the Annual Meeting of the Pioneer Society, Centerville, MI).

27. S. Packard, 1983, "Restoring oak ecosystems" (*Restoration and Management Notes* 11:5-16).

Orange Lichen

Orange or sunburst lichen (*Xanthoria parietina*) is common in the Lake Superior basin and the northern hemisphere. It tolerates pollution and has a taste for nitrogen. It is said to preferentially colonize places where birds and mammals defecate.

Consider the Lilies

1. Climate Central citing the National Oceanic and Atmospheric Agency annual report for 2012. (For additional information see the National Climate Data Center's "National overview: annual 2012" http://www.ncdc.noaa.gov/sotc/national/2012/13#over, accessed June 2012).

2. S. Green, L.S. Kalkstein, D.M. Mills and J. Samenow, 2011, "An examination of climate change on extreme heat events and climate-mortality relationships in large U.S. cities" (Weather, Climate and Society 3:281-292, online journal of the American Meteorological Society, http://dx.doi.org/10.1175/WCAS-D-11-00055.1, accessed June 2012).

3. S. Saunders, D. Findlay, T. Easley and T. Spencer, 2012, "Doubled trouble: more Midwestern extreme storms" (Rocky Mountain Climate Organization and Natural Resources Defense Council, Louisville, CO. http://www.rockymountainclimate.org/images/Doubled%20Trouble.pdf, accessed June 2012).

Bird Migration, Belief, and Science

1. Although Aristotle was right about cranes, he wasn't about other birds. Jim's brother, Richard Armstrong at the University of Houston, notes: "Aristotle declared that summer Redstarts annually transform themselves into Robins in winter. He also thought summertime Garden Warblers change into Blackcaps. These miraculous transmutations were treated as a matter of fact for hundreds of years, and not just on the authority of Aristotle. Observation seemed to coincide with the explanation in this case: Redstarts migrate to sub-Saharan Africa at a time when Robins, who breed farther north, come to winter in Greece. Since the species were never completely present at the same time, the explanation seemed plausible." (*See* Aristotle's *The History of Animals*, Book I, Part 49B and Book VIII, Part 16, in which he wrote "A great number of birds also go into hiding; they do not all migrate, as is generally supposed, to warmer countries.")

What Laura Saw: Making a Little Home on the Extreme Great Plains

1. J. Spaeth, 1987, *Laura Ingalls Wilder* (Twayne Publishers, Boston, MA), 1.

2. J.E. Miller, 1998, *Becoming Laura Ingalls Wilder* (University of Missouri Press, Columbia, MO), 219.

3. Spaeth, *Laura Ingalls Wilder*, 23.

4. Cited in D.M. Miller, 2002, *Laura Ingalls Wilder and The American Frontier: Five Perspectives* (University Press of America, Lanham, MD), 49.

5. Miller, *Becoming Laura Ingalls Wilder*, 199-200.

6. Miller, *Becoming Laura Ingalls Wilder*, 219.

7. Cited in Miller, *Wilder and American Frontier*, 49.

8. Miller, *Becoming Laura Ingalls Wilder*, 112.

9. W.J. Parton, M.P. Gutmann and D. Ojima, 2007, "Long-term trends in population, farm income, and crop production in the Great Plains" (*BioScience* 57:737-747).

10. C.A. Woodhouse and J.T. Overpeck, 1998, "2000 years of drought variability in the central United States" (*Bulletin of the American Meteorological Society* 79:2693-2714); for western Minnesota and the eastern Dakotas, also see K.A. Chapman, A. Fischer and M.K. Ziegenhagen, 1999, *Valley of Grass: Tallgrass Prairie and Parkland of the Red River Region* (North Star Press, St. Cloud, MN).

11. Parton, 2007.

12. Spaeth, *Laura Ingalls Wilder*, 23.

13. Spaeth, *Laura Ingalls Wilder*, 1.

14. D.S. Wilcove, 2008, *No Way Home: The Decline of the World's Great Animal Migrations* (Island Press, Washington, D.C.).

15. J. Lockwood, 2003, "The death of the super hopper" (*High Country News*, http://www.hcn.org/issues/243/13695, accessed July 31, 2008).

16. C .Bormar, 2008, "The Rocky Mountain locust: extinction and the American experience" (National Center for Case Study Teaching in Science New York, University at Buffalo: http://www.sciencecases.org/locusts/locusts.asp, posted 2003, accessed August 4, 2008).

17. Lockwood, 2003.

18. Miller, *Becoming Laura Ingalls Wilder*, 45.

19. Chapman, 1999.

20. Cited in Miller, *Wilder and American Frontier*, 40.

21. Miller, *Becoming Laura Ingalls Wilder*, 74.

22. U.S. Census Bureau, 2006, "United States percent change in population, 2000-2006" (Population Estimates Program, U.S. Bureau of the Census, Washington, D.C.); D.E. Popper and F.J. Popper, Jr., 1987, "The Great Plains: from dust to dust" (*Planning* 53:12–18).

23. Parton, 2007.

24. Parton, 2007.

DEFINING THE GREAT PLAINS

The boundary of the Great Plains varies depending on the source (Rossum and Lavin 2000). Based on topography, the eminent cartographer Erwin Raisz (1957) included all of the Ingalls family's homes outside the Big Woods as part of the "Interior Plains," an opinion underscored by recent topographic analysis using satellite imagery (Thelin and Pike 1991). This region is characterized by flat topography broken by river valleys, a continental climate prone to frequent, extreme drought, and soils with a deep, organic-rich A-horizon created by the growth and death of grasses over millennia. When the Ingalls left the Big Woods and entered these great plains somewhere in southeast Minnesota, they saw nearly continuous grasslands that were, as recently as the 1830s, grazed by immense numbers of ungulates and set on fire almost every year by Indians. Open savannas and more closed-canopy woodlands were largely confined to fire-protected river valleys. Narrower interpretations of the great plains included that of N.M. Fenneman (Fenneman and Johnson 1946) who considered the 100th meridian a significant climatic factor which more or less divided the tallgrass prairie from the mixed grass prairie. Easterners think of the tallgrass prairie as an anomaly in the eastern deciduous forest biome, leading them also to narrowly define the great plains. Canadians, however, seeing only the small northern edge of the great plains, take a broad view, like Raisz, and consider it all the same region (Bostock 1967), as do meteorologists (Woodstock and Overpeck 1998). We take a broad view of the Great Plains as the Ingalls would have experienced it: easily traversed flat land, magnificent soil, little impediment to cultivation, and the ever-present threats of drought and extreme winters due to a mid-continental location in the lee of the Rocky Mountains.

H.S. Bostock, 1967, "Physiographic regions of Canada (1:15,000,000 scale)" (Geological Survey of Canada, Ottawa, Canada).

N.M. Fenneman and D.W. Johnson, 1946, "Physical divisions of the United States (1:7,000,000 scale)" (US Geological Survey, US Government Printing Office, Washington, D.C.).

E. Raisz, 1957, "Landforms of the United States (1:8,870,000 scale)" (Ginn and Company, Boston).

S. Rossum and S. Lavin, 2000, "Where are the Great Plains? A cartographic analysis" (*Professional Geographer* 52:543-552).

G.P. Thelin and R.J. Pike, 1991, "Landforms of the conterminous United States. A digital shaded-relief portrayal (Miscellaneous Investigations map I-2206, 1:3,500,000 scale)" (US Geological Survey, Washington, D.C.).

SIGNIFICANT EVENTS IN THE LITTLE HOUSE SERIES

1836	Charles Ingalls born, New York state.
1867	Laura Ingalls born near Pepin, southwest Wisconsin.
1869	Ingalls family moves to Osage Reservation, northeast Kansas (*Little House on the Prairie*).
1871	Ingalls family returns to Pepin, Wisconsin (*Little House in the Big Woods*).
1874	Ingalls family moves to Walnut Grove, southwest Minnesota (*On the Banks of Plum Creek*).
1870s-1880s	Rocky Mountain locust plagues the Ingalls in Walnut Grove and pioneers elsewhere on the Great Plains.
1870s-1890s	Periodic, multi-year droughts on the Great Plains.
1876	Ingalls family moves to Burr Oak, northeastern Iowa. Laura did not write about this time when her family worked for wages at an inn.
1878	Ingalls family moves back to Walnut Grove, Minnesota.
1879	Ingalls family moves to De Smet, eastern South Dakota (*On the Shores of Silver Lake*).
1880-1881	Extreme winter on the Great Plains (*The Long Winter*).
1882-1885	Laura teaches (*Little Town on the Prairie, These Happy Golden Years*).
1885-1890	Laura marries Almanzo Wilder and they live in De Smet (*The First Four Years*).
1890-1891	Laura and Almanzo live with Almanzo's parents in Spring Valley (southeast Minnesota), move to Westfield (Florida), and return to De Smet.
1891-1894	Laura and Almanzo live in De Smet.
1894	Laura and Almanzo move to Rocky Ridge Farm, Mansfield in the well-watered Missouri Ozarks where they live for the rest of their lives.

1932-1971	Little House books published by Harper Collins: *Little House in the Big Woods* (1932), *Little House on the Prairie* (1935), *On the Banks of Plum Creek* (1937), *By the Shores of Silver Lake* (1939), *The Long Winter* (1940), *Little Town on the Prairie* (1941), *These Happy Golden Years* (1943), *The First Four Years* (1971).
1957	Laura dies. Almanzo died in 1949.

One Hundred Forty Years of Planning Open Space and Why Is It Not Quite Right?

1. This number is, of course, open to debate, but Peter Vitousek and colleagues pointed out in 1997 that, with 5.8 billion people living on Earth (7.2 billion in 2013 and predicted 9.6 billion in 2050), we required that 40 percent of the Earth's total output of green matter from converted sunlight and carbon dioxide be put to direct human use. This is the land only. Open water used by people is less, but increasing. With a projected population in a moderately conservative growth scenario of 11 billion in 2100, unless we become more efficient, there will not be enough arable cropland to support us. Consequences for the other life forms on the Earth are not even part of this equation. *See* P. Vitousek, H.A. Mooney, J. Lubchenco and J.M. Melillo, 1997, "Human domination of Earth's ecosystems" (*Science* 277:494-499).

2. For further information on this, see R. Costanza, R. d'Arge, R. de Groot, S. Farberk, M. Grasso, B. Hannon, K. Limburg, S. Naeem, R.V. O'Neill, J. Paruelo, R.G. Raskin, P. Suttonkk and M. van den Belt, 1997, "The value of the world's ecosystem services and natural capital" (*Nature* 387: 253-260) and G.C. Daily, (editor), 1997, *Nature's Services: Societal Dependence on Natural Ecosystems* (Island Press, Washington, D.C.).

3. For some of these facts, consult G.K. Meffe and C.R. Carroll, 1997, Principles of Conservation Biology, 2nd Edition (Sinauer Associates Inc., Sunderland MA). A definitive statement on the loss of natural ecosystems is provided by R.F. Noss, E.T. LaRoe III and J.M. Scott, 2001, "Endangered ecosystems of the United States: a preliminary assessment of loss and degradation" (USGS Biological Service, Washington, D.C.). On the other hand, good things are happening too, such as improved water quality in Lake Erie, the Cuyahoga River, and other notoriously polluted places of the 1970s, and the recovery of the Eastern Deciduous Forest as told by B. McKibben, 1995, "An explosion of green" (*The Atlantic* (April), Washington, D.C.).

4. Where sewers are at hand, a typical urban lot is 40x120 feet or 1/10 acre, while many suburban lots are 65x150 feet or nearly ¼ acre.

5. For evidence see, for example, R.W. Burchell and S. Mukherji, 2003, "Conventional development versus managed growth: the costs of sprawl" (*American Journal of Public Health* 93:1534-1540).

6. The US EPA estimates that transportation accounts for 31 percent of the carbon dioxide emissions in the United States, exceeded only by electrical generation at 38 percent.

7. These declines have been monitored since 1966 when the U.S. Fish and Wildlife Service began its Breeding Bird Survey across America as reported by J.R. Sauer, J.E. Hines and J. Fallon, 2005, "The North American Breeding Bird Survey, results and analysis 1966–2004, version 2005.2" (USGS Patuxent Wildlife Research Center, Laurel, MD). For recent results see http://www.mbr-pwrc.usgs.gov/bbs/bbs.html.

8. European buckthorn (*Rhamnus cathartica*) which overtakes woodlands, preventing tree regeneration and crowding out wildflowers, is a well-known example.

9. In R.F. Noss and A.Y. Cooperrider, 1994, *Preserving Nature's Image* (Island Press, Washington, D.C.), some cited studies suggest that 75 percent open space across a landscape is the critical

threshold for sensitive wildlife, but the actual number depends on local moderating or exacerbating factors. For stream health, 10 percent connected impervious cover—rooftops and pavement draining directly to sewers—is a threshold of noticeable change, while at 25 percent CIC a stream is afflicted by "urban stream syndrome"—not a good thing. See C.J. Walsh, A.H. Roy, J.W. Feminella, P.D. Cottingham, P.M. Groffman and R.P. Morgan II, 2005, "The urban stream syndrome: current knowledge and the search for a cure" (*Journal of the North American Benthological Society* 24:706-723).

10. Several studies have been published on these benefits and savings: by the U.S. EPA, Chicago Wilderness, Trust for Public Lands, and Applied Ecological Services, to name a few.

11. There is a large and growing body of research on this topic, called "edge effects"—the impact of human-influenced land on adjacent wild and semi-wild land.

PHOTO CREDITS

The images in this book reflect the character of the Upper Midwest and Great Plains. Despite the fairly level landscape, the forests, fields, lakes, rivers, and sky prove there is beauty and mystery everywhere. Even in the side-view mirror of a car.

Kim Chapman: Trempealeau (Cover), Crosby Lake (Notes From an Urban Birder), Forest (Standing by the Pine), Lake & Sky (Unconscious Loyalty to Untamed Landscapes), Tahquamenon (Tribal Take on Environmentalism), Prairie Horizon (Working from Memory), Oak Savanna (The Landscape of Nostalgia), Road in Woods (Vanishing Act), Magnetic Rock and Rushford From Bluffs (Consider the Lilies), Pasque Flower (Shakespeare's Birthday), Snow and Oak (Now Winter Nights)

Shutterstock: Bees (The Echo of the Bees), Sandhill Cranes (Bird Migration, Belief, and Science)

Ladislav Hanka: Fields Going Wild, Reclaiming the Night, Reseeding the Fields (From the Darkness, Light), Red-bellied Woodpecker and Honey-Comb (Still Talking After All These Years)

iStockphoto: Blue Mounds (Prairie and the Land of Imagination), Blackberries (Blackberries), Rear View Mirror (Lost in Space), Farm House (What Laura Saw), Combine in Suburbs (Land Certification), Reel Mower Blades (Mowing the American Lawn), Air Photo (One Hundred Forty Years of Planning

Jim and Kim at Trail Center, Gunflint Trail, northern Minnesota.

ABOUT THE AUTHORS

Kim Alan Chapman (right) has worked as a conservationist, consultant, teacher, and ecologist for thirty years. He holds degrees in biology and conservation biology from Kalamazoo College, Western Michigan University, and the University of Minnesota. Among his publications, his favorite is *Valley of Grass*, from North Star Press, which won a Minnesota Book Award. He lives with his wife, a graphic designer and singer, with visits from daughter and son, in St. Paul, Minnesota.

James Armstrong (left) learned nature in his suburban backyard and the northern Great Lakes wilderness. Educated formally at Western Michigan University, Northwestern, and Boston University, he teaches English at Winona State University in Minnesota and served as that city's first poet laureate. His first book of poetry, *Monument in a Summer Hat*, was published by New Issues Press, and his second, *Blue Lash*, by Milkweed Editions. He lives in Winona with his wife, also a teacher, and two daughters.

"The Echo of the Bees"; "Standing By the Pine: The Poet and 'Truest Use'" and "Lost in Space" first appeared in *Orion* magazine. "Fishing for Inspiration"; "Consider the Lilies"; and "Now Winter Enlarges as We Snug in Houses" were originally guest columns in the Winona Daily News. "Hill Prospect of Kalamazoo," "Kalamazoo County by Air," "Heron" and "Dump" appeared in *Monument in a Summer Hat*, New Issues Press (1999). "Orange Lichen," "Oligotrophic," "Bleak House" and "The Boiler" appeared in *Blue Lash*, Milkweed Editions (2005). The essay "What Laura Saw: Making a Little House on the Extreme Great Plains" was published in the 2010 *Proceedings of the North American Prairie Conference*. Images of *Fields Going Wild, Reclaiming the Night, Reseeding the Fields* and the photograph of the worked-on bee hive frame are used with the permission of Ladislav Hanka.